STRATEGIES FOR REAL-TIME SYSTEM SPECIFICATION

By

Derek J. Hatley   Imtiaz A. Pirbhai

Dorset House Publishing
353 West 12th Street
New York, New York   10014

Library of Congress Cataloging-in-Publication Data

Hatley, Derek J., 1934–
    Strategies for real-time system specification.

    Bibliography: p.
    Includes index.
    1. Real-time data processing.   2. System design.
I. Pirbhai, Imtiaz A., 1953–   . II. Title.
QA76.54.H38   1987   004'.33   87-50801
ISBN 0-932633-11-0
ISBN 0-932633-04-8 (pbk.)

CREDITS
Text: The text was set by Braun-Brumfield, using Century Schoolbook. The graphics
were prepared by the authors using Macintosh Plus and MacDraft.
Cover Design: Jeff Faville, Faville Graphics
Back Cover: Hatley photo: Bultman Studios, Inc.; Pirbhai photo: Stewart Auer

Distributed in the United Kingdom, Ireland, Europe, and Africa by John Wiley &
Sons Ltd., Chichester, Sussex, England.

Printed in the United States of America

Library of Congress Catalog Card Number 87-50801

ISBN: 0-932633-11-0

To Sue

DJH

To my father,
Baba Anwar Shah Taji,
and in memory of my mother

IAP

Acknowledgments

First and foremost, we thank Wendy Eakin, our editor and publisher, who gently but firmly led these two neophyte authors through the rigors of writing a book. You too should thank her, dear Reader: For most of our careers we have worked on or with engineering specifications and standards, and if you are at all familiar with those kinds of documents, you will understand that she is all that stands between you and total boredom.

Many people have contributed in many ways to the work presented here, and while we can mention only a few, we thank you all. Bruce Chubb, Angelo Dimitriou, Rex Morin, and Rod Wierenga gave management support for development and introduction of the requirements method. Dave Bulman sat in on the method's original conception, and, with his great knowledge and experience, helped us sift out the good ideas from the bad. The original Methods Team consisted of Kathy Hornbach, Bill Kelly, Martie Lorenz, John McCreary, and George Wood. Don Morrow remains the preeminent practitioner of the method itself, while John TenCate is master of the art of transforming the resulting model into a real system. Linda Goggins succeeded in the enormous task of coordinating and compiling the first (manual) application of the method. Kent McPherson performed some miracles with LATEX, the document preparation system for this book, to make it work the way we wanted.

Tim Petersen, Irv Reese, Dick Schoenmann, and Peter Sutcliffe provided the management support needed for the development of the architecture method, as well as support for the further expansion and acceptance of both the requirements and architecture methods in the user community.

Dan Bacon, Rodney Bell, James Bouhana, Bob Doering, Peter Hruschka, Lou Mazzucchelli, Don Morrow, Rick Swanborg, Tony Wasserman, and Bob Weisickle reviewed various drafts of the book and improved it immeasurably with their insights.

Finally, we give a very special acknowledgment to Paul Gartz. Paul has been an enthusiastic champion of these methods, and an inspiration to the rest of us working on them. His aggressive canvassing on behalf of the methods has been responsible for their acceptance by management and the industry.

Contents

List of Figures   xi

Foreword   xix

Preface   xxi

PART I: The Overall Strategy   1

1 Overview   3
- 1.1   The Birth of the Requirements Model 4
- 1.2   The Birth of the Architecture Model 6
- 1.3   Compatibility of the Models 7
- 1.4   Applicability of the Models 7
- 1.5   The System Life Cycle 8

2 The Role of the Methods   11
- 2.1   Structured Methods: What They Are 11
- 2.2   System Requirements Model 13
- 2.3   System Architecture Model 19
- 2.4   System Specification Model 24
- 2.5   The Development Life Cycle 26
- 2.6   Structured Methods: What They Are Not 30
- 2.7   Summary 30

PART II: The Requirements Model   33

3 Overview   35
- 3.1   The Structure of the Model 37

4 The Process Model   **41**
    4.1   Data Context Diagrams   41
    4.2   Data Flow Diagrams   44
    4.3   Leveling and Balancing   46
    4.4   The Numbering System   47
    4.5   Data Flows   49
    4.6   Data Stores   51
    4.7   Process Specifications   51
    4.8   Interpreting the Process Model   54
    4.9   Summary   56

5 The Control Model   **59**
    5.1   Control Context Diagrams   59
    5.2   Control Flow Diagrams   61
    5.3   Control Flows   64
    5.4   Data Conditions   66
    5.5   Control Stores   67
    5.6   Control Specifications   67
    5.7   Process Controls   70
    5.8   Summary   72

6 Finite State Machines   **74**
    6.1   Combinational Machines   76
    6.2   Sequential Machines   78
    6.3   Incorporating Finite State Machines into CSPECs   85
    6.4   Summary   92

7 Timing Requirements   **93**
    7.1   Repetition Rate   94
    7.2   Input-to-Output Response Time   94
    7.3   Summary   96

8 Requirements Dictionary   **98**
    8.1   Primitive Attributes   98
    8.2   Group Structure 100
    8.3   Dictionary Data Bases 102
    8.4   Summary 102

9 Requirements Model Interpretation and Summary   **106**
    9.1   The Requirements Model Interpreted 106
    9.2   Requirements Model Summary 108

PART III: Building the Requirements Model 111

10 Overview **113**
  10.1 Model Users and Builders 113
  10.2 The Sources of Requirements 114
  10.3 The Model Building Process 115

11 Getting Started **118**
  11.1 User Requirements Statements 118
  11.2 Separating Data and Control 119
  11.3 Establishing the System Context 123
  11.4 Partitioning the Top Levels 126
  11.5 Summary 129

12 Developing the Model's Structure **130**
  12.1 Abstraction and Decomposition 130
  12.2 The Seven-Plus-or-Minus-Two Principle 131
  12.3 Grouping and Decomposing Processes 132
  12.4 Grouping and Decomposing Flows 133
  12.5 Naming Processes and Flows 140
  12.6 Use of Stores 142
  12.7 Functionally Identical Processes 142
  12.8 De-emphasizing the Control Model 143
  12.9 Control Intensive Systems 144
  12.10 The Dilemma of Detail: Requirements Versus Design 145
  12.11 The Final Product 147
  12.12 Summary 148

13 Preparing Process Specifications **150**
  13.1 The Role of Process Specifications 150
  13.2 The Different Types of PSPECs 151
  13.3 Some Important Signal Conventions 154
  13.4 Structured English 157
  13.5 Annotating with Comments 158
  13.6 Summary 158

14 Preparing Control Specifications **160**
  14.1 Avoiding Control Specifications 160
  14.2 Combinational Control 161
  14.3 Sequential Control 167
  14.4 Multi-Sheet CSPECs 172

14.5   Fitting CSPECs In   175
14.6   Summary   178

15 Defining Timing   **179**
15.1   Timing Overview   179
15.2   Response Time Specification   180
15.3   Summary   182

16 Managing the Dictionary   **183**
16.1   Flow Types   183
16.2   Dictionary Symbols   187
16.3   Summary   188

PART IV: The Architecture Model   191

17 Overview   **193**
17.1   Requirements-to-Architecture Template   194
17.2   Architecture Model Symbols   197

18 Architecture Diagrams   **200**
18.1   Architecture Context Diagrams   200
18.2   Flows and Interconnects   201
18.3   Architecture Flow Diagrams   202
18.4   Architecture Interconnect Diagrams   208
18.5   Summary   211

19 Architecture Dictionary and Module Specifications **213**
19.1   Architecture Module Specification   214
19.2   Architecture Interconnect Specification   217
19.3   Timing Requirements   219
19.4   Architecture Dictionary   220
19.5   Summary   221

20 Completing the Architecture Model   **222**
20.1   Allocation to Hardware and Software   222
20.2   The Hardware and Software Architectures   223
20.3   The Complete Architecture Model   225

PART V: Building the Architecture Model   227

21 Overview   **229**
    21.1   Architecture Development Process 230
    21.2   Systems Come in Hierarchies 231

22 Enhancing the Requirements Model   **234**
    22.1   Input and Output Processing 234
    22.2   User Interface Processing 237
    22.3   Maintenance and Self-Test Processing 239
    22.4   The Complete Enhanced Requirements Model 242
    22.5   Technology-Independent Versus Technology-Nonspecific . . . 243
    22.6   Organizational Implications 245
    22.7   Summary 247

23 Creating the System Architecture Model   **248**
    23.1   Architecture Context Diagram 248
    23.2   Architecture Flow and Interconnect Diagrams 249
    23.3   Example of AFD and AID Mapping 251
    23.4   Model Consistency and Balancing 254
    23.5   The Complete Architecture Model 256
    23.6   Summary 257

24 Creating the Hardware and Software Architecture Models   **258**
    24.1   Hardware and Software Partitioning 260
    24.2   Applying the Template to Software Requirements 263
    24.3   Developing the Software Architecture 266
    24.4   The Hardware and Software Architecture Process 268
    24.5   Summary 269

25 Architecture Development Summary   **270**
    25.1   Partitioning the Modeling Process 270

PART VI: Examples   275

26 Automobile Management System   **277**
    26.1   Problem Statement 277
    26.2   Requirements and Architecture Development 279
    26.3   Requirements Model 281
    26.4   Architecture Model 301

27 Home Heating System **308**
    27.1   Problem Statement 308
    27.2   Requirements Model 311
    27.3   Architecture Model 321

28 Vending Machine **323**
    28.1   Customer Dialogue 323
    28.2   Requirements Model 325
    28.3   Architecture Model 334

APPENDIX A: Standard Symbols and Definitions **339**
    A.1   Introduction 339
    A.2   Standard Symbols 339
    A.3   Requirements Model 343
    A.4   Architecture Model 357

APPENDIX B: Making the Models into Documents **367**
    B.1   Organizing the Models 367
    B.2   Military Standards 370

APPENDIX C: Information Modeling: The Third Perspective **373**

References **377**

Index **379**

List of Figures

A Map of the Book xxii

1.1   The universal hierarchy of systems   4
1.2   The total system life cycle   9

2.1   Vending machine DFD 13
2.2   Vending machine PSPEC 14
2.3   Composite data entries from vending machine dictionary 14
2.4   Vending machine CFD 15
2.5   Vending machine CSPEC 16
2.6   Primitive control entries from vending machine dictionary 17
2.7   The structure of the requirements model 18
2.8   Vending machine AFD 20
2.9   Vending machine AMS 20
2.10 Vending machine architecture dictionary entries 21
2.11 Vending machine AID 21
2.12 Vending machine AIS 22
2.13 Augmented vending machine architecture dictionary 22
2.14 The structure of the architecture model 23
2.15 The formation of the system specification 24
2.16 Requirements-to-architecture iterative loop 25
2.17 System, software, and hardware specification structure 26
2.18 Overlapping systems development phases 27
2.19 Development life cycle spiral 28

3.1   Composite chart of the requirements model 38

4.1   The process structure (highlighted) 42
4.2   Data context diagram 43
4.3   Data flow diagram 44

4.4   Transaction centers   46
4.5   Four levels of data flow diagrams superimposed   47
4.6   Leveling, numbering, and parent/child relationships   48
4.7   Data flows   49
4.8   Splitting flows between levels   50
4.9   Two examples of process specifications   53
4.10   The structures of structured English   55
4.11   The primitive network   57

5.1   The control structure (highlighted)   60
5.2   Control context diagram   61
5.3   Control flow diagram   62
5.4   Variations on CSPEC bars   63
5.5   Comparison between discrete and continuous signals   65
5.6   A data condition   66
5.7   The model as a feedback control loop   69
5.8   Process controls   71
5.9   Controlling a transaction center   72

6.1   Decision table for a heating system   77
6.2   Condensed decision tables for a heating system   79
6.3   Rotary combination lock: a sequential machine   80
6.4   State transition diagram   81
6.5   State transition table   83
6.6   State transition matrix   84
6.7   State transition matrix (alternate form)   84
6.8   Combinational CSPEC, with its DFD and CFD   86
6.9   Sequential CSPEC, with its DFD and CFD   88
6.10   Block diagram of composite CSPEC   89
6.11   Composite CSPEC   90
6.12   Typical multi-sheet control specification   91

7.1   Response time specifications   95
7.2   Timing diagram to supplement the response time
       specification   96

8.1   Typical primitive continuous signal definitions   99
8.2   Typical primitive discrete signal definitions   99
8.3   Requirements dictionary symbols   101
8.4   Dictionary listing   103
8.5   Indented explosion of a large group flow   104

9.1   Primitive network with control structure 107

11.1   Signal and process categories 121
11.2   Typical PSPEC: a primitive requirements statement 123
11.3   Assuming the worst: all conceivable functions included 124
11.4   Functions reduced after checking system scope 125
11.5   Diagram with a first-cut control flow 126
11.6   Composite top-level data and control flow diagram 127
11.7   DFD 0: Control & Monitor Auto 127
11.8   CFD 0: Control & Monitor Auto 128

12.1   Correction of uneven flow distribution 134
12.2   Correction of clustered processes 135
12.3   Splitting and merging data flows 136
12.4   Decomposing data flows 136
12.5   Splitting off unused flows 137
12.6   Flows with common members 137
12.7   Multiple flows 138
12.8   Two-way flows 138
12.9   The half-arrow convention 139
12.10 A flow tree 139
12.11 Functionally identical processes 143
12.12 Composite chart of the model for control intensive system . . . 146

13.1   A PSPEC with equations 152
13.2   A tabular PSPEC 153
13.3   A flight profile used in a PSPEC 154
13.4   Geometrical relationships used in a PSPEC 155
13.5   Continuous, discrete-valued, and time-discrete signals 156

14.1   A full decision table 163
14.2   A reduced decision table 164
14.3   An ambiguous set of input combinations 165
14.4   Alternative representation of transaction center control 166
14.5   Data flow diagram showin throttle control 170
14.6   Control specification showing throttle control 172
14.7   A multi-sheet state transition matrix 173
14.8   Organization of a composite CSPEC 174
14.9   A floating CSPEC 177

15.1   Dictionary, response time, PSPEC, and CSPEC timing
       specifications 180

16.1 Flow types and their attributes 184

17.1 Architecture model components 194
17.2 Requirements template 194
17.3 Architecture template 195
17.4 Architecture template for the Automobile Management System 196
17.5 Architecture model layering 197
17.6 Architecture module symbol 198
17.7 Information flow vector symbol 198
17.8 Information flow channel symbols 199

18.1 ACD for a flight management system 201
18.2 ACD for the Automobile Management System 202
18.3 AFD for a flight management system 203
18.4 AFD for a data acquisition subsystem 204
18.5 Architecture template for a flight management system 204
18.6 Architecture template for a data acquisition subsystem 205
18.7 AFD 0: Automobile Management System 205
18.8 AFD layering 206
18.9 AFD 2: Shaft Interface Module 207
18.10 AFD 5: Throttle Interface Module 207
18.11 AID for a flight management system 209
18.12 Redundancy of architecture modules 209
18.13 Redundancy of architecture channels 210
18.14 AID 0: Automobile Management System 211
18.15 AID 2: Shaft Interface Module 211

19.1 Architecture model support components 213
19.2 Architecture module specification 215
19.3 A DFD, CFD, and their CSPEC to be allocated 215
19.4 Splitting CSPECs for allocation 216
19.5 Traceability matrix for the Automobile Management System . . 217
19.6 Interconnect channel and corresponding AIS 218
19.7 A typical AIS 219
19.8 Partial architecture dictionary for the Automobile Management System 221

20.1 Partitioning between hardware and software 223
20.2 System, hardware, and software requirements hierarchy 224

20.3 System, hardware, and software architecture hierarchy 224
20.4 A vertical slice through the architecture model 226

21.1 Hierarchical nature of natural systems 232
21.2 Hierarchical nature of systems development 232

22.1 Outside-in approach to architecture development 235
22.2 Input and output buffers for the requirements model 236
22.3 Input and output processes for the Automobile Management
     System 237
22.4 Enhancements to the Automobile Management System DFD
     for user interface processing 238
22.5 DFD/CFD for the driver interface process 239
22.6 User interface buffer to the requirements model 240
22.7 Enhancements for maintenance and self-test buffer 241
22.8 Maintenance processing added to the requirements model . . . 241
22.9 Enhanced DFD for Automobile Management System 242
22.10 Enhanced CFD for Automobile Management System 243
22.11 Architectural enhancements to the requirements model 244

23.1 ACD for the Automobile Management System 249
23.2 Generic DFD/CFD/CSPEC 250
23.3 AFD 0: Automobile Management System 251
23.4 AID 0: Automobile Management System 252
23.5 Architecture module specification for the Automobile
     Management System 253
23.6 Architecture interconnect specification for the Automobile
     Management System 253
23.7 Architecture dictionary for the Automobile Management
     System 254
23.8 Architecture development process 256

24.1 Hierarchical nature of the Automobile Management System . . 258
24.2 DFD of requirements allocated to the automobile management
     computer module 259
24.3 CFD of requirements allocated to the automobile management
     computer module 260
24.4 AID for automobile management computer hardware
     configuration 262
24.5 Requirements allocated to hardware 262
24.6 Enhanced hardware requirements 262
24.7 AFD for shaft interface module 263

24.8   AID for shaft bus receiver 263
24.9   Enhanced DFD for the automobile management computer
        software 265
24.10   Enhanced CFD for the automobile management computer
        software 266
24.11   A structure chart 267
24.12   Software development structure 268
24.13   Hardware and software architecture development process 269

25.1   Iterative process for developing system requirements and
        architecture 271
25.2   System modeling process 272
25.3   Hardware and software partitioning process 273
25.4   Hardware and software modeling process 273
25.5   Application of requirements and architecture modeling to large
        systems 274
25.6   Integrated system, hardware, and software model 274

A.1   Data flow: A solid arc with a name 340
A.2   Control flow: A dashed arc with a name 340
A.3   CSPEC bar: A short unlabeled bar 340
A.4   Process: A circle with a name and a number 341
A.5   Store: A pair of parallel lines containing a name 341
A.6   Terminator: A rectangle containing a name 342
A.7   Architecture module: A rounded rectangle containing a name
        and number 342
A.8   Information flow vector: A solid or dashed line with a name . . 343
A.9   Architecture information flow channels 343
A.10   Components of the requirements model 344
A.11   Sample data context diagram 345
A.12   Sample control context diagram 346
A.13   Sample data flow diagram 347
A.14   Data flow diagram naming and numbering rules 348
A.15   Sample control flow diagram 349
A.16   DFD and CFD naming and numbering 349
A.17   Samples of process specifications 350
A.18   Process specification naming and numbering rules 351
A.19   Generic CSPEC for combinational system 351
A.20   Sample CSPEC for combinational system 352
A.21   Generic CSPEC for sequential system 353
A.22   Sample CSPEC for sequential system 354

A.23 Illustration of flow decomposition in the requirements
      dictionary 357
A.24 Components of the architecture model 358
A.25 Architecture template 358
A.26 Sample architecture context diagram 359
A.27 Sample architecture flow diagram 360
A.28 AFD naming and numbering rules 361
A.29 Sample architecture interconnect diagram 362
A.30 Sample architecture module specification 363
A.31 Sample architecture interconnect specification 364
A.32 Example of enhancements to dictionary 365

C.1   Requirements projections of a system 374
C.2   Architecture template with three requirements projections . . . 375

Foreword

"Most systems people use the term *real-time* rather loosely," the young manager said. We were seated over dinner with three members of her staff and some other managers who took part in the day's seminar. "They say they've got a real-time constraint when they're worried about impatient insurance brokers or bankers sitting in front of their terminals. A real-time system, in their minds, is just one that needs to be 'quick as a bunny.' If they fail to meet that constraint, their users might be inconvenienced or even annoyed. When we use the term, it means something rather different."

Her co-workers began to smile, knowing what was coming. "We build systems that reside in a small telemetry computer, equipped with all kinds of sensors to measure electromagnetic fields and changes in temperature, sound, and physical disturbance. We analyze these signals and transmit the results back to a remote computer over a wide-band channel. Our computer is at one end of a one-meter long bar and at the other end is a nuclear device. We drop them together down a big hole in the ground and when the device detonates, our computer collects data on the leading edge of the blast. The first two-and-a-quarter milliseconds after detonation are the most interesting. Of course, long before millisecond three, things have gone down hill badly for our little computer. We think of *that* as a real-time constraint."

I had been lecturing that day on the use of data flow modeling techniques for system specification. There had been the odd question about the use of such techniques for real-time systems, and my (typically glib) answer was that the techniques were applicable, though perhaps not totally sufficient. After all, my own earliest work with data flow modeling had been at Bell Labs and at La CEGOS Informatique, in both cases working on real-time systems. Or were those real-time systems? Maybe they were really just systems that needed to be 'quick as a bunny'? The young manager's graphic example had left me in some doubt.

It has always been clear that something more than the basic tools of structured analysis are needed to specify timing and synchronization requirements. In the simplest case, that "something" could be as trivial as a set of textual annotations, perhaps directly on the data flow diagrams. But for even slightly more complicated cases, there is the possibility of linked timing and ordering constraints that may involve a dozen or more system components. There has been a need for a systematic way to deal with such constraints.

Over the last few years, I began to hear favorable reports of some real-time modeling techniques called the Hatley/Pirbhai Extensions. This multi-perspective approach combined data flow decomposition with model components constructed in control- and information-space. The result appealed to me as a specification technique that was not only applicable, but for most cases sufficient for real-time systems. I contacted the developers and started to try out their extensions.

The act of writing a Foreword is a kind of endorsement. It says, if nothing else, "Read this book, it couldn't hurt." In this case, I can be considerably more positive than that. I can tell you that I learned valuable new techniques from Hatley and Pirbhai, and that I apply them regularly on real-world real-time applications.

October 1987   Tom DeMarco
Camden, Maine   The Atlantic Systems Guild

Preface

This book describes two methods for specifying, respectively, the requirements for and the design structure of software-based systems. Although the methods grew up around real-time embedded systems, systems of all types and sizes have benefited from them, largely because of their flexibility and adaptability. The methods can be viewed as an integrated toolkit from which all the tools are compatible, but only those that are useful for the particular job need be used.

The subject of this book is neither computer science nor software. Although the vast majority of the systems to which the methods are applied will in fact be implemented using software in digital computers, the methods do not address how to write that software or how to design that hardware. What the methods do address is how to specify the *problems* that the hardware and software must solve.

Organization and audience of the book

The book is intended for a wide range of readers. We assume that you are involved, or at least interested, in software-based systems, but that your needs may range from just a general understanding to an in-depth working knowledge. We have tried to organize the book to make it easy for you to select those parts that are of specific interest to you and to avoid those that are not.

The figure on the following page shows the layout of the book. Part I provides an overview from which everyone will benefit. Parts II and IV describe *what* the methods are, and if you only need to understand the specifications resulting from their use, then these two parts are enough for you to read. If you need to *prepare* specifications, then you will also need to read Parts III and V, which describe *how* to use the methods. Part VI contains examples of the application of the methods, and we conclude the book with appendices and a brief reference list.

Decide what your area of interest is—requirements analysis, design, or both—and what depth of understanding you need—general familiarity, use of

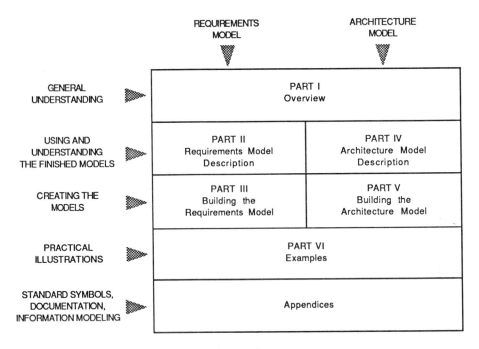

A Map of the Book

the completed specifications, or building the specifications—and it will be clear from the figure which parts of the book you should read.

Derek J. Hatley
Wyoming, Michigan

Imtiaz A. Pirbhai
Seattle, Washington

PART I
The Overall Strategy

Chapter 1

Overview

For more than a decade, there has been growing dissatisfaction with conventional strategies for systems development, and an increasing number of proposals for replacing them with new, more formal approaches. The problem is that conventional development methods cannot cope with the size and complexity of the systems we are now able to implement. These system characteristics are possible because of the ever-increasing capacity and capability of computer hardware. Systems having up to a million lines of high-order source code are already commonplace, and others are on the horizon that will require ten or more times that amount.

The inadequacies of the development methods were first apparent in large business and commercial systems, but as digital technology came into use in real-time embedded systems, they too became subject to the same problems. We are past the stage of wondering whether formal development methods are really needed. The question is, Can we keep pace with the capabilities of the technology using the methods we already have? What further extensions and improvements can we make to them? Can we devise better and more comprehensive methods?

A problem with past system specification methods has been that they each tend to address only one aspect of the system, whereas systems actually have many aspects, all of which need to be addressed. The methods described in this book seek to overcome this problem by addressing a number of these aspects in an integrated manner. From the functional requirements point of view, they address the aspects of processing, control, and timing. From the physical requirements point of view, they address the architectural specification of the system, and most importantly, they take account of the hierarchical and iterative nature of systems and of systems development. Figure 1.1 illustrates how the whole universe may be thought of as a hierarchy of systems. Any individual system may itself be expressed as such a hierarchy, and the progression down through its levels involves defining the requirements

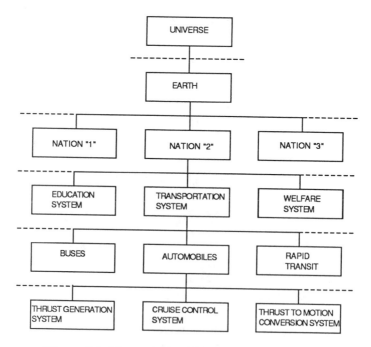

Figure 1.1. The universal hierarchy of systems.

for the level below, then making decisions on the architecture or design of that level to meet those requirements, then repeating this procedure for the next level down, and so on. This perspective makes clear the adage that one person's requirements are another person's design: a cause of considerable confusion in earlier development methods, but an integral part of the methods addressed here.

Before we delve into the details of the methods, we will give a brief historical account of their development. This will help you understand the situations that create the need for such methods, and will give you some insight into what it might take to introduce them into your own organization.

1.1   The Birth of the Requirements Model

The requirements specification model described in this book evolved at a major avionics systems development company. This evolution started in late 1982, and culminated two years later in the successful Federal Aviation Administration certification of a complex real-time, embedded avionics system for a commercial airliner. The system is now in widespread use in the airline industry.

At the time, the development effort was the largest we had ever undertaken. Previously, we had been without formal procedures for integrating the efforts of our system and software developers: We had depended on their individual communications with each other, and on the abilities of a few overworked lead engineers, in order to keep the various subsystems consistent.

There comes a point at which this just won't do, a point at which the interactions *between* the subsystems are at least as complex as the subsystems themselves. Faced with this dilemma, and with the very real threat of a major disaster if we did not improve our performance, we investigated the formal development methods that already existed. We found a fairly mature set of methods that had been developed in the 1970s for large mainframe business applications, and that had been successfully applied in that field.

Several of the existing requirements definition methods were capable of representing the information processing parts of our systems, but they could not handle the complex control structures that large real-time systems also typically include. Since these control structures can be represented using finite state machine theory, we decided that we needed to integrate an established requirements definition method with finite state machine theory in a unified structure, and to do it so as to retain the benefits of both.

The requirements definition method that seemed to have the most merit was DeMarco's structured analysis [4], so we chose this as the starting point. One of the greatest merits of the DeMarco method is its attention to human readability and understandability through the use of graphics. In addition, it shares with most other requirements definition methods the attributes of information abstraction, built-in self-consistency checking, and the ability to be self-indexing.

Because the project was already underway, we needed a requirements definition method immediately. During just two weeks of brainstorming and trial and error, we found the approach we were looking for—a way to partition a large finite state machine into pieces corresponding to the pieces of a structured analysis—and the requirements model described in this book was born. One week later, a group of development engineers took the first class in the new method. That first teaching effort was not a polished presentation, but the substance was there. As we gained experience in its use, we made some further improvements in our emerging method, but, surprisingly, it has never needed any fundamental changes.

The existing and widely used structured design method [11,19] was applicable (with very little modification) to the design definition of our real-time systems.

Introducing the model

The approach we took to introduce our new methods was contrary to that advocated by methods experts, who advise that methods be introduced on a small, low-visibility project. We did not have (and have never had) such a project, and in fact introduced the method on the largest, most critical project we had ever undertaken. To offset the risks in this situation, we established a Methods Team—a group of six people whose sole role was to make the methods work. The team members prepared and taught classes, provided consultation, solved problems as they arose, made improvements to the methods, and investigated ways to automate them.

If critical projects are the only kind your shop, too, ever has to work on, and you are about to introduce revolutionary new development methods, we recommend this approach of dedicating a team to support them.

It would be misleading to suggest that the requirements and design definition methods alone were responsible for the success of the project. We made a number of other changes at the same time: For example, a large scientific computer was dedicated to the project; each system and software engineer was provided with an interactive terminal; an efficient, modular working environment was installed; we scaled the project using the Putnam model [15]; and we used a more detailed and comprehensive progress tracking procedure than we had ever used before. The relative contributions of the individual factors are hard to judge, but their combined effect was greatly improved productivity.

One of the earliest decisions made with regard to the requirements model was to make it freely available to anyone wishing to use it, rather than to copyright it, or treat it as proprietary information. Our rationale was first, that our business is avionics, not development methods; second, that it would be to our advantage to have the rest of the industry follow our lead; and further, that it would be particularly advantageous to have automated tool developers embed our method in their tools. As a result of this early decision (and because of the success of the requirements model in its first application), the method has become widespread in the industry. Many diverse companies are using it, and there are currently at least six automated CASE tool developers [21] supporting it (some more completely than others—we neither endorse nor recommend against these or any other CASE tools; you must evaluate them relative to your own needs and environment). In addition, there are seminars [20] available giving instruction in the use of both the requirements and the architecture models. This popularity has given rise to constant demands for more available information on the method, and these demands provided our principal motivation for writing this book.

1.2   The Birth of the Architecture Model

While this change in approach to the development of one major avionics system was taking place, the airframe manufacturer that needed the system was wrestling with an even broader problem—that of multiple system integration. Because land-, sea-, air-, and space-based vehicles are now filled with complex interacting systems, the problems of handling this complexity have moved up a level from subsystems within a system to systems within a vehicle.

The issues at this level have a different nature, however. The *total* vehicle with all its embedded systems may be considered to be one supersystem. The power of modern technology can allow unconventional partitionings of this supersystem. Many previously separate functions might be included in one system, or functions that traditionally have been performed by analog processing might now be done digitally. The resulting systems must fit into a well-defined physical structure, interconnected by communication buses with rigid protocols, and they must meet many requirements beyond their basic functionality, such as safety, reliability, and maintainability. Frequently, the systems will be developed by different contractors, so the issue of precise interface definition becomes paramount.

This scenario, in which functional requirements at one level must be rigorously allocated to a physical structure with nonfunctional requirements added, gave rise to the architecture model, described in Parts IV and V.

1.3   Compatibility of the Models

The requirements and architecture models complement each other well. Processes in the requirements model can be allocated to slots in the architecture model, and this procedure can be repeated many times over going down through increasing levels of detail. Similarly, in the upward direction, the vehicle itself may be considered to be just one system within a network of systems, such as the air traffic control for a region. Again, the functional requirements for this larger system may be defined using the requirements model, and then allocated to the physical communications network using the architecture model. This leveled repetition of functional requirements definition, followed by physical allocation, is fundamental to the nature of large systems development.

1.4   Applicability of the Models

Although the methods were developed around avionics systems, the technology explosion has reached all areas of industry, and systems of unprecedented complexity are appearing in manufacturing, process control, and even in the very business applications in which the original methods were first applied. The methods described in this book are applicable in any of these areas, and indeed have gained acceptance in applications including communications, instrumentation, medical systems, process control, and military systems. The need for the methods is much more a function of size and complexity than of application area.

1.5 The System Life Cycle

Before studying the requirements and architecture methods, we must under-stand what purpose they serve. One way to illustrate this is to look at what the methods do and where they fit in the total system life cycle. This is shown in Figure 1.2 in which the development levels correspond to the hierarchical levels of Figure 1.1

The figure illustrates that the requirements and architecture models ap-ply throughout all levels of systems development and both are applied at each level. A set of requirements is generated at a given level, using the requirements model. These requirements are allocated to physical units or modules using the architecture model. The requirements for each unit are then expanded to more detail, and the whole process is repeated at the next level.

Of course, most projects will only deal with perhaps one or two of these iterative cycles, but on the other hand, most projects fit into a larger pic-ture—they may be part of a complete aircraft, or of a manufacturing plant, or of a communication network—in which many more cycles will occur. It is good to have an understanding of the larger framework in which your project fits.

The final level, at which implementation is to take place, may require modification to the architecture model, or may require a language-dependent representation (Ada PDL, for example), depending on the language or imple-mentation needs.

While we do not address testing activities in this book, we have found that structured development proves to be very beneficial in this area. Having the system defined both functionally and physically in a layered hierarchy of processes and units leads to a similar organization of the test procedures. The testing can proceed very methodically from the bottom up, verifying the func-tionality and the structure at each level up to the top.

Some caveats

Some key points illustrated in Figure 1.2 need to be emphasized:

- The life cycle does *not* end at the point of system delivery, as is so often implied: It continues on into the service phase, usually for much longer than the development and build phases. It is customary for modifica-tions and upgrades to occur while the system is in service. This is illus-trated in Figure 1.2 via the loop from System in Service through De-ploy System and Field Issues and back to the development cycle. These changes, together with the system maintenance cost, can make the cost during service much higher than during development. The benefits of

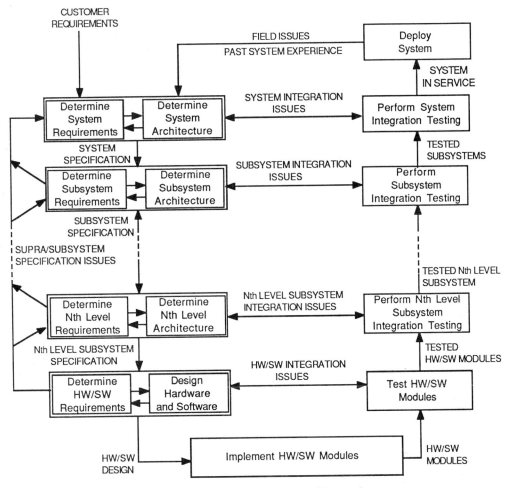

Figure 1.2. The total system life cycle.

formal methods are most obvious at the development phase, but in fact, their benefits can be multiplied many times over during the service phase because of the ease with which changes can be made after the original developers are gone.

- Contrary again to common misconceptions, the development does *not* occur in simple sequential steps. There is extensive overlap, feedforward, and feedback between each phase and its neighbors. The process is, in fact, iterative, both within each phase and over multiple phases. The requirements and architecture models record their respective definitions regardless of the order in which they are done. As we shall show in the chapters that follow, everything is traceable between levels and between phases so risk of confusion due to iterative updates is minimized.

- In large, software-intensive systems, the activities of defining the requirements, the architecture, and the hardware and software design are (or should be) much more extensive than the actual implementation. In fact, with the advent of tools that will generate code automatically from requirements statements, we are rapidly approaching the point at which, for all intents and purposes, the definition *is* the implementation. The two methods exist specifically to support this front-end definition activity.

- Systems themselves, and the process of developing them, are leveled hierarchies. In the extreme, we can consider the whole universe, the elementary particles of which it is composed, and every structure in between, as one huge leveled hierarchy of systems, as was shown in Figure 1.1. The particular systems in which we are interested fall somewhere in this range, and the points we choose to call "top level" and "implementation" are quite arbitrary. This perspective makes it clear why there is so much confusion over the definitions of "requirements" and "design." The fact is that one person's requirement is another person's design, depending on the particular interests of those people relative to the hierarchy. The methods exactly reflect this hierarchical nature of large systems.

Chapter 2

The Role of the Methods

In this chapter, we give you a complete but brief look at everything to be described in the rest of the book. This serves two purposes: Readers who simply want a general idea of what the methods are about will get it by reading just this chapter, while those who intend to delve deeper will get a good overview of what is to come. We deliberately introduce concepts and diagrams here without complete explanations; the diagrams and other constructs used in these methods are designed to be intuitively meaningful and we would like you to use your intuition to understand them before getting into the detailed whys and wherefores.

2.1 Structured Methods: What They Are

We define "structured methods" as consisting of modeling tools and techniques that illuminate certain aspects of the desired system during the specification process. Different methods are appropriate at each of the different specification phases.

Structured methods are useful for any type of system, such as real-time, data processing, and process control. The important point to note is that they are *systems,* not simply random groupings of hardware and software components, or strings of 1s and 0s along with some transistors and LSI chips—they are systematic groupings of components put together to behave as a whole.

The components that make up a system—both hardware and software components—are highly interrelated, and, in order to successfully perform their intended function, they must integrate well. The system specification process, therefore, must define the system as a whole, as well as its partitioning into hardware and software components. It must define *what* problem the system is to solve (its requirements) and *how* that system is to be structured

11

(its architecture or design structure). A third aspect that must be covered, but that is beyond the scope of this book, is the actual implementation of the design structure—the hardware construction and software coding. These are both major disciplines in their own right.

What and how

As an analogy of the use of the methods, we use the real-life example of a town with a river that often overflows during the springtime mountain thaws, causing flooding, and dries every summer, causing severe water shortages. These problems have several possible solutions, including these three:

- The town could abandon its current location and move somewhere with an adequate water supply and no flooding.

- A canal could be dug to divert the river around the town, and a water pipeline run in from a nearby city.

- A dam and reservoir could be built upstream from the town to regulate the flow of water to prevent flooding and to provide an adequate supply for use in the summer months.

The third option might seem to be the solution of choice, but further analysis of considerations such as cost and available resources might make any of the alternatives viable.

As this example shows, there is a need to capture what the problem is and then trade off the options to find the best solution. Similarly, in specifying a system and its hardware and software components, we need to capture *what* problem the system is to solve, and through a tradeoff process determine *how* to solve it. To state the problem and to capture its solution (analogous to defining the system's requirements and architecture), we build the two models of the system on paper: the requirements model and the architecture model. The requirements model is built as a technology-independent model of the system's essential requirements [9] and the architecture model is a technology-dependent model of the system's structure.

What are these models, and what aspects of a system do they illuminate? As a quick overview to familiarize you with some of the terms and the appearance of the models, we illustrate them in the following sections using a vending machine as an example system. Figures 2.1 through 2.6 illustrate the requirements model and Figures 2.8 through 2.13 illustrate the architecture model.

2.2 System Requirements Model

The system requirements are captured through an integrated model that views the system from two aspects: its information processing (functional) behavior, and its control (state) behavior. A third viewpoint, which is summarized in Appendix C, is information modeling or data modeling [16].

The following paragraphs summarize the process and control models which represent the first two aspects.

The process model

The data flow diagram (DFD) is the primary tool depicting functional requirements. It partitions these requirements into component functions, or processes, and represents them as a network interconnected by data flows. Its main purpose is to show how each process transforms its input data flows into output data flows, and to show the relationships between those processes. For example, the DFD in Figure 2.1 shows a vending machine's six functions and the interconnections between them.

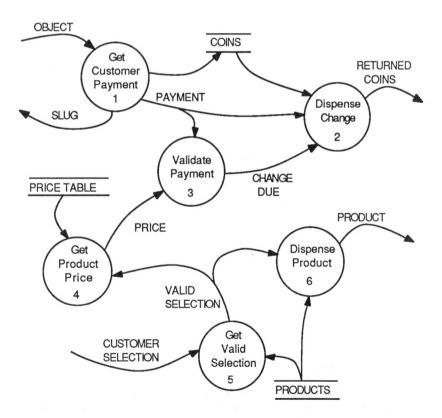

Figure 2.1. Vending machine DFD.

Two additional tools support the DFD: a process specification (PSPEC or process spec) for each primitive process, and a requirements dictionary (RD) that specifies every data flow. Processes that are not primitive are broken down into more detailed DFDs and do not have PSPECs.

Figure 2.2 shows a PSPEC for process 3 on the vending machine DFD, and a part of its dictionary appears in Figure 2.3. The dictionary notation is explained in Part II.

```
PSPEC 3 : VALIDATE PAYMENT
INPUTS :        PRICE, PAYMENT
OUTPUTS :       SUFFICIENT PAYMENT, CHANGE DUE

If PAYMENT ≥ PRICE then
        Issue SUFFICIENT PAYMENT = Yes
        Issue CHANGE DUE = PAYMENT - PRICE
Otherwise
        Issue SUFFICIENT PAYMENT = No
```

Figure 2.2. Vending machine PSPEC.

```
OBJECTS = COINS + SLUGS

COINS = QUARTERS + NICKELS + DIMES

PRODUCTS = [ SODA | GUM | CANDY ]
```

**Figure 2.3. Composite data entries
from vending machine dictionary.**

PSPEC 3 shows an output SUFFICIENT PAYMENT which, because it is a control flow, is not shown on the DFD. Instead, it appears out of process 3 on the control flow diagram (CFD), shown later in Figure 2.4.

One further component, not illustrated here, is the response time specification. These components together capture the functional requirements of the system.

The control model

Data flow diagrams illustrate what functions the system is to perform, but do not tell us under what circumstances it will perform them. In the vending machine example, we would probably want to prevent the customer from making a selection without entering coins, and to prohibit a product from being dispensed from the machine until the customer's selection and payment have been validated. Other factors or conditions that influence the enabling and disabling of processes on the DFD might also be important to identify.

A useful analogy is that of the action of a catalyst in a chemical process. A catalyst makes a chemical reaction happen without taking part in the reaction: It simply acts as a facilitator. In this same way, we need facilitators that will make the processes on the DFD "happen." Just as the catalyst enables a chemical reaction, we need to enable and disable the processes on the DFD under some specific circumstances: to specify the catalyst in our requirements model.

Two tools serve this purpose: control flow diagrams, which show the flow of catalysts (control signals) in our system, and control specifications (CSPECs or control specs), which indicate how the catalyst action (control processing) takes place. Figure 2.4 is a CFD for our vending machine system;

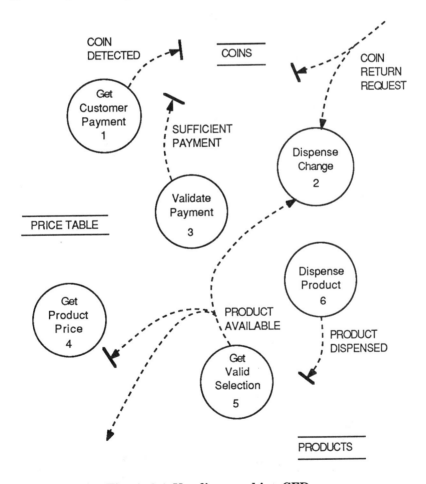

Figure 2.4. Vending machine CFD.

the processes on the CFD are the same as those in Figure 2.1, but this time we show the control signals associated with each process, represented as dashed arcs. Figures 2.5 and 2.6 show the CSPEC and additional dictionary entries respectively, for the vending machine.

CSPECs contain diagrammatic and tabular representations of finite state (FS) machines. The control signals flowing to and from the CSPEC bars on the CFDs are the inputs and outputs of these FS machines. Figure 2.5 shows

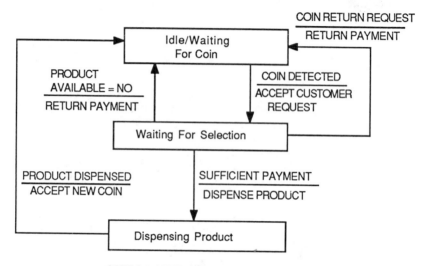

CSPEC 0: VEND PRODUCT: Sheet 1 of 2

Control Action \ Process Activated	Dispense Change 2	Dispense Product 6	Get Valid Selection 5
Accept Customer Request	0	0	1
Return Payment	1	0	0
Accept New Coin	0	0	0
Dispense Product	1	1	0

CSPEC 0: VEND PRODUCT: Sheet 2 of 2

Figure 2.5. Vending machine CSPEC.

```
COIN RETURN REQUEST = \ User request for coin
                        return\
                      2 Values: True, False.

PRODUCT AVAILABLE = \ Product  availability
                      status\
                    2 Values: Yes, No.
```

**Figure 2.6. Primitive control entries
from vending machine dictionary.**

one example consisting of two diagrams: a state transition diagram (STD) and a process activation table (PAT). State transition diagrams show the states of the system and how they are influenced by control signals. They respond to events represented by control flows and show the corresponding action that the system must take. Events and actions are represented on STDs as "Event/Action" labels on each of the transitions between the states. Process activation tables show the circumstances under which the processes on a DFD are enabled and disabled. The actions from an STD enter a PAT, which enables and disables the appropriate processes. Like the DFDs and PSPECs, the CFDs and CSPECs are supported by the requirements diction- ary, which contains the definition of all the control signals in the system.

Processes that are not controlled from a CSPEC are "data triggered," that is, they are enabled each time there is sufficient data at their inputs to per- form the specified function. The functions of the system, as represented in a DFD, are modeled independently of when they are supposed to be enabled or disabled; the control requirements of the system then act as the catalyst that makes the system functions happen.

Requirements model summary

The whole system requirements model is a cohesive statement about the sys- tem's data flow (shown in the DFDs), data processing (shown in the PSPECs), control flow (shown in the CFDs), and control processing (shown in the CSPECs). These components interconnect with each other as shown in Figure 2.7.

The components illustrated, and the chapters in which they are explained in more detail, are described and listed below:

- Data flow diagrams decompose the system and its functions (Chapters 4 and 12).

- Process specifications specify in concise terms each detail of the sys- tem's functional requirements. Control flows generated inside PSPECs through tests on data flows are called "data conditions." They flow on

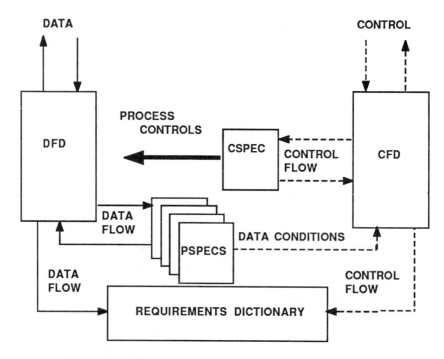

Figure 2.7. The structure of the requirements model.

CFDs, not DFDs, where they are treated as any other control flows (Chapters 4 and 13).

- Control flow diagrams map control flows along the same paths as the data flows may travel; the bar symbol indicates CSPEC interfaces. CFDs mirror the processes and stores of DFDs, but do not show data flows (Chapters 5 and 12).

- Control specifications specify control processing—controls for the processes on the DFD. They are made up of various components, some of which you have seen in the earlier part of this chapter (see also Chapters 5 and 14).

- The response time specification defines the limits on response time allowed between events at the system input terminals and the resulting events at the system output terminals (Chapters 7 and 15).

- The requirements dictionary completes the requirements model. It contains an alphabetical listing of all the data and control flows on the DFDs and CFDs along with their definitions (Chapters 8 and 16).

The requirements model is built as a layered set of DFDs and CFDs with associated PSPECs and CSPECs. Each successive level of diagrams and specifications expresses a refinement of the higher-level diagrams.

2.3 System Architecture Model

Is the requirements model a sufficient statement of the system's specification? To answer this question, we need to see if the model provides all the information we need to design the system. Part of this information is the definition of *what* the vending machine is to do, and the requirements model can certainly answer questions on that. Consider, for example, the question, Can customers request their payments be returned without making a selection?

The CSPEC STD shows that upon receiving a Coin Return Request, the system goes back to the Waiting For Coin state; the PAT in the CSPEC shows that the Return Payment action enables the Dispense Change process. But if, instead, we asked, How does the customer request the return of payment and by what mechanism is this request fulfilled? we find that the requirements model cannot provide an answer, so the answer to our question is, No, the requirements model alone is not a sufficient system specification.

Going back to our flooding river example, we first identified the problem, then saw several ways to solve it. Similarly, for the specification of systems, we need to capture not only *what* the system requirements are, but also *how* the system will fulfill those requirements.

The means for capturing this system mechanization is the architecture model, whose principal purposes are

- to show the physical entities that make up the system

- to define the information flow between these physical entities

- to specify the channels on which this information flows

These purposes are fulfilled using diagrams, supported by textual specifications and a dictionary.

Architecture flow diagrams and module specifications

The architecture flow diagram (AFD) is the primary tool depicting the system architecture. It shows the physical partitioning of the system into its component pieces, or modules, and the information flow between them. Its main purpose is to allocate the functional processes of the requirements model to physical units of the system, and to add more processes as needed to support the new physical interfaces. Figure 2.8 shows an AFD containing the main

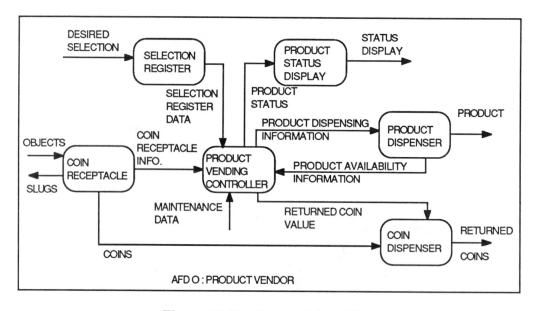

Figure 2.8. Vending machine AFD.

physical units of the vending machine system; the requirements model data processes, PSPECs, and CSPECs are divided into groups that are allocated to these architecture modules.

Just as DFDs are supported by PSPECs and a requirements dictionary, so the AFDs are supported by architecture module specifications (AMSs) and an architecture dictionary (AD). Module specifications define the inputs, outputs, and processes allocated from the requirements model for each architecture module. The architecture dictionary contains the data and control flow definitions of the requirements dictionary, plus the allocation of these flows to architecture modules. Figures 2.9 and 2.10 show a sample AMS and partial architecture dictionary for the vending machine example.

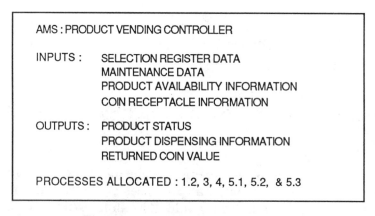

Figure 2.9. Vending machine AMS.

FLOW NAME	COMPOSED OF	ORIGIN MODULE	DESTINATION MODULE
OBJECTS	[COINS | SLUGS]	EXTERNAL	COIN RECEPTACLE
COINS	QUARTERS + NICKELS + DIMES	COIN RECEPTACLE	PRODUCT VENDING CONTROLLER
PRODUCTS	⎡ SODA ⎤ ⎢ CANDY ⎢ ⎣ GUM ⎦	PRODUCT DISPENSER	EXTERNAL

Figure 2.10. Vending machine architecture dictionary entries.

Architecture interconnect diagrams and specifications

In addition to the physical entities and the information flow between them, we need to capture *how* the information flows from one architecture module to another, and for this we use the architecture interconnect diagram (AID). The AID shows the actual physical information channels between the AFD's architecture modules and to and from the environment. The AID is supported by architecture interconnect specifications (AISs), textual specifications that specify the characteristics of the communication channels. Figures 2.11 and 2.12 show an AID and AIS for the vending machine example.

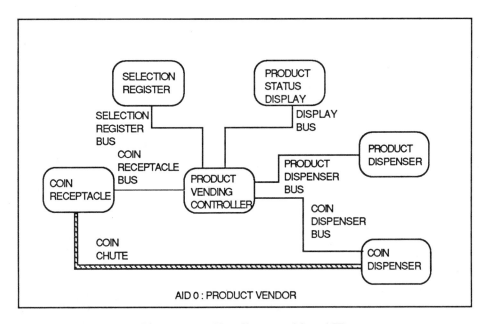

Figure 2.11. Vending machine AID.

AIS : PRODUCT DISPENSER BUS

The information on this bus will be sent
as a discrete signal containing 8 serial
bits. The product information will be encoded
into the 256 combinations.

The characteristics of this bus will be

High = 5 +/- 0.2 Volts
Low = Ground

Figure 2.12. Vending machine AIS.

The architecture dictionary also captures the allocation of data and control flows to specific interconnect channels. Figure 2.13 shows an example of
flows allocated to communication channels.

FLOW NAME	COMPOSED OF	ORIGIN	DESTINATION	CHANNEL
OBJECTS	[COINS | SLUGS]	EXTERNAL	COIN RECEPTACLE	EXTERNAL
COINS	QUARTERS + NICKELS + DIMES	COIN RECEPTACLE	PRODUCT VENDING CONTROLLER	COIN RECEPTACLE BUS
PRODUCTS	SODA CANDY GUM	PRODUCT DISPENSER	EXTERNAL	EXTERNAL

Figure 2.13. Augmented vending machine architecture dictionary.

Architecture model summary

After building the architecture model for the system, we can answer the
questions that could not be answered by the requirements model alone. The
complete *system specification model,* consisting of the requirements and architecture models, specifies both *what* the system is to do, and *how* its design
will be structured.

The system architecture model is a cohesive statement of the system's
physical configuration in terms of the architecture modules, the information
flow between them, and their interconnects, as illustrated in Figure 2.14.

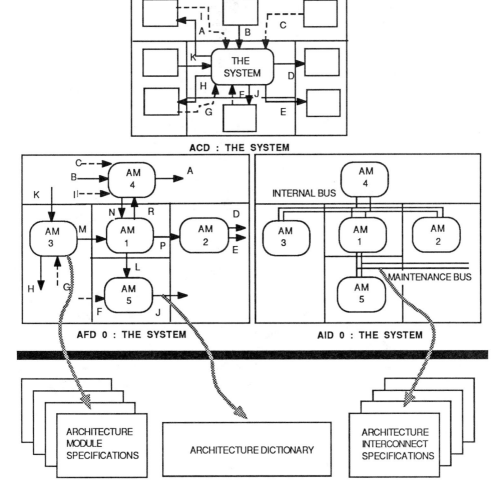

Figure 2.14. The structure of the architecture model.

The component relationships illustrated, described in detail in Parts IV and V, are

- The architecture flow diagram shows the physical configuration of the system, in terms of its architecture modules and all the information flow (data and control).

- The architecture interconnect diagram shows the physical interconnect of the system components, in terms of the channels by which information flows between the architecture modules.

- The architecture module specification captures the allocation of requirements from the requirements model to specific architecture modules.

- The architecture interconnect specification captures the characteristics of the channels by which information flows between the modules.

- The architecture dictionary is an enhancement of the requirements dictionary. It captures the allocation of all the data and control flows to architecture modules and the channels on which they flow.

The system architecture model consists of a layered set of AFDs and AIDs and their associated AMSs and AISs. Each successive layer refines the configuration defined by the higher-level diagrams.

2.4   System Specification Model

Figure 2.15 illustrates the requirements and the architecture models together forming the total system specification model. The two component models are shown side-by-side to emphasize that they cannot be developed sequentially, that is, we cannot completely develop one and not think about the other. The system requirements and architecture are interrelated and must be developed in parallel.

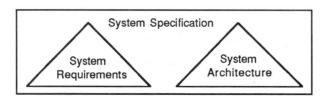

**Figure 2.15. The formation of the system
specification.**

As the flooding river example showed, a given set of requirements can have many possible solutions depending on the decisions and tradeoffs made when transforming a technology-independent requirements statement into a technology-dependent architecture model. It is these decisions and tradeoffs that cause the iterations between the requirements and architecture models implied by Figure 2.16.

In developing the architecture model, we allocate the requirements model to architecture modules and add the following:

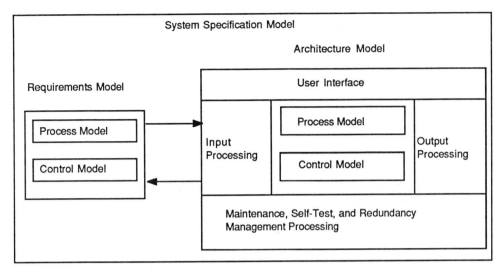

Figure 2.16. Requirements-to-architecture iterative loop.

- user interface processing

- input processing

- output processing

- maintenance, self-test, and redundancy processing

Why does the transformation process add more viewpoints? Any system has to be accessed by users, whether people or other automated systems. This access requires that we have specific interfaces between the system and its environment. The architecture model resolves these interfaces in the form of user interface processing.

In the case of the vending machine example, this means resolving the mechanics of how the customer enters coins, makes product selections, and receives the selected products. The system-to-maintainer interface specification defines maintenance and self-test processing, which, for the vending machine, is the mechanism by which the system maintainer loads new products, empties the coin box, and changes product prices. The system-to-system interface identifies input and output processing, but since the vending machine is a stand-alone system, it does not have any, and being a noncritical system, neither does it have any redundancy requirements.

Overall, then, the transformation of the system requirements model into an architecture model is an iterative process that resolves all the interfaces and allocates the requirements to architecture modules through tradeoffs and design decisions. The result is a fully integrated system specification covering both the functional requirements and the physical design.

2.5   The Development Life Cycle

Iterative development

The iterative nature of the specification process, described in the previous section, is contrary to the traditional view of the systems development life cycle. In this traditional view, the development life cycle is pictured as a sequential set of finite duration activities, or as a waterfall, in which activity flows from one level of development to the next without ever returning.

This view obscures the true nature of systems development: It has always been an iterative process in which any given step can feed back and modify decisions made in a preceding one. Failure to recognize this fact has been a major difficulty in project management, giving an erroneous feeling of warmth (We are done with requirements! We can proceed with design!).

We need techniques, then, that support the iterative nature of systems development. An integrated set of structured methods provides this support naturally because the models provide visibility and consistency throughout the entire system definition. Changes fed back from later stages of development become easy to incorporate, and their impact easy to assess.

In the specification of any system, we establish the requirements and the architecture for the system as a whole, for the hardware, and for the software, as shown in Figure 2.17. The techniques covered in this book can be used for all of these purposes.

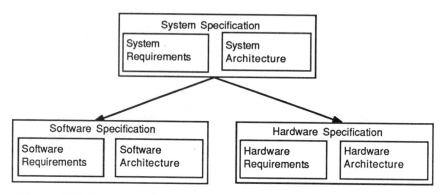

Figure 2.17. System, software, and hardware specification structure.

Hierarchical representation

The models create a hierarchical layering of system specifications, consistent with the hierarchical nature of systems in general. By layering the specifications in this manner, we are able to stabilize the upper levels, which helps in the later development of lower levels. There are usually constraints on the higher system levels that can be incorporated early in the specification process, establishing the "big picture" before proceeding on into more detail.

The life cycle diagram shown in Figure 2.18 takes into account the iterative and concurrent nature of the development process, and the hierarchical layering of systems. This model more accurately represents what actually happens, or should happen, during systems development.

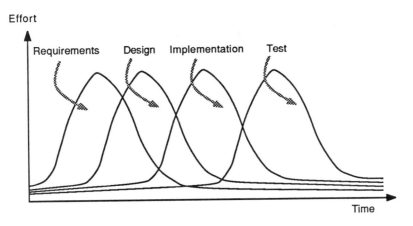

Figure 2.18. Overlapping systems development phases.

The diagram shows that all the life cycle activities start concurrently, and vary in effort and scope as the development proceeds. Initially, the major activity is requirements definition, with less, but not zero, effort on the other activities.

The need for early testing activities

You might wonder why we would want to devote any time to testing up-front. There are several reasons. Traditionally, testing and maintainability have been afterthoughts, but over the whole system life cycle they are as important as any of the other factors. So, while we gather functional and architectural requirements, we should also be gathering testing and maintainability requirements. The second reason for doing up-front testing is that the test equipment needs to be specified and designed early in the cycle so that it will be ready in time for system test. A third reason is that the best time to give active thought to verification and validation of the functional and architectural requirements—what criteria we will need to test that these requirements have been correctly implemented—is while compiling them.

This model of the life cycle shows that defining the requirements does not just end abruptly, but that new requirements appear, and existing requirements change, as the development proceeds.

The total life cycle

The development of a system requires many iterations of activities that were thought of as "phases" in the waterfall life cycle model. Each iteration requires varying degrees of effort and emphasis on these different activities. As shown in the life cycle model of Figure 2.18, the early iterations require more effort on system specification, while progressively later iterations require more emphasis on implementation and testing.

Figure 2.19 [1] shows two views of the iterative life cycle model of Figure 2.18. Systems development starts with a statement of the goals and objectives of the system, followed by the first iteration that might result in a feasibility report, and finally, through many iterations, an operational system will result.

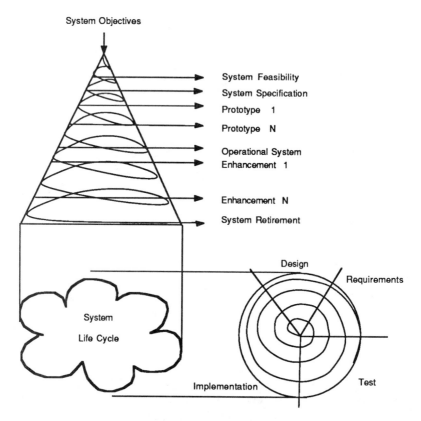

Figure 2.19. Development life cycle spiral.

Although this might be the end of the *development* life cycle of the product, it is certainly not the end of the *product* life cycle. Once an operational system has been produced, that system must be enhanced or modified based on changing customer requirements. Thus, during the product life cycle beyond delivery of the operational system, there may be several other iterations of the product development activities. These iterations continue until the product is retired and no longer maintained, or it is redeveloped with new functionality, using new technology.

The requirements and architecture methods support this iterative nature of systems development. At the uppermost levels, during the early stages of establishing product feasibility and system specification, the methods can be used to perform system requirements partitioning and architecture allocation. They can also be used for specification of the detailed hardware and software components.

Several benefits result from applying the methods early in the development process:

- The early partitioning and allocation of the system leads to systematic identification of critical functions and units, which can then be prototyped or otherwise evaluated.

- The impact of enhancements and modifications that will be made to the system specification after system delivery becomes more visible and the planning of these changes becomes more manageable.

- As the system is modified or enhanced, the methods provide the traceability to better implement and test the modified system.

The point here is that the systems development process is not ended with the delivery of an operational system, and the total life cycle cost of a system is not just the initial development cost but the total cost expended until the system is retired. How the initial development is conducted can have far-reaching impact on the total system life cycle cost. The methods can help reduce this total cost by effectively, accurately, rigorously, and unambiguously capturing the system's specification, which not only benefits the development life cycle but the entire product life cycle.

Development life cycle summary

At every phase of the life cycle, we are specifying requirements and architecture of one level of the system or another. The methods allow us to produce a layered set of specifications, rather than a single specification, corresponding to the layers of the system hierarchy. At the same time, it is important to recognize that we are developing complete systems, not separate pieces of hardware, or software, or processes. It is essential, therefore, that the deliverables—system, software, or hardware specifications—integrate to provide a consistent, rigorous, and unambiguous view of the entire system and its component pieces.

The strategies described in this book not only provide these deliverables, but also ensure traceability between them.

2.6 Structured Methods: What They Are Not

Structured methods are not the cure to everything that ails systems development. We are not suggesting that these methods alone can or should be construed as any guarantee of a perfect systems development process. Other activities such as scheduling, resource allocation, project-tracking methods, and sound management techniques should and must be carried out as before. Structured methods are just one possible set of tools from which to choose when developing a system. A project or program team must decide how and why they are going to use them, so that there is a clear understanding of the role they will play in the systems development life cycle.

The methods will not do your thinking for you, but their built-in consistency checks and organized structure will help you find discrepancies and incompleteness in your thinking. They will not deliver your implemented system: *You* must make sure it is implemented properly. Beware of letting formal methods sway you into thinking that the systems development process somehow ends with the delivery of structured documentation. This is not so. The methods must be used in conjunction with other activities to deliver a system to the user, and you must judge how they best fit into that process.

The best way to view the methods is as a tool box. Use whatever you need whenever you need it. But before you decide to use anything from the tool box you must decide what it will do for you. Don't use a hammer to chop wood!

2.7 Summary

- The methods detailed in this book are the requirements model and the architecture model, which describe *what* the system must do and *how* the design will be structured. The book does not address the actual system implementation.

- The requirements model consists of data flow diagrams, process specifications, control flow diagrams, control specifications, timing specifications, and a requirements dictionary.

- The architecture model consists of architecture flow diagrams, architecture interconnect diagrams, architecture module specifications, architecture interconnect specifications, and an architecture dictionary.

- The architecture model adds nonfunctional requirements beyond the functional ones included in the requirements model.

- The systems development process is iterative both on the micro and macro scales. Contrary to the traditional view, most development activities should take place in parallel, and interact with each other.

- Structured methods are tools that assist in certain parts of the development process. They do not replace good, established project management practices.

PART II

The Requirements Model

Chapter 3

Overview

Our strategy is to establish what the desired end product is, before describing how to produce it. Consequently, in Part II, we describe in detail the completed requirements model, as it would be received by the user, and in Part III, we describe *how* to construct the model. The principal tools of the requirements model are flow diagrams: graphical models of signal flows and processes acting on those flows. Flow diagrams consist of data flow diagrams and control flow diagrams. The former are essentially the same as the DFDs of DeMarco [4]; the latter are similar to DFDs but with some important and unique differences.

The other components of the requirements model are process specifications and the requirements dictionary (which are similar to DeMarco's mini-specifications and data dictionary), and control specifications (which are unique to this method).

You might wonder why we are describing here those parts of the method that have been described so often, and so well, before. The answer is, first, that we want the book to stand alone as a complete description of the whole method. Second, the earlier descriptions allowed a commendable degree of flexibility in the ways the method could be used. This has resulted in many different conventions being adopted in its use. It is therefore important to explain the particular conventions *we* have adopted in extending the method. If you have already been using "basic" structured analysis, you might very well find that some of our conventions are quite different from yours.

Key features of the method are

- It is a purely abstract model of the requirements, not a physical model of the design. It thus represents *what* has to be designed, not *how* to design it.

35

- It is diagrammatic, exploiting our ability to absorb visual information more effectively than textual or verbal information ("a picture is worth a thousand words").

- It hides unnecessary detail at any given level, and provides for progressive decomposition from that level down—the information hiding, abstraction, and decomposition principles put forward by Parnas [13]—thus allowing presentation of the requirements from a top-level overview down to the most intricate detail.

- It meets the needs of large, complex systems, including real-time systems, for representation of a process structure and a control structure. It does this by integrating DeMarco's structured analysis with finite state machine theory. Neither of the methods alone can meet these needs.

- It has built-in consistency checks within and between all its components. This feature of structured analysis has been extended to the whole structure, taking the guesswork out of the rigor and consistency of the model.

- It is self-indexing, another feature of structured analysis that has been successfully extended. It is easy to find your way around the resulting model without referring to page or paragraph numbers (although formal documentation requirements usually force us to keep these numbers).

The first of these features—the abstract nature of the model—deserves special emphasis, because it seems to be the one that newcomers to the method find hardest to grasp. Perhaps the best way to approach it is to understand the motivation for wanting such a feature, and this is best understood by reviewing the history of structured methods development.

Although structured methods generally represent their subject matter in a top-down fashion, the methods themselves have evolved in a bottom-up fashion. As software-based systems grew larger and more complex, the first obvious problem to be overcome was unmanageable and incomprehensible code. The need to solve this problem gave rise to structured programming in the form of constraints on module size, entry and exit points, branching, and so on. It also gave rise to high order languages, and, more recently, to program design languages.

Structured programming improved the quality of the code within individual modules, but still, as systems continued to grow in size and complexity, the interactions *between* the modules became as complex as the earlier code had been. Structured design methods, in which modules are constrained to communicate with each other in an organized way, were developed to deal with this complexity. These methods improved the quality of the software structure external to the modules, such that if both structured design and structured programming methods were conscientiously applied, the resulting system would work exactly as the designer intended.

Unfortunately, it still often happens that what the designer intended is not what the user wanted! The reason for this is that as the technology allows us to make systems that have ever larger capacity and complexity, the requirements themselves for such systems become large, complex, and difficult to describe and understand. Thus, the need was established for a method to represent the functional requirements of a system in an organized and understandable way, and in a way that is entirely independent of the eventual design and implementation of the system. Given such a model, various designs can be developed and compared without changing the requirements representation.

DeMarco's structured analysis method was designed to meet this need for data processing systems, and the extended structured analysis method described here was designed to meet the need for more general systems.

The model does, unfortunately, have a machine-like appearance; moreover, we are used to models that *are* intended to represent the actual design structure or implementation. As should now be clear, this is *not* the intent here. Again, it is a purely abstract model, with highly idealized properties, whereby each of its processes is independently data triggered and infinitely fast—unlikely characteristics for a real system. These properties are deliberately chosen for the very reason that we *can* ignore the constraints of the physical world, and concentrate exclusively on the required functionality.

As we build a requirements model, we follow this separation principle by including those characteristics that are of concern to the users, and deliberately excluding those that are not. The latter are left to the designer, and the moment we allow them to migrate into the requirements model, then we are including items that are *not* requirements; in so doing, we are placing unnecessary and artificial constraints on the designer.

We will remind you of this property at appropriate places throughout Parts II and III to emphasize its importance in each aspect of the model.

3.1   The Structure of the Model

Figure 3.1 is a composite chart, which enlarges on the diagram of Figure 2.7, and illustrates how the major components of the requirements model relate to each other. We will describe the major roles and relationships of these components before going into their individual details in the following chapters.

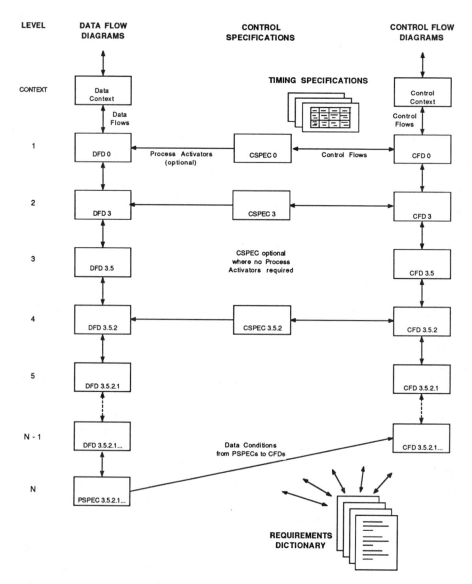

Figure 3.1. Composite chart of the requirements model.

At the top of Figure 3.1 are the data context diagram and the control context diagram. These show, respectively, the data and the control signals flowing between the system and the external entities with which the system must communicate. They also show the overall function of the system in the form of a single process. These diagrams represent the highest-level, or most abstract, view of the requirements, and show the central role the system is required to perform within its external environment.

Next (below the context diagrams in Figure 3.1) are two more flow diagrams—the level 1 DFD and CFD. They too represent the overall function of the system in graphical form, but in somewhat more detail than the context diagrams.

Below the level 1 diagrams are level 2 diagrams. For purposes of illustration, the figure shows just one DFD and one CFD at level 2, but, in fact, each of the several subprocesses on the level 1 diagrams may have its own level 2 DFD and CFD, so there will be several diagrams at this level. Just as the level 1 diagrams represent a more detailed statement of the system's purpose, so the level 2 diagrams represent more detailed statements of the purposes of the subprocesses on the level 1 diagram.

Similarly, level 3 diagrams decompose the processes and signal flows on the level 2 diagrams into more detailed statements, with a further multiplication of the number of diagrams. This decomposition continues level by level, each step revealing finer and finer details of the originally stated system's purpose.

The decomposition ends, for any given subprocess on the DFD side, with a concise statement of the purpose of a process using simple text, equations, tables, or diagrams. This statement constitutes a process specification, as illustrated at the bottom of the column of DFDs. A process that is described by a process specification is called a functional primitive, or just a primitive.

On the CFD side, the decomposition parallels that of the DFDs, but some of the control signals flow to and from control specifications, shown in the center column of Figure 3.1. The CSPECs describe the finite state machine functions of the system, which we will discuss in Chapter 6. Each CSPEC is associated with a specific CFD—the one adjacent to it in the diagram. It will usually control processes, but only those in the specific DFD adjacent to it in the figure. This close association of a DFD, CFD, and CSPEC is an important part of the structure and self-consistency properties of the requirements model.

The system input-to-output timing requirements are shown in the timing specification, shown between the context and level 1 diagrams (and detailed in Chapter 7). These specifications simply list events that are detected at the system inputs (the system stimuli), the corresponding events that are required to occur at the system outputs (the system responses), and the timing constraints within which the system must generate these responses.

Finally, Figure 3.1 shows the requirements dictionary. Although it is shown outside the main structure, the RD serves a vital role throughout the model since it contains precise definitions of all the data and control flows in all their levels of decomposition.

The remaining chapters of Part II describe each component of the method in detail, but it is important not to lose track of how they fit into the overall structure of Figure 3.1 as you study them.

For the purposes of this description, we refer to the DFDs and PSPECs as the *process model,* the CFDs and CSPECs as the *control model,* and the two of them with the requirements dictionary and timing specifications as the *requirements model.* This is in keeping with the evolution of the methods: The process model corresponds to the classical structured analysis model; the control model is the part we added, derived from finite state machine theory; and the requirements model is the complete, integrated combination of the two.

Chapter 4

The Process Model

The composite chart of Figure 3.1 is repeated in Figure 4.1 with the process model highlighted. As we summarized in the last chapter, and can see from Figure 4.1, this model consists of data flow diagrams and process specifications. Its purpose is to specify the information processing requirements of the system.

4.1 Data Context Diagrams

Context diagrams are just special cases of data and control flow diagrams, but they serve such a special and important role in the model that they merit special attention. They identify the external entities (typically, other systems, operators, users, communication channels, and so on) with which we require the system to communicate, and state the major purpose of the system in the form of a single system process. Context diagrams are of major importance because they summarize the central requirement to accept certain inputs, perform some actions on these inputs according to the stated system purpose, and so generate certain outputs.

As we saw in Figures 3.1 and 4.1, the data context diagram (DCD) shows the data flowing between the system being specified and the external entities with which it must communicate. The control context diagram (CCD) shows the same information for control flows (we will discuss the distinction between data and control flows later).

An example of a data context diagram is presented in Figure 4.2. The DCD consists of terminators, data flows, and a single process; these are its only components. The process is shown as a circle or bubble. Terminators (sometimes referred to as "externals") are shown as rectangles, and represent the external entities with which the system must communicate. They are also called sources and sinks depending on whether they transmit or receive

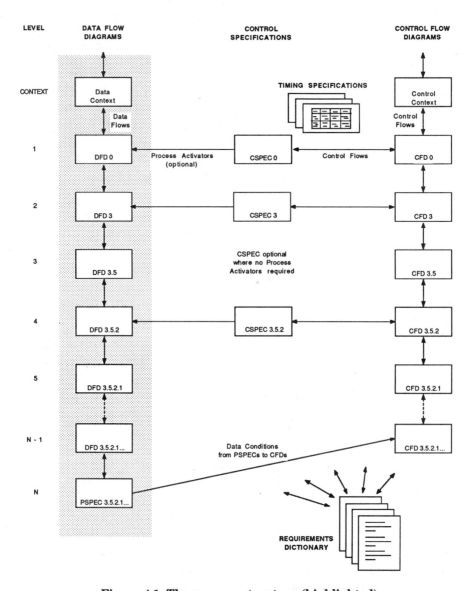

Figure 4.1. The process structure (highlighted).

data. Data flows are the communication links between the terminators and the process, and are shown as directed arcs. You will notice that some of the terminators in the diagram appear to be unused—they are not connected to anything. In fact, they *are* used in the associated control context diagram, and are shown in the DCD as a useful reminder of that fact. We will examine each of the components of a DCD in detail.

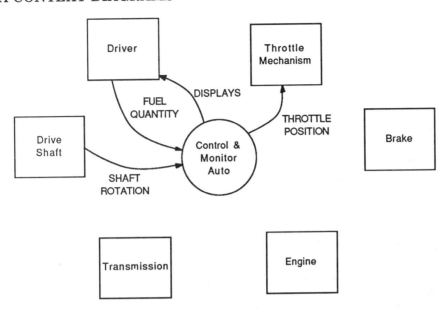

Figure 4.2. Data context diagram.

The context process

The single process in a context diagram represents the whole system to be specified. Its symbol is a circle containing a descriptive name for the central role of the system, such as Control & Monitor Auto or Perform Flight Management. As with all process names, this name represents the pure logical function of the system or process, that is, without regard to its eventual physical form. In conventional structured analysis, this logical form is followed by a physical analysis using essentially the same model, but here we replace that approach with the architecture model described in Parts IV and V. The requirements model, then, represents the pure functional requirements while ignoring the design and implementation; the architecture model takes this pure functional statement and develops a particular design structure from it.

System inputs and outputs

The flow arcs show the names and directions of data that flow to and from the system process. These arcs represent the data flows that will eventually appear at the input/output terminals of the implemented system. The model so far, then, illustrates that the system is to receive certain data, transform that data according to the brief function statement in the context process, and so produce the stated output data.

The term "data flow," or sometimes just "data" or "flow," is used here in a rather broad sense. The methods are general enough to cover any kind of process acting on any kind of object. The objects may include, for example, materials on a manufacturing plant's conveyor system, written information provided by a bank customer, data manually entered into a computer terminal, analog electrical signals into an autopilot system, or digital data signals on a data communication link. They are all categorized as data flows from the point of view of this model.

Terminators

The terminators (sources and sinks) show the external entities from and to which the data flows; that is, the entities with which the system is required to interface. In Figure 4.2, they are Drive Shaft, Throttle Mechanism, Driver, and so on. These entities may be anything with which communication is possible—computers, automated manufacturing systems, pilots, bank customers, telephone switching networks, and so on. What they have in common, apart from communicating with our system, is that they are *outside the scope of our system*. This highlights a central role of context diagrams: They divide the universe into objects and processes that are part of our system (that is, contained in the context process), and those that are outside of it.

4.2   Data Flow Diagrams

Figure 4.3 illustrates a data flow diagram. It contains processes, data flows, and data stores, but not terminators. The processes and data flows are simi-

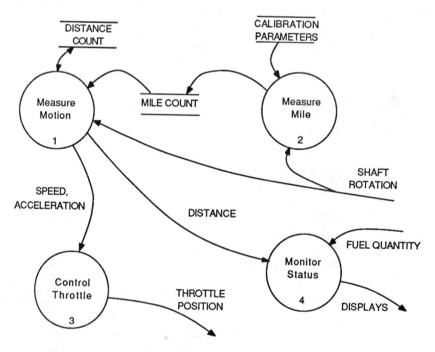

Figure 4.3. Data flow diagram.

lar to those on the data context diagram. Data stores represent data stored for later use by a process, and are indicated by pairs of parallel lines with names between them. Because of its appearance, the DFD is frequently called a bubble diagram or bubble chart.

Every DFD in a leveled set is a decomposition of a process at the next higher level, and is assigned the same name and number as that process. For example, the DFD in Figure 4.3 is a decomposition of the context process in Figure 4.2. The process is decomposed into subprocesses, and its input/output flows into subflows. In addition, new flows are introduced between the subprocesses. It is important to emphasize that these subprocesses and subflows do *not* make *new* statements about the system; they simply make more *detailed* statements about it.

A DFD is referred to as the child of the process it decomposes; conversely, that process is the parent of the DFD. In referring to multi-level DFDs, the analogy is extended to grandparents, grandchildren, ancestors, descendants, and so on.

Processes

The purpose of a process is simply to produce its outputs from its inputs according to the action implied by its name. At any given level of abstraction, this transformation is stated to a corresponding level of abstraction, but the combination of all its descendant decompositions eventually states the transformation in exact detail.

The names of processes represent actions, and they always start with a verb followed by an object on which that verb acts—for example, Predict Fuel At Destination, or Find Remaining Account Balance. Data flows, on the other hand, are objects, and their names—such as Sensor Data, or Account Balance—*never* contain verbs.

Transaction centers

There is a particular structure of processes and flows that may constitute all or part of a DFD, and that occurs often enough to merit a special name and special mention. It is called the transaction center, and two forms in which it may occur are shown in Figure 4.4. It occurs when one of several alternative actions is to be taken on one set of data, such as deciding whether to enter a customer's deposit into a checking, savings, or IRA account, or whether to make a loan payment with it. The action of a transaction center could be as simple as setting a discrete-valued signal to one of its several different values.

The control of transaction centers sometimes needs special attention, and this will be discussed in Section 5.6.

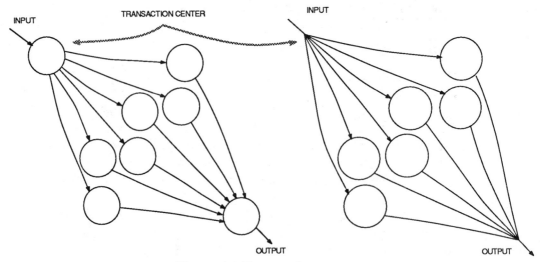

Figure 4.4. Transaction centers.

4.3   Leveling and Balancing

Since a DFD and its parent process represent the same information at different levels of detail, their inputs and outputs must be identical. The sources and destinations of these inputs and outputs are therefore not labeled on the DFD, and appear to be flowing from and to nowhere (see Figure 4.3). In fact, their sources and destinations can be found simply by referring to the parent process. In other kinds of diagrams, conventional block diagrams, for example, off-page connectors are used, but these are not needed in data flow diagrams.

This decomposition of DFDs into increasingly detailed diagrams is called leveling, and is illustrated in Figure 4.5, where four levels of decomposition are superimposed. If you imagine all the higher-level bubbles in this figure stripped away, it becomes clear that the set of diagrams *could* be shown as a single network of all the primitives. The higher-level diagrams are abstractions of that single network, merely collecting together the primitive processes into ever larger groups. Figure 4.6 shows the same four diagrams separated out, with additional information discussed in the following section.

As is stated above, a correct parent/child pair must have the same input and output data flows. If there is a discrepancy between the two, then a flow has been shown that either does not come from anywhere or is not used anywhere. This is equivalent to contradictory statements in different parts of a traditional narrative document in which there is usually no sure way of finding the contradiction. In DFDs, checking for such inconsistencies is a straightforward procedure, which can either be done manually or can be au-

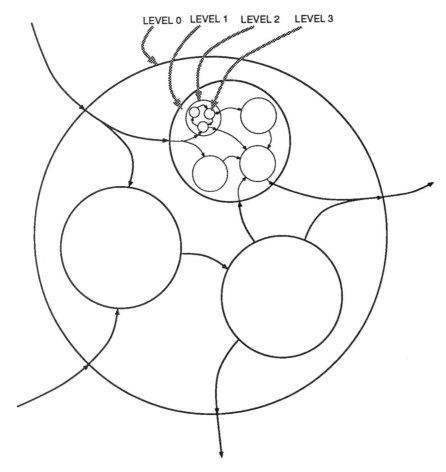

Figure 4.5. Four levels of data flow diagrams superimposed.

tomated. This procedure is known as *balancing,* and is one of the principal self-consistency checks of the requirements model.

4.4 The Numbering System

As we have seen in Section 4.2, each process is assigned a name descriptive of its function; it is also assigned a number, consisting of the number of its parent process with one more digit added. Thus, the child diagram of process 3.2.4 "Manage Flight Plan," is labeled "DFD 3.2.4 Manage Flight Plan," and its processes have numbers 3.2.4.1, 3.2.4.2, 3.2.4.3, and so on. In practice, the processes are often labeled simply .1, .2, .3, and so on, since it is understood that they are prefixed by the DFD number. Figure 4.6 illustrates the numbering system.

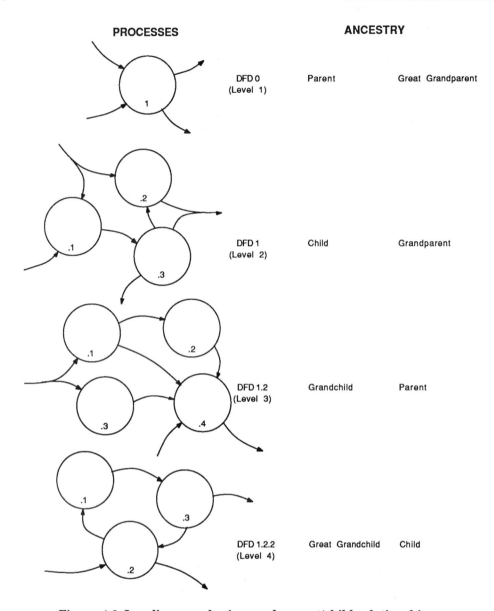

Figure 4.6. Leveling, numbering, and parent/child relationships.

By convention, the single process in a context diagram is assigned the number 0 (though this number is usually not shown), and hence the level 1 DFD is also numbered 0. Processes on a level 1 DFD have single-digit numbers: 1, 2, 3, and up. Level 2 DFDs inherit the single-digit numbers of their parent processes, while their processes have two-digit numbers. Processes on DFD 2, for example, are numbered 2.1, 2.2, 2.3, and so on. Thus, the number of digits in the process numbers in a given DFD is the same as the level number of that DFD—a very convenient way to identify the level of a flow diagram. The number of digits in the DFD number is one less than the DFD's level number.

Figure 4.6 illustrates these level and process numbering conventions, as well as the parent/child relationships.

4.5 Data Flows

Data flows may represent anything from a single item of information to a group of any number of items. When the flow represents a group, its name is descriptive of that whole group. Group flows decompose into subgroups and eventually into primitive, single-item flows. The parent/child analogy used with DFDs is used also with data flows: The subgroups of a group are its children and the group flow is their parent. Figure 4.7 shows examples of ways to group and decompose data flows.

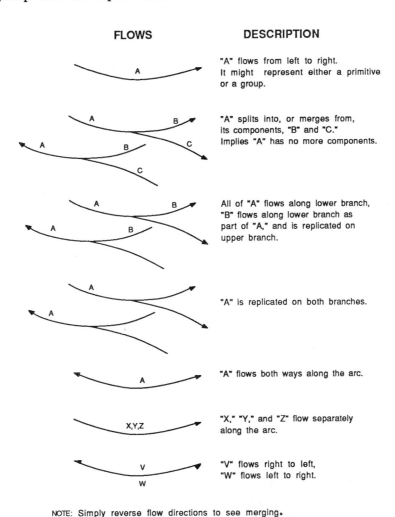

FLOWS   DESCRIPTION

"A" flows from left to right.
It might   represent either a primitive
or a group.

"A" splits into, or merges from,
its components, "B" and "C."
Implies "A" has no more components.

All of "A" flows along lower branch,
"B" flows along lower branch as
part of "A," and is replicated on
upper branch.

"A" is replicated on both branches.

"A" flows both ways along the arc.

"X," "Y," and "Z" flow separately
along the arc.

"V" flows right to left,
"W" flows left to right.

NOTE: Simply reverse flow directions to see merging.
All the flow branching variations may also occur
between levels.

Figure 4.7. Data flows.

Group flows are frequently decomposed as they pass from a parent to a child diagram, as illustrated in Figure 4.8. In such cases, on the child diagram, the subflow name will be followed by the parent flow name in parentheses to identify the source on the parent diagram, as shown in the figure. Occasionally, a flow may decompose in the upward direction, that is, while passing from a child to a parent diagram. In such cases, the child flows will appear on the parent diagram and will reference the parent flow on the child diagram.

Flows may also decompose and combine on a single diagram by splitting and merging the flow arcs. The trunk will be labeled with the parent name and the branches with the names of the children. Splitting and merging of arcs can also show one flow going to or from more than one place. In such cases, the trunk is labeled and one or more of the branches is not, implying that a branch carries the same data as the trunk. Figures 4.7 and 4.8 demonstrate these splitting and merging principles. Note that no processing takes place at the branch and merge points. Members of group flows are not combined in any way, so they are free to separate at will. The reason for grouping them, and for using the branching and merging constructs, is to condense the information and de-clutter the diagram.

Where there are several ungrouped flows in the same direction between two processes, they are sometimes shown on the same arc with their names separated by commas or some other convenient delimiter, as illustrated by the flow labeled X, Y, Z in Figure 4.7. This is done when the flows are unrelated, and therefore cannot be grouped together under a single descriptive name.

Where flows move in opposite directions between the same two processes, the half-arrow convention may be used. In Figure 4.7, "V" flows in the direction marked by a half-arrow that is shown on the same side of the arc as the name "V." Flows in the other direction, and their half-arrow, are shown on the other side of the arc, as in our example in which "W" flows from left to right.

All data flows—groups, subgroups, and primitives—are exactly defined in the dictionary as described in Chapter 8. This provides a second principal self-consistency check within the requirements model. Whereas processes are verified for consistency by balancing from the context level all the way

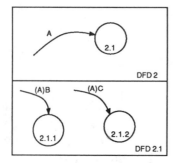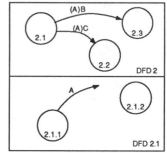

Figure 4.8. Splitting flows between levels.

to the PSPECs, data flows are verified by cross-checking that every one is defined in the dictionary and that the definitions for groups and subgroups are consistent with each other.

4.6 Data Stores

The third and final component of a DFD is the data store. Referring back to Figure 4.3, we see that DISTANCE COUNT, CALIBRATION PARAMETERS, and MILE COUNT are data stores. In this method, we use the convention that a data flow is present and can be read and reread any number of times by a receiving process until its source process stops generating it. The contents of a data store, on the other hand, are present, and can be read and reread any number of times by a receiving process, *until they are replaced by new data arriving at the store.* The store thus has the effect of sustaining the output of a process until it produces a new output. For example, consider a store containing an aircraft's flight plan. Usually, the plan will be updated prior to each flight. This stored data will be read many times during the flight, and will then be updated again prior to the next flight.

The above conventions differ somewhat from those used for traditional structured analysis, where both data flows and data stores have destructive readout. Nondestructive readout has proved to be a more useful convention and is closer to the physical reality in a computer.

Data stores are named with the data they contain, following the same naming conventions in every respect as are applied to data in a data flow. Unlabeled flows to or from a store carry the whole data group of the store. Flows carrying subgroups of the stored data are labeled with the subgroup names (note the close correspondence with branching and merging data flows). Data stores may be read-only (constants), read-write (data produced by a process for later use), or both. Write-only stores would serve no useful purpose, so they are not used.

Consistent with the nonredundancy principal of the requirements method, a given data store appears on one DFD only. If its outputs or inputs are used on other diagrams, they flow there as data flows in the usual way. Sometimes, however, on that one DFD, a store may appear more than once—this is done to simplify a complex diagram, for example, to keep the flow lines short.

4.7 Process Specifications

The decomposition of a process continues until a level is reached at which the process can be described concisely and briefly in a process specification, or PSPEC. These processes are called functional primitives or just primitives. The principle is that at some point there is little room left for ambiguity or confusion, and we revert to a narrative definition that may consist of little more than an expansion of the name of the process. PSPECs are almost always less than one page long, and are often only a few lines long. Primitive processes may occur at any level, and often occur at different levels within a single model.

A PSPEC is the child of the process it describes, so the principles of leveling and balancing apply just as they do for parent and child DFDs. A primitive process and its PSPEC share the same inputs and outputs. Every input to the process is used within some expression in the specification, which shows how every output from the process is generated. No other flow names appear in the PSPEC; however, it is sometimes necessary to use simple internal variables to link a series of equations together, for example, or to use well-known physical and mathematical constants. Thus, the purpose of the PSPEC is to show how its outputs are generated from its inputs. It does nothing more and nothing less.

In traditional structured analysis, the basic tool of a process specification is structured English, described later in this section, but engineering systems often require PSPECs to contain equations, tables, diagrams, or charts, which leave little or no room for misinterpretation. If the process requires a large table of data or a large set of equations, such data often will be put in an appendix and referenced in the PSPEC.

Examples of typical PSPECs are shown in Figure 4.9. Note that comments sometimes are included at the end of a PSPEC. While the PSPEC proper is absolutely concise and unambiguous, comments are less formal and include background material to help the user better understand the underlying purpose of the PSPEC. Comments normally are distinguished from the main body of the specification by some convenient convention, such as preceding and following the statement with an asterisk, or putting them in a labeled Comments field.

Process specifications define all the processing required by the user or customer. They may contain further requirements that are of no direct interest to the customer, but that are necessary for the system to work. In other words, they contain all the information necessary for the designer to know *what* to do without saying *how* to do it. For example, a customer requirement might be stated as, Make an optimum estimate of the aircraft's position given the particular navigation sensors on board. This might turn out to require, for example, a sixth-order Kalman filter. The software designer would not be expected to know this, so the filter parameters must be derived by the analyst. The numerical algorithms for implementing the filter, however, would be left to the designer.

Structured English

The intent of structured English is to combine the rigor of a programming language with the readability of English. Certain types of words are pre-

PSPEC 1; Measure Motion

For each pulse of SHAFT ROTATION:

add 1 to DISTANCE COUNT

then set:

$$\text{DISTANCE} = \frac{\text{DISTANCE COUNT}}{\text{MILE COUNT}}$$

At least once per second, measure pulse rate of SHAFT ROTATION in pulses per hour, and set:

$$\text{SPEED} = \frac{\text{Pulse rate}}{\text{MILE COUNT}}$$

At least once per second, measure rate of change of SHAFT ROTATION pulses in pulses per hour per second, and set:

$$\text{ACCELERATION} = \frac{\text{Rate of change}}{\text{MILE COUNT}}$$

PSPEC 2; Measure Mile

Each time activated, start counting SHAFT ROTATION pulses.

While LOWER LIMIT $\leq$ pulse count $\leq$ UPPER LIMIT

set MILE COUNT = pulse count

otherwise

set MILE COUNT = DEFAULT COUNT

Sets MILE COUNT to the count of shaft rotation pulses if that number is within the range that reasonably represents a measured mile. Otherwise sets it to the default value.

Figure 4.9. Two examples of process specifications.

ferred, and grammatical structures are limited to very simple ones. This simplicity, together with their brevity, ensures that the specifications are unambiguous.

The types of words used are

- command verbs applied to an object (transitive, imperative verbs)

- data flow names

- prepositions and conjunctions needed to show logical relationships

- commonly understood mathematical, physical, and technical terms

- other words, as needed to meet the goals of the specification, as sparingly as possible

- mathematical equations

- illustrations such as tables, diagrams, and graphs

The structures are simple, single-entry, single-exit constructs:

- concurrency: more than one activity takes place simultaneously

- sequence: activities occur in a specified time sequence

- decision: a branch in the flow of activities is made based on the results of a test on an input

- repetition: the same activity is repeated until some specified limit or result is reached

The examples in Figure 4.10 illustrate the structures, using capitalization of flow names, and indentation to show subordination.

4.8 Interpreting the Process Model

We have now described the complete process model as originated by DeMarco [4] and others, including the particular conventions we have chosen to adopt. We have still to describe the rest of the requirements model—those parts that depart from traditional structured analysis and are unique to this method— but before doing so, we will take a look at the meaning of the data flow model. Later, in Section 9.1, we will take a similar look at the complete requirements model, to see what *it* means, and, in particular, how it affects the meaning of the basic data flow model.

Concurrency:

> Calculate NAVAID DISTANCE as great circle distance from
> > AIRCRAFT POSITION to NAVAID POSITION.
>
> Calculate ALT DIFFERENCE as
> > AIRCRAFT ALTITUDE − NAVAID ALTITUDE.
>
> Set RADIO FREQUENCY to NAVAID FREQUENCY.

Note that structured English is nonprocedural; the above specification does *not* imply that the three statements must be done in any particular order. If a particular sequence is required, it is specifically stated using the following constructs.

Sequence:

> Find INTEREST DUE as
> > RATE × INSTALLMENT PERIOD × PRINCIPAL.
>
> Next, subtract INTEREST DUE from ACCOUNT BALANCE.
>
> Next, issue REMAINING BALANCE as ACCOUNT BALANCE.

Decision:

> If ALTITUDE is greater than TRANSITION ALTITUDE, then:
>
> > set SPEED to MACH,
>
> otherwise:
>
> > set SPEED to AIRSPEED.

Repetition:

> For each member of SELECTED NAVAIDS:
>
> > Compute great circle distance between
> > > AIRCRAFT POSITION and NAVAID POSITION,
> >
> > then save result in NAV DISTANCE ARRAY in
> > > order of distance.

Figure 4.10. The structures of structured English.

A set of DFDs is a model of the requirements of a system, not a representation of the system's implementation. The model is highly idealized in that it is assumed to be data triggered and infinitely fast: Whenever data sufficient for a given process to perform its task appears at its inputs, then it *will* perform that task, and do so instantaneously. The implementation, on the other hand, almost certainly will *not* be data triggered, and will *certainly* not be infinitely fast. These characteristics were chosen deliberately to separate us from the problems of design and implementation, such as processing delays, timing budgets, foreground and background processing, and so on, and to allow us to concentrate on the pure requirements. Of course, these design and implementation considerations must be addressed eventually, but not at the requirements definition phase.

The process model assumes neither sequential nor parallel processing. Processes are free to operate in parallel as long as their data is available to do so. If the implementation calls for sequential processing, this will become an additional design constraint to be dealt with at design time.

The process model can be thought of as a huge network of primitive processes linked together by their data flows. You can visualize this by looking back at Figure 4.5—the diagram superimposes four levels of decomposition, and by thinking of it with the higher-level bubbles removed. The idea is further illustrated in Figure 4.11, in which a large primitive network is shown with its terminators attached. This cluttered representation is not very useful, but it does help us to understand what the model really represents. It is also a useful illustration of just how idealized the model really is. Each one of those primitive processes can be thought of as an independent, infinitely fast, data triggered processor; it certainly does not represent a likely configuration for the real physical system.

4.9 Summary

- A data context diagram partitions the world into two parts: One part consists of the information and processes that are within the scope of our system; the other consists of everything that is outside of that scope. A DCD also shows the information flow across the boundary between the two parts.

- Data flow diagrams illustrate the information flow and processing within our system.

- A given DFD expands on the information represented by its parent process; as a whole, a set of DFDs represents requirements statements at increasing levels of detail.

- The inputs and outputs of a process and its child DFD must match. Verifying that this is so is called balancing and is a principal consistency check of the method.

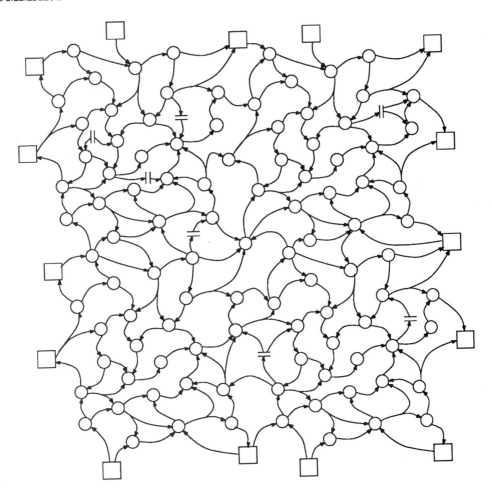

Figure 4.11. The primitive network.

- Starting with the context process, processes are progressively decomposed into more detailed diagrams: a procedure called leveling. A numbering system goes hand-in-hand with the leveling procedure, and makes the model self-indexing.

- Data flows represent the flow of information into and out of the system, and between processes. This information decomposes in parallel with the levels of detail of the DFDs.

- Data stores retain information from a flow after the source has ceased sending it. The information can then be used repeatedly until replaced by new information.

- Process specifications are brief, concise, narrative descriptions of the functions of processes at the lowest level of decomposition—primitive processes. Their traditional form is structured English, but equations, tables, diagrams, and other forms are frequently used, especially in engineering applications.

- The process model is an abstract, idealized, data triggered, infinitely fast model, intended to represent requirements, not the design or implementation.

Chapter 5

The Control Model

We are now ready to address the control structure of the requirements model—the control flow diagrams and control specifications illustrated in Figure 3.1, and repeated here in Figure 5.1 for convenience. CFDs and CSPECs are closely associated with each other and with the data structure. Overall, the purpose of the control structure is to determine what the process structure must do under any given external or internal conditions or operating modes.

Within the process structure, such decisions are restricted to the lowest level—the decision construct inside the PSPECs. The decisions made by the control structure are typically at higher levels of the model; they determine major changes in the system's operating mode, and involve turning on and off large groups of processes. The control structure also receives information about the status or mode of external systems, and transmits similar information about itself. The components of the control structure—control context diagrams, control flow diagrams, and control specifications—are described in detail in the following sections.

5.1 Control Context Diagrams

Control context diagrams are identical to data context diagrams, except that they contain control flows instead of data flows. An example—the partner of the DCD of Figure 4.2—is shown in Figure 5.2.

Control flows are shown with broken lines to distinguish them from data flows; their characteristics are described later, in Section 5.3. Like DCDs, CCDs show communications to and from the outside world. Each has a single process representing the system to be specified, and one or more (usually more) terminators. The usual convention, as illustrated in Figures 4.2 and 5.2, is to show all the system terminators on both the data and control con-

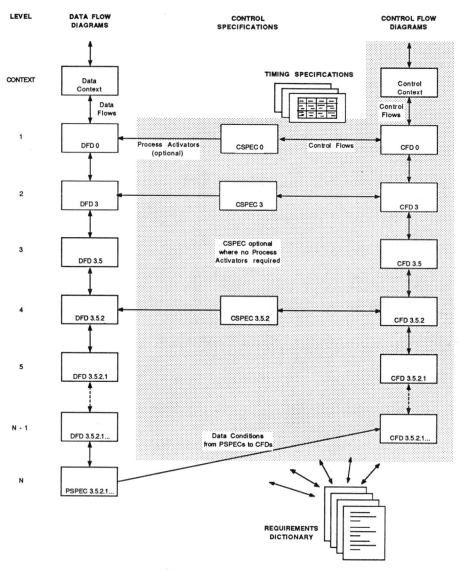

Figure 5.1. The control structure (highlighted).

text diagrams, even if some of them are associated only with data flows or only with control flows. This can result in some terminators on either of the context diagrams being shown with no flows attached, but they are left in anyway as a reminder that they exist.

The single process in each of the two context diagrams for a given system are, in fact, one and the same—they both represent the one system to be specified. The control context diagram establishes the control information interface between the system and the environment, while the data context dia-

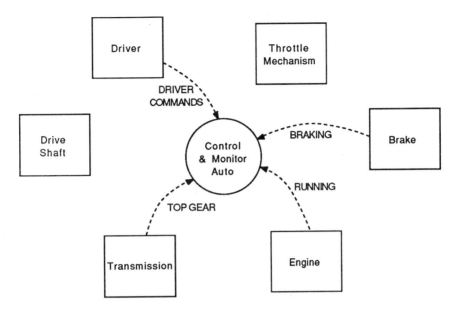

Figure 5.2. Control context diagram.

gram establishes the data information interface. Since both the processes and the terminators are identical, it follows that the two context diagrams (and, as we shall see, every associated DFD and CFD pair) *could* be superimposed and drawn as one, but there are advantages to keeping the control and data structures separate. Obviously, then, the 'two" processes have the same name, and the same number: 0 (recall Section 4.4).

5.2   Control Flow Diagrams

Control flow diagrams share the naming, numbering, leveling, and balancing properties of DFDs, as well as the parent/child relationships of DFDs, as described in Chapter 4. In addition, CFDs include a special symbol (a short solid bar) signifying their interface with a CSPEC, which we describe later in this section.

Figure 5.3 shows a control flow diagram that is the partner of the DFD of Figure 4.3. Since the processes on the two context diagrams are the same, so are their children, the level 1 diagrams; they share the same name and are numbered DFD 0 and CFD 0. Furthermore, their subprocesses are also the same—process 1 on DFD 0 is the same process, and has the same name, as process 1 on CFD 0. They differ only in that the former carries the data flows, and the latter carries the control flows.

We have found that new users of the model tend to have common misconceptions about CFDs. The processes on a CFD do *not* represent processing of

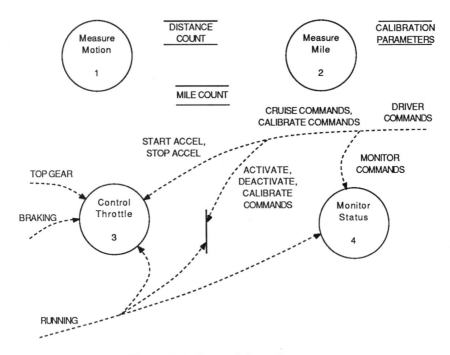

Figure 5.3. Control flow diagram.

the control flows entering it—this is done by the CSPECs; neither do they represent the states of the system—these (as we shall see in Section 5.6 and Chapter 6) are contained within the CSPECs; and finally, the control flows entering the processes do *not* activate or deactivate those processes—this is done by process activators also within the CSPECs.

CFDs simply constrain the control flows to follow the same routing rules that data flows must follow; that is, they can only pass between properly paired parent and child diagrams. A major difference lies in the fact that, whereas the internal sources and destinations of data flows are primitive processes, those of control flows are CSPECs.

Elsewhere in the literature, the term "control flow diagram" is sometimes used synonymously with "state transition diagram" (which is discussed in Chapter 6). As you must now realize, this is *not* its meaning in this method. Here, the term is used because the diagram it describes is very similar to a DFD, so it is very appealing to give correspondingly similar names to the two diagrams. State transition diagrams appear only in CSPECs in this method, and are never referred to as control flow diagrams. We decided the descriptive benefits of our special use of "control flow diagram" outweigh the occasional confusion it might cause.

Like their parents—the context diagrams—DFD 0 and CFD 0 *could* be combined into one, but, except in the case of very simple systems, we choose to keep them separate to keep their separate roles distinct and to limit the amount of information on a single diagram. Decomposition of processes into

DFDs and CFDs continues exactly in parallel, just as it does at level 1. DFD decomposition terminates when all the processes are primitives. CFD decomposition terminates in a CSPEC, but not in association with primitive processes, as we shall see in more detail later in this chapter.

In the types of system to which this method has usually been applied, CFD decomposition always terminates before that of the associated DFDs. In some control intensive systems, however, they may go down to the same level, or CFDs may even decompose further than DFDs.

CFD to CSPEC interface

An obvious major difference exists between DFDs and CFDs: Some flow arcs on CFDs terminate in a short line or bar symbol. These bars indicate flows to and from the associated CSPEC, as distinct from those to and from the parent process. A PSPEC is only associated with a primitive process, which by definition is at the lowest level of decomposition, whereas a CSPEC is associated with *a paired CFD and DFD* at *any* level in the structure, and its inputs and outputs flow from and to the CFD. This is illustrated in the composite chart, Figure 5.1. To indicate this "sideways" flow, we use the bar symbol.

Figure 5.4 shows the various ways in which CSPEC bars can be used.

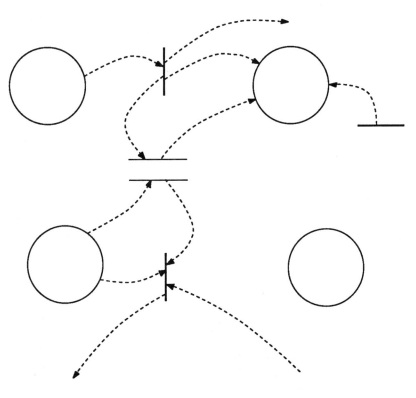

Figure 5.4. Variations on CSPEC bars.

Notice that several bars can appear on one diagram, but that they are all associated with the same CSPEC. For this reason, the bars do not need any labels. All the flows entering and leaving all the bars on CFD 3.5, for example, go to and from CSPEC 3.5.

Control flow diagrams contain processes, which are the very same ones as in the DFDs, and so need no further discussion. They also contain control flows and control stores, which are discussed in the following sections.

5.3   Control Flows

As we have stated, control flows are graphically distinguished from data flows by representing them with broken, instead of solid, lines. Their extrinsic properties, that is, those that relate to their use on the flow diagrams, are identical to those of data flows. Thus, all the properties illustrated in Figure 4.7 apply to control flows as well as to data flows. Their *intrinsic* properties, however, are different, in that primitive control signals are *always* discrete-valued, whereas data signals may be either discrete-valued or continuous-valued, and, in fact, are usually the latter. Figure 5.5 illustrates the difference between these two properties, showing an example of each as it would typically vary with time.

Mathematicians go through considerable anguish in their attempts to rigorously define the differences between continuous and discrete variables, but we do not intend to be that precise. For our purposes, the following two-part definition is sufficient:

- Discrete signals may take on one of a finite number of known values that need not have any particular relative order, and

- Continuous signals may take on one of an arbitrarily large number of ordered numeric values.

Thus, in Figure 5.5, the first diagram shows a time/magnitude plot of a continuous signal. Other than changes in scale factor, there is no other way this diagram can be drawn. The second and third diagrams show the same discrete variable with a different ordering of its values. The information conveyed by the two diagrams is identical. Such a rearrangement of the continuous variable values would result in a meaningless diagram.

Continuous signals usually represent a continuous physical quantity, such as airspeed or pressure, whereas discrete signals usually represent some unique mode or condition, such as flight phase (takeoff, climb, cruise, descent) or valve condition (open, closed, jammed). Like data flows, control flows are defined in the requirements dictionary, as discussed in Chapter 8.

We will discuss how signals are designated as data or control in Chapter 11. For the moment, remember that all control signals are discrete; data signals are usually continuous, but some are discrete; and some discrete signals are designated as *both* data and control.

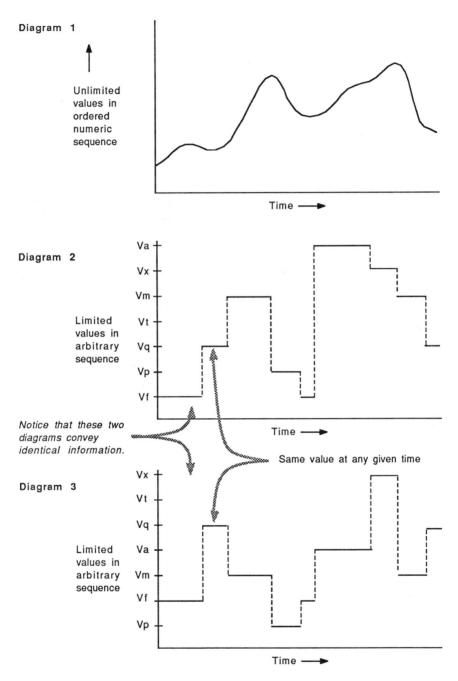

Figure 5.5. Comparison between discrete and continuous signals.

From the user's point of view, the important distinction between data and control signals is that the former appear on DFDs and are used in PSPECs, whereas the latter appear in CFDs and are used in CSPECs.

5.4 Data Conditions

Referring back to the composite diagram in Figure 5.1, we see information flowing from a PSPEC in the data structure across to the control structure. This information consists of control flows that are derived from data. These control flows provide the only link from DFDs to CFDs, and they are given a special name, *data conditions*. In spite of this special role, there is nothing special about their *intrinsic* properties, which are identical to those of all other control signals.

Note that the control model deals with control that occurs at a high level in the system, where major processes may be turned on and off according to the operating mode. At the computer programming level, the term "control" refers to branching and conditional statements that are often direct functions of data. In the control model, this kind of control is just a part of the detailed processing inside a PSPEC.

Figure 5.6 illustrates a PSPEC that generates a data condition and the associated DFD and CFD. The data condition, though generated in the child

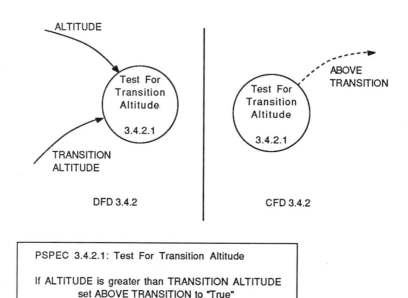

Figure 5.6. A data condition.

PSPEC of a primitive process, does not appear as an output from that process on the DFD, but *does* appear out of the corresponding process on the CFD.

This behavior of data conditions requires that we slightly modify the balancing principle described in Section 4.7. To verify that a PSPEC balances, we must check both its DFD *and* its CFD, as the figure illustrates.

5.5 Control Stores

Control stores have exactly the same role in CFDs as data stores have in DFDs: They store control flows after the sources of those flows have ceased producing them. A given store may be unique to a DFD, unique to a CFD, or used both in a DFD and in its associated CFD. In this last case, it has the same name on both diagrams, and the usual principle applies: The name is descriptive of all signals in the store; in this case, there are both data and control signals.

Everything stated about data stores in Section 4.6 applies also to control stores:

- They retain their content until it is overwritten.

- Their names are the names of the information they contain.

- Unlabeled flows to and from the store carry all the store's information.

- Flows carrying subgroups of the stored information are labeled with the subgroup names.

- Stores may be read-only, read-write, or both.

- A given store only appears on one CFD, but may appear more than once on that diagram.

Data stores appear on DFDs and control stores appear on CFDs; their symbols are identical so no special illustration of control stores is needed.

5.6 Control Specifications

Control specifications represent the finite state machine behavior of the system, which we will discuss in Chapter 6. Before looking inside these specifications, it is important to understand how they fit into the overall structure of the model. First, their intrinsic purpose is exactly the same as that of

PSPECS: precisely to show how their outputs are generated from their inputs. PSPECs and CSPECs, however, differ in the way they carry out their purposes, and differ greatly in the role they play in the overall structure, as is evident from Figure 5.1 and the discussion below.

Referring once again to Figure 5.1—the composite chart of the control model—we see that CSPECs provide the link from the CFDs to the DFDs. Their inputs are control flows from the CFDs, and some of their outputs control processes in the DFDs. They have other outputs, which feed back into the CFDs as control flows.

Each CSPEC has the same name and number as the DFD and CFD with which it is associated. Its control flow inputs and outputs all come from and go to that CFD via the bar symbol, which specifically represents that particular CSPEC. Any processes the CSPEC controls are on its associated DFD. By verifying that these relationships have in fact been satisfied, the important self-consistency and numbering principles of the flow diagrams and PSPECs are carried through to the CSPECs too.

The one-to-one relationship between CSPECs and CFDs produces another advantage: Just as flows to and from the parent process do not need labels such as off-page connectors (because there is no ambiguity as to where they go), neither do the flows terminating in bars need them, because they all go to and from the one CSPEC.

Continuing to refer to Figure 5.1, we see that a CSPEC is *always* associated with a CFD (and usually with a DFD), but the converse is not true. A CSPEC is present only where process control is required on the associated DFD, or where some control signals are to be converted, through a finite state machine, into new control signals.

The simple, close relationships between DFD, CFD, and CSPEC allow us to organize a complex specification into simple groups of items with well-defined relationships between those groups. An associated DFD, CFD, and CSPEC (all with the same name and number, and closely related to each other) are usually grouped together in the completed specification, making it easy for the user to move back and forth between them. These groups are arranged in numerical order (or sometimes in top-down order of levels), and the numbering system then makes it equally easy to move up and down levels, between parent and child groups.

Control specifications, then, close the loop we have been building throughout this part of the book. The whole requirements model can be considered a feedback control loop, as illustrated in Diagram 2 of Figure 5.7, analogous to the traditional feedback control diagram of Figure 5.7, Diagram 1. We have data flows entering our model through the DFDs; some processes in the data structure produce control signals (the data conditions described in Section 5.4), which feed into the control structure; signals from the CFDs drive the CSPECs; and the CSPECs control some of the processes on the DFDs. The primary purpose of the CSPECs is to modify the response of the

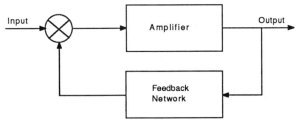

Diagram1: Traditional Feedback Control Amplifier

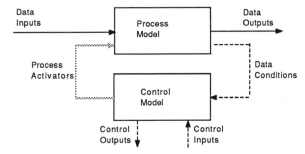

Diagram 2: The Requirements Model as a Feedback Controller

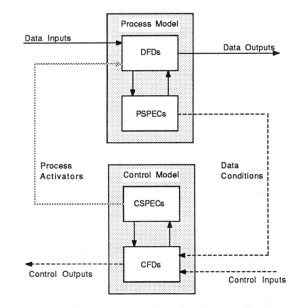

Diagram 3: The Symmetry of the Requirements Model

Figure 5.7. The model as a feedback control loop.

data processor (that is, the whole collection of data processes) according to past and present conditions both within and outside the system. CSPECs also convey information about those conditions to the outside world. Diagram 3 of

Figure 5.7 is simply a rearrangement and enlargement of Diagram 2, illustrating the symmetry of the model.

As you saw in Chapter 2, CSPECs contain representations of finite state machines—state transition diagrams, state transition matrices and tables, and decision tables. These will all be discussed in depth in Chapter 6.

5.7 Process Controls

Process controls are control outputs from CSPECs that have the special purpose of activating and deactivating processes. They therefore have only two values: On and Off. Process controls are defined inside the CSPECs, where they are assigned the names of the processes they control. It is easy to find those processes as they are all on the one adjacent DFD, so the process controls are not shown on either the DFDs or the CFDs.

Figure 5.8 shows parts of two CSPECs and their associated DFDs. The CSPECs determine whether their process controls are On or Off, and the corresponding processes are activated or deactivated accordingly.

We chose to call the CSPEC outputs that control processes "process activators" because it is convenient to represent everything in terms of positive logic—when the logic function is True, the activator is On, and the process is active. We might have called them "process deactivators"—there is a sound argument for doing so. When a process is activated, it exhibits its "default" data triggered, infinitely fast behavior, as described in Section 4.8, so in a sense the activator is doing nothing. When a process is deactivated, the model behaves differently from the traditional structured analysis model, so we must be sure we understand this behavior. The convention chosen is that when a process is deactivated, it does nothing, and its outputs are null (just as they are when it has insufficient inputs to do its job). Deactivating a process is just like temporarily deleting it, and all its outputs, from the system. Other conventions might have been possible—like inhibiting processes receiving its outputs, or maintaining the outputs present at the time it was deactivated—but the one chosen has proved simple and useful.

The lower DFD in Figure 5.8 is a descendant of a process in the upper one, and it, too, has some process controls acting on it. This brings up an important property of process controls in a leveled set of DFDs: A process is active only when it *and all its ancestors* are active. Looking at it the other way round, when a process is *deactivated*, all its descendants are also deactivated. This is true even for any of its descendants that do not themselves have process controls. The rationale behind this convention is perhaps easier to understand if you recall that the descendant DFDs of a process are contained within that process; it seems reasonable that when a process is turned off, everything inside it is turned off also.

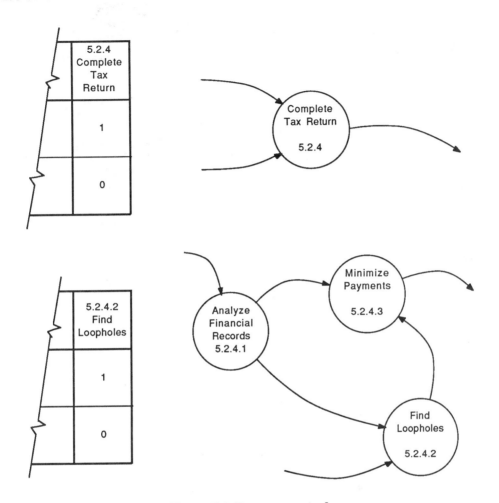

Figure 5.8. Process controls.

When all its ancestors are active, a process without a process control is considered to be always active, that is, it responds to its data inputs on demand, in the usual way.

Transaction center control

The control of transaction centers is sometimes treated differently from the control of other types of processes. A transaction center often has many branches, with simple, primitive processes on each branch. Writing a separate PSPEC and having a separate process activator for each branch can be cumbersome. Instead, the transaction center is "collapsed" into a single process, and the CSPEC references the branches within that process, indicating which of them are active. Figure 5.9 shows a collapsed transaction center controlled from a CSPEC.

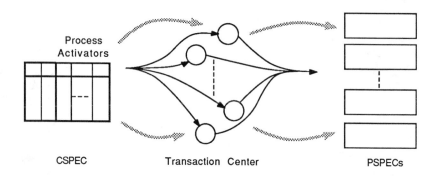

Diagram 1: The Standard Arrangement

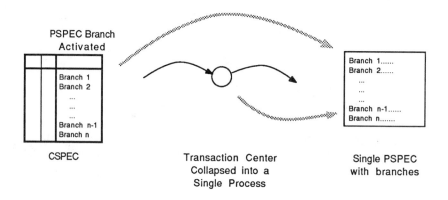

Diagram 2: The Condensed Arrangement

Figure 5.9. Controlling a transaction center.

5.8 Summary

- Control context diagrams duplicate the division of the world shown in data context diagrams, but they show control information instead of data passing between the system and the outside world.

- Control flow diagrams are paired with DFDs, and mimic their processes. They contain control flows instead of data flows.

- Some control flows enter and leave CSPECs, and this is shown by a bar symbol on the CFD.

- Control flows are represented by broken lines, and, like data flows, are either primitive or group flows. Primitive control signals are always discrete, whereas primitive data flows may be continuous or discrete (usually the former).

- Data conditions are control signals generated within PSPECs through tests on data. They cross over from the data to the control structure, thus providing one of the two links between the two.

- Control stores are exactly analogous to data stores, except that they contain control signals. They may or may not be associated with data stores on the corresponding DFDs.

- Control specifications contain the finite state machines needed to represent that type of behavior of the system. Their inputs are control flows from the CFDs, and their outputs are process activators and control flows entering the CFDs.

- Process controls are generated from the logic in the CSPECs, and activate and deactivate process on the corresponding DFD. They provide the other link between the data and control structures.

- The control structure is integrated with the process structure in such a way that it inherits all the leveling, numbering, and balancing properties.

Chapter 6

Finite State Machines

Large, complex systems, and especially real-time systems, have the property that past and present events, both external and internal, change their behavior. These changes are more fundamental than producing a different output value from a computation when the corresponding inputs change; the computations themselves may change, or stop altogether—the system may behave like an entirely different processor from one time to another. This kind of behavior is hard to represent with a process model alone, but the finite state machine model is very well-suited to it, and when combined with the process model, the two together become a very powerful means for representing virtually any system requirements.

The main purpose for having a control model at all is to represent those system requirements that have finite state machine behavior, so it is worth discussing in greater detail the nature of this behavior. Accordingly, we will now look inside control specifications at the finite state machines they contain.

Machines may be categorized into continuous and finite state types. We have already discussed continuous and discrete signals in Section 5.3, and there is a close association between these and the two types of machines.

Continuous machines, also known as analog machines, are characterized by continuous-valued inputs, outputs, and internal elements. PSPECs represent continuous machines in the requirements model. Despite their predominantly continuous characteristics, they are able to receive and produce discrete-valued signals also. We have seen this in the specific case of data conditions in Section 5.4.

Finite state machines are characterized by discrete-valued inputs, outputs, and internal elements. Continuous machines usually process continuous signals, but can also process discrete signals, whereas finite state machines can *only* process discrete signals.

We should note here that most systems today will, in fact, be implemented on digital computers, which are entirely finite state. You might therefore question why we draw the distinction between the two types of machine.

The answer is twofold: First, the model we are developing here is a model of the *requirements,* and does not recognize the particular implementation chosen. In principle, the system could just as well be implemented on an analog computer. Second, the two types of signals and machines are indeed treated differently in a digital computer. Continuous signals typically represent continuous physical quantities, such as airspeed or flow rate, and are represented by digital words having a numeric interpretation of the *magnitude* of the signals. In particular, they have a most and least significant bit. Changing the least (or even the several least) significant bits would rarely have any noticeable effect on the system outputs. Discrete signals, on the other hand, represent modes or operating states of the machine, such as flight phase or valve condition, and are represented by digital words with a purely symbolic interpretation. The idea of magnitude does not apply: No bit is any more or less significant than any other, and changing any one of them is likely to change the whole operating mode of the system.

Thus, although the digital computer is, strictly speaking, entirely finite state, when it is performing data processing functions, it is treated as if it were continuous.

Finite state machine categories

Just as machines in general can be categorized as continuous and finite state, finite state machines can, in turn, be categorized as combinational and sequential. The outputs of a combinational machine are uniquely determined by its current inputs; past inputs have no influence. The outputs of a sequential machine are determined by both its current and past inputs. Another way to say this is that sequential machines contain memory, while combinational machines do not. These two types are discussed in Sections 6.1 and 6.2.

Most nontrivial systems are sequential machines overall. A flight management system, for example, will have a flight plan loaded into it before takeoff, which will influence its outputs throughout the flight. This is clearly a case of current outputs being influenced by past inputs. In spite of the overall sequential nature of systems, it turns out that in the requirements analysis, the various parts of a system usually can be divided into three groups, which can be represented by continuous machines, combinational machines, and sequential machines respectively. Since this division represents increasing degrees of complexity, it is worth doing in such a way as to minimize the more complex parts.

6.1   Combinational Machines

A combinational machine is defined as a finite state machine whose outputs
are determined entirely by its current inputs. Expressing this in mathematical notation, we would write the equation:

$$\{y_i\} = \mathbf{f}\{x_j\}$$

where $\{y_i\}$ is the set of outputs and $\{x_j\}$ is the set of inputs, and $\mathbf{f}$ is a combinational logic function.

Many examples of combinational machines occur in everyday life; they
are by no means all exotic systems. An example is a luggage lock with three
numbered thumbwheels:

$$\boxed{\;\boxed{2}\quad \boxed{5}\quad \boxed{3}\;}$$

When the thumbwheels are set to the proper digits, the lock opens. It has no
memory, so is not affected by how the wheels get to their final position. This
information can conveniently be represented in the form shown below, called
either a decision table or a truth table:

Control Input			Control Output
Wheel Settings			Lock Status
Wheel 1	Wheel 2	Wheel 3	
7	8	6	Lock Open
Any other combination			Lock Closed

In the special case in which all the inputs and outputs are binary, the
function $\mathbf{f}$ can be expressed using Boolean equations. For example,

OPEN VALVE = $\overline{\text{PRESSURE OVER LIMIT}} \cdot \overline{\text{VALVE JAMMED}}$
SOUND ALARM = PRESSURE OVER LIMIT $\cdot$ VALVE JAMMED

Here there are two inputs, PRESSURE OVER LIMIT and VALVE JAMMED, both of
which have the values True and False, and two outputs, OPEN VALVE and
SOUND ALARM, both of which have the values On and Off. The message is that
the valve is to be opened if the pressure is not over-limit and the valve is not
jammed; an alarm is to be sounded if the pressure is over-limit and the valve
is jammed.

In the usual case, many of the inputs and outputs have more than two
values, and, although Boolean equations can still be used in theory, they are
cumbersome, and the more common approach is to use decision tables (DTs).

As shown above and in Figure 6.1, a decision table is simply a tabular arrangement of all the combinations of the input signal values with the required values of the output signals for each combination. The input signal names are shown at the top left of the table with their values listed under them. Usually, the left-most signal has each of its values listed once, the second signal has each of its values repeated once for each value of the first, the third has each of its values repeated once for each combination of the values of the first two, and so on. Other arrangements are sometimes used, but the main principle is that all the combinations of the input values are covered somewhere in the table.

The output signal names are shown at the top right of the table. Under them are shown the values they are required to take on for each of the com-

INPUTS			OUTPUTS	
MODE	TEMPER-ATURE	PRESSURE	HEATER	PUMP
Idle	High	High	Off	Off
		Low	Off	Off
	Low	High	Off	Off
		Low	Off	Off
Auto1	High	High	Off	Off
		Low	Off	On
	Low	High	On	Off
		Low	On	On
Auto2	High	High	Off	Off
		Low	Off	On
	Low	High	On	Off
		Low	On	Off

Figure 6.1. Decision table for a heating system.

binations of input signal values. Whereas all combinations of input signal values are covered, the output signal values may or may not all be used, depending on the needs of the system.

An important, and in practice almost universal, variation in the use of decision tables is the appearance of "don't care" conditions in both the inputs and outputs. It frequently occurs that some combinations of input signal values either cannot occur in practice, or if they do, the results are inconsequential. In such cases, the corresponding entries in the decision table may be left blank or given an appropriate symbol (d/c, ø, or −, for example). Another frequent occurrence is that several very similar input combinations produce the same output. There are limitless variations on the format of the tables that take advantage of situations like these by condensing many of the separate combinations into one row. Figure 6.2 illustrates some of these possibilities. Note that the first table in this figure is a fully condensed version of Figure 6.1. From the user's point of view, the principle is always the same: The output values shown on the right are required to occur when the input values on the same row exist.

6.2 Sequential Machines

A sequential machine is defined as a finite state machine whose outputs are determined both by its current and its past inputs. In other words, the machines contain memory. This memory is represented in the form of states. A sequential machine is always in one of its specified states. In any given state, certain "events"—combinations of input signal values—will cause the machine to change its state, or to produce outputs, or both. The outputs of sequential machines are referred to as "actions." For the moment, we will refer to the inputs and outputs simply as events and actions; we will discuss how they are converted from and to control flows later in this chapter.

Again, as with the discrete versus continuous debate, theoreticians enjoy long philosophical discourses on the exact meaning of state. For our purposes, it is synonymous with the mode or condition of the machine, such as Climb, Cruise, Descent; Standby, Auto, Manual. Later examples will further illustrate its practical meaning.

In mathematical notation, we represent the sequential nature of the model by using an index, N, to identify the Nth input set, output set, and state:

$$\{y_i\}_N = \mathbf{f}[\{x_j\}_N, q_N]$$
$$q_{N+1} = \mathbf{g}[\{x_j\}_N, q_N]$$

Where: $\{y_i\}_N$ is the Nth set of outputs,

$\{x_j\}_N$ is the Nth set of inputs, and

q_N is the Nth state.

$\mathbf{f}$ and $\mathbf{g}$ are combinational logic functions indicating that the current output and the next state are both functions of the current input and current state.

INPUTS			OUTPUTS	
MODE	TEMPER-ATURE	PRESSURE	HEATER	PUMP
Idle			Off	Off
Auto1	High	High	Off	Off
Auto1	High	Low	Off	On
Auto1	Low	High	On	Off
Auto1	Low	Low	On	On
Auto2	High	High	Off	Off
Auto2	High	Low	Off	On
Auto2	Low		On	Off

INPUTS				OUTPUTS
MASTER ENABLE	HEAT REQUEST 1	ENABLE ALL	ENABLE 1	ACTIVATE 1
Off				Off
	Off			Off
Heat	On	On		On
Heat	On	Off		On
Heat	On	Off	Off	Off

Figure 6.2. Condensed decision tables for a heating system.

Like combinational machines, sequential machines do not have to be complex. An example is a rotary combination lock, shown in Figure 6.3. This type of lock remembers the sequence in which you turn the dial, and will only open if the sequence and the numbers selected are correct. A useful way to illustrate this procedure is with the state transition diagram, also shown in Figure 6.3.

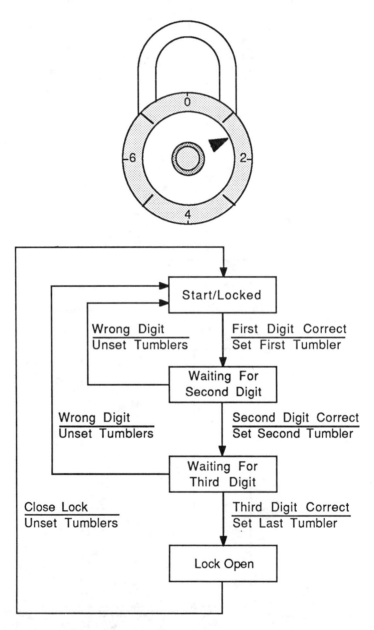

Figure 6.3. Rotary combination lock: a sequential machine.

State transition diagrams

The most familiar representation for a sequential machine is the state transition diagram, of which Figure 6.4 is an example.

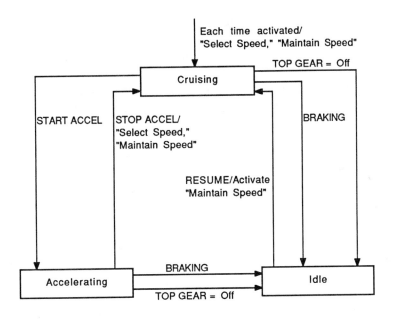

Figure 6.4. State transition diagram.

STDs have the following four components:

states	represented by rectangular boxes containing the names of the states they represent, for example, CLIMB, CRUISE, DESCENT; STANDBY, AUTO, MANUAL
transition arcs	represented by lines, with arrowheads showing the direction of the transition
events	shown, by their names, as labels on the arcs of the transitions they cause
actions	shown, by their names, adjacent to the events that cause them; the two are separated by a line

$$\text{EVENT/ACTION} \quad \text{or} \quad \frac{\text{EVENT}}{\text{ACTION}}$$

Normally, one of the states is identified as the start state, which the machine will be in when turned on. Alternatively, the machine may be set to a desired initial state by some external startup process. The start state is either labeled as such, or a transition arc is shown entering it, but not coming from any other state.

In any given state, when an event occurs that is associated with a transition from that state, the machine will go to the state indicated by that transition arc, and will simultaneously perform the associated action. If an event occurs that is not associated with a transition from that state, nothing happens.

Transitions sometimes return to the state they left. This is done when, in a given state, an event is required to cause an action, but not to change the state. The converse can also occur: An event changes the state, but does not produce an action.

A machine with n states would have n^2 transitions if every state could make the transition to every other state (including itself), but this is rarely the case in practice. Most machines allow only a few of these transitions to occur.

There are two well-known sequential machine models: Mealy and Moore [2,7]. In the Mealy model, the actions are associated with the transitions. In the Moore model, the actions are functions of the current state only, which is a simpler arrangement, but less flexible. In the requirements model, we use a hybrid approach: The usual convention is to drive the output actions from the transitions, but where convenient, they can be driven by the states as well. Thus, an output from a CSPEC containing the state transition diagram of Figure 6.3 might be Unset Tumblers originating from some of the transitions. Another output might be Lock State with values Start/Locked, Waiting For Second Digit, Waiting For Third Digit, and Lock Open.

An important convention used in this model is that the actions, although they are associated with the transitions, which are transient in nature, are assumed to continue in effect until the next transition occurs. This means that a process activated by a particular action will remain activated continuously, and will continue to respond to changing data inputs until the next transition. This convention goes hand-in-hand with the convention discussed in Section 5.7 that processes are active only while their activators are on. They are *not* activated by "switching them on" and deactivated by "switching them off"—the convention adopted by Ward and Mellor [18], which implies that the process itself has memory.

State transition tables and matrices

The STD is the most expressive representation of a sequential machine for relatively simple cases, but quickly becomes incomprehensible when the number of states and/or transitions becomes large. Two alternative representations are used to accommodate these more complex cases: the state transition table (STT) and the state transition matrix (STM). Both represent exactly the same information as the STD, but can be made arbitrarily large without becoming unmanageable.

Figure 6.5 shows the state transition table for the STD of Figure 6.4. It consists of four columns. The first column contains a list of each of the states. The second column shows, for each current state, all the events that cause transitions from it. The third shows the action (if any) associated with each transition. The fourth shows the state to which each transition goes. This table can be extended over as many pages of the specification as necessary, so the size of the machine is not an obstacle, but it can be difficult to get a clear picture of the machine's operation from this representation.

Current State	Event	Action	Next State
Start	Each Time Activated	"Select Speed," "Maintain Speed"	Cruising
Cruising	TOP GEAR = Off	-	Idle
	BRAKING	-	Idle
	START ACCEL	-	Accelerating
Idle	RESUME	"Maintain Speed"	Cruising
Accelerating	BRAKING	-	Idle
	TOP GEAR = Off	-	Idle
	STOP ACCEL	"Select Speed," "Maintain Speed"	Cruising

Figure 6.5. State transition table.

Figure 6.6 shows the state transition matrix for the STD of Figure 6.4. Here, the states are listed on the left side of the matrix, and the events along the top. Each element in the matrix shows the action (if any), and the next state (if any), caused by the event above that element when the machine is in the state on the left of that element. This representation, too, can be extended over multiple pages. It has the advantage of providing a quick visual check of what happens if a given event occurs while the machine is in a given

Event \ State	Each Time Activated	TOP GEAR = Off	BRAKING	START ACCEL	RESUME	STOP ACCEL
Start	"Select Speed," "Maintain Speed" / Cruising					
Cruising		Idle	Idle	Accelerating		
Idle					"Maintain Speed" / Cruising	
Accelerating		Idle	Idle			"Select Speed," "Maintain Speed" / Cruising

Figure 6.6. State transition matrix.

state. It also has the advantage that all possible combinations of states and events are shown, providing a form of completeness check. This same attribute, however, often causes the matrix to be quite sparse (since it is usual for many transitions not to be allowed), and therefore to take up a lot more space than the table. Despite this disadvantage, this representation of sequential machines is the one most frequently used in the requirements model.

Other arrangements of the matrix form are possible, one of which is shown in Figure 6.7 for the STD of Figure 6.4. Here, the current state is shown on the

From State \ To State	Cruising	Idle	Accelerating
Start	Each Time Activated / "Select Speed," "Maintain Speed"		
Cruising		TOP GEAR = Off / BRAKING	START ACCEL
Idle	RESUME / "Maintain Speed"		
Accelerating	STOP ACCEL / "Select Speed," "Maintain Speed"	TOP GEAR = Off / BRAKING	

Figure 6.7. State transition matrix (alternate form).

left, and the next state along the top. Each element shows the event and action associated with a transition from the state on the left to the state above. Here, all combinations of states are shown, so this matrix too provides a completeness test, but different from that of the previous matrix. The form of matrix of Figure 6.7 has the same disadvantage of sparseness as the previous form, plus another: There is sometimes more than one transition between one pair of states, so multiple entries might be needed in a single element.

6.3   Incorporating Finite State Machines into CSPECs

So far, this chapter has dealt with finite state machines as a separate topic, independent of the requirements model. This is appropriate, because automata theory, of which finite state machines are a part, is an independent and well-established mathematical and engineering discipline that has been around for a long time—much longer than the structured methods. It has been used extensively for many years in such applications as digital machine design. One of its great attractions as a component of these methods is that it is based on a solid and mature theoretical foundation, as well as being very applicable to the representation of system control structures.

So how do we use this discipline in the requirements model? We have already had a glimpse of the answer in our composite chart of the method, Figure 3.1, and in Section 5.6. The answer is that the finite state machines we have been describing all reside inside the CSPECs. We have seen that the inputs to a CSPEC come from the associated CFD via the bar symbol, and that their outputs either go back to the same CFD, also via the bar symbol, or they control processes on the associated DFD. These inputs and outputs are, in fact, the inputs and outputs of finite state machines contained within the CSPECs.

Combinational control specifications

Figure 6.8 shows a decision table embedded in a CSPEC with parts of the associated DFD and CFD. Notice that all the inputs to the decision table appear also on the CFD as arcs entering bar symbols. Some of its outputs are control flows, which appear as arcs leaving bar symbols on the CFD. Other outputs control processes on the DFD, as indicated by the names and numbers of these processes at the top of the decision table's output columns. These process control outputs are always binary, and signify that when the input signal conditions cause that output to be True, the corresponding process is enabled, and behaves as if it were a normal, data triggered process. When those input conditions cause the output to be False, the process is disabled and produces no outputs, regardless of its inputs. It is as if the process and its outputs had been temporarily removed from the model. (If, like the authors, you are an electrical engineer, you might prefer to think of this as equivalent to the high impedance state of a tri-state driver.)

Decision tables that are used to activate processes are referred to as process activation tables or PATs. Figure 6.8 also illustrates a special variation

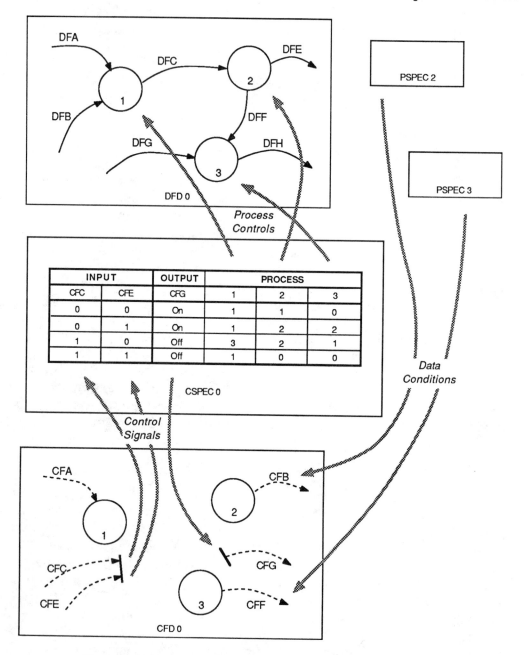

Figure 6.8. Combinational CSPEC, with its DFD and CFD.

used in PATs. Instead of using just the usual binary output values of 0 and 1, some rows in the table contain 0, 1, 2, 3, and so on. The 0 has the usual meaning: False or Off. The sequence 1, 2, 3 indicates that when the input criteria for that row become True, the processes are activated in that sequence. This construct is used where it is important that certain process outputs are available before others start their tasks, but where this is not clearly implied by the data flows. Any step in the sequence may activate any number of processes. There might, for example, be one 1, three 2s, one 3, and two 4s.

Sequential control specifications

Figure 6.9 shows a state transition diagram embedded in a CSPEC with parts of the associated DFD and CFD. Where sequential control is used, the simplest form a CSPEC can take is to contain just a single STD—this is also the least usual form in practice. As we shall discuss later, in the requirements model, sequential machines usually are used in combination with combinational machines, but here, to illustrate the principles involved, we shall describe the simple form shown in Figure 6.9. From this point on, most of our examples will show sequential machines in matrix form.

By studying the events and actions on the STD as well as the control signals flowing into and out of the bar symbols on the CFD, you will see that the inputs to the bar symbols are the STD events, and that the outputs from them are the STD actions. Remember the convention we described in Section 6.2 whereby the outputs (actions) from a sequential machine are assumed to remain in effect until the next transition occurs. This translates into control signals out of the CSPEC remaining in effect for the whole duration between transitions.

The STD of Figure 6.9 could be replaced by an exactly equivalent state transition table, or state transition matrix, at the discretion of the model builder. The meaning of the model would not change at all. In fact, in the large, complex systems to which these methods are most often applied, the STM is the most popular representation; the STT is rarely used.

Composite control specifications

In CSPECs, sequential machines are usually used in combination with combinational machines; that is, STMs usually are used in combination with decision tables. Figure 6.10 shows an example of how this combination fits together. The CSPEC inputs enter decision table(s), where they are converted into the form needed to represent the events to drive the STM. The STM then produces its output signals (the actions), the signals enter further decision tables, these decision tables convert the signals into the process controls and control signals needed by the rest of the model. When decision tables are

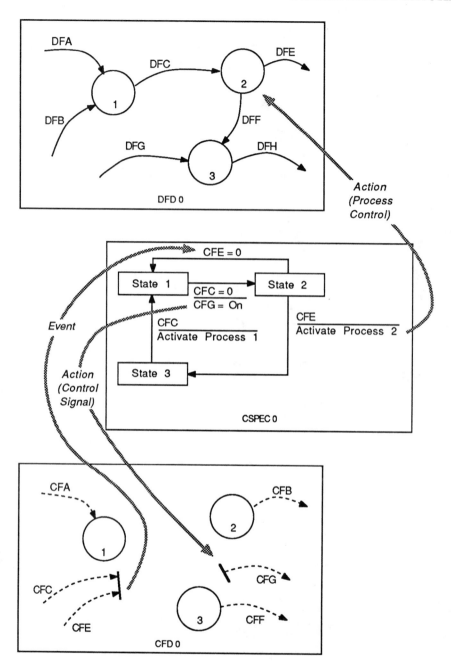

Figure 6.9. Sequential CSPEC, with its DFD and CFD.

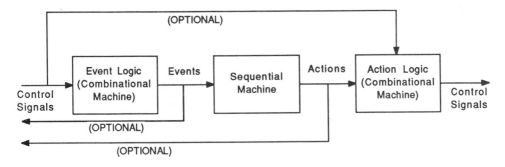

Figure 6.10. Block diagram of composite CSPEC.

used in these roles, they are often called the event logic, and the action logic, respectively. As shown in Figure 6.10, the configuration is quite flexible, with a number of optional links and outputs. Figure 6.11 shows an actual composite CSPEC with all these components.

Multi-sheet control specifications

As we have stated, the structure of the requirements model is founded on the structure of the basic DeMarco structured analysis method [4]. The naming and numbering conventions of structured analysis are carried over to the CFDs and CSPECs, and the leveling and balancing principles are extended to the whole structure. A direct outcome of these principles is that no more than one CSPEC can be associated with one DFD. In other words, we have chosen to put all the logic to control one DFD into one CSPEC. This logic, however, might be arbitrarily large and complex, depending on the characteristics of the system being modeled, so it might not all fit on one standard-size sheet of paper. We must, therefore, accept the fact that a CSPEC can take up more than one page in the specification, and this, indeed, is frequently true in practice. It is the only component of the method with this property. This outcome is typical of system design: Constraining one parameter (in this case, allowing only one CSPEC per DFD) causes another parameter to expand (multiple sheets per CSPEC).

In a multi-sheet CSPEC, the sheets need to "communicate" with each other: For example, outputs from a decision table on one sheet might be used as inputs to a decision table or STM on another sheet. Thus, we have signals that are internal to a CSPEC and that might not be used anywhere else in the model. This, too, is different from any other component of the method.

Because a multi-sheet CSPEC can become quite complex within itself, the following conventions are used to organize it:

- Each sheet carries the name and number of the whole CSPEC, and, in addition, follows the well-known "sheet *m* of *n*" convention, so we know how many sheets to expect and can check that they are all there.

INPUT		EVENT		
CFA	CFB	EV1	EV2	EV3
0	0	On	Off	Off
0	1	Off	Off	On
1	0	On	Off	Off
1	1	Off	On	Off

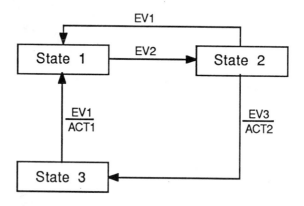

ACTION	OUTPUT		
	CFC	CFD	CFE
ACT1	Off	On	Standby
ACT2	On	Off	Ready

*NOTE: Trace the events from the event logic
to the STD, and the actions from the
STD to the action logic.*

Figure 6.11. Composite CSPEC.

- If the CSPEC is a composite one, as illustrated in Figures 6.10 and 6.11, the diagrams are arranged in the sequence shown in those figures: event logic, sequential machine, and action logic.

- If a CSPEC is more than three or four sheets long (and they are sometimes much longer), then a users' guide is included describing the general layout of that CSPEC, and listing the sheet(s) on which each input, each output, and each internal signal appears.

Figure 6.12, shown on this page, illustrates some of these conventions.

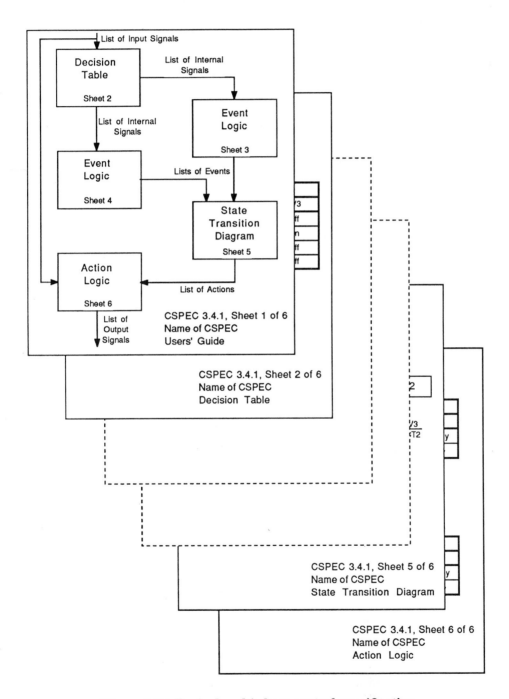

Figure 6.12. Typical multi-sheet control specification.

6.4 Summary

- Machines in general may be divided into continuous (analog) and finite state types.

- Finite state machines can deal only with discrete-valued information.

- FS machines, in turn, may be divided into combinational (having no memory) and sequential (having memory) types.

- Combinational machines are characterized by an input set, a transfer function, and an output set, and are represented by Boolean equations, or more commonly by decision tables.

- Sequential machines are characterized by an input set, a set of states, a transfer function, a next-state function, and an output set. They are represented by state transition diagrams, tables, or matrices.

- State transition diagrams consist of states, transitions, input events, and output actions. State transition tables and matrices consist of exactly the same information, but present it in a different format.

- CSPECs contain finite state machines. In practice, a CSPEC might contain several of the above objects; typically, the inputs and outputs of a sequential machine pass through combinational machines.

- The CSPEC is the only component of the requirements model that may comprise several sheets. The sheets are numbered, and a users' guide to the CSPEC may be included.

Chapter 7

Timing Requirements

Timing is one of the most critical aspects of modern real-time systems. Often, the system's response must occur within milliseconds of a given input event, and every second it must respond to many such events in many different ways. Typically, the system is embedded in a vehicle or in a larger system, so size, processing capacity, and memory capacity are limited. Achieving these critical timing requirements under these constraints becomes very difficult, and is a major challenge for the designer.

Fortunately, the fact that the requirements model carefully separates requirements definition from design, as discussed in Chapter 3, means we, as requirements analysts, do not have to address the problems of *how* to achieve this performance. We need only to address the problems of how to accurately and unambiguously specify *what* the system must do. Armed with this specification, and with the performance characteristics of the processor(s) they have to work with, the designers can go about their difficult task with confidence.

This separation of requirements from design has a particularly dramatic impact in the timing area. The reason is that from the requirements point of view, we are only concerned with *external* timing. The users are concerned only that the system will respond overall to a certain stimulus within certain time constraints, but whether that response was achieved through a background or foreground task, how it was scheduled relative to other tasks, what the internal port-to-port timing was, and what kind of executive controller was needed to achieve it, are issues that do not concern them.

Notice that the idealized properties of the model support this approach very well. We can blithely ignore response times *within* our model, because it is infinitely fast. The moment an input stimulus occurs, the corresponding output is instantly present. This allows us to concentrate on the central purpose of the model, which is to represent the required functionality of the system. The hardware and software constraints within which the designer has to work will be provided as a set of processor and language characteristics, and the external timing by our timing specifications. The problem the designer has to solve, then, has three parts: the functional requirements to be provided, the constraints of the hardware and programming language, and the constraints of the external timing specification. It is a distinct advantage to the designer to have these three parts of the puzzle clearly separated.

From the requirements point of view, then, timing relates *only* to the signals at the system interface, those signals included on the context diagrams. This rather simple timing picture has just two aspects: repetition rate and input-to-output response time. Both aspects are discussed in the sections that follow.

7.1 Repetition Rate

The particular repetition rate with which we are concerned when specifying functional requirements is the *required recomputation rate* of external primitive outputs—primitive outputs that are contained in the context diagram flows. The repetition rates of internal signals are left to the discretion of the designer, unless they are necessary parameters of the required function.

The bus on which the external signals flow may require a repetition rate that is different from the required recomputation rate. For example, operational considerations might dictate that, for a smooth, comfortable ride for the passengers in a commercial jet, the lateral steering commands should be updated every 200 milliseconds. The bus specification, on the other hand, might call for the lateral steering commands to be transmitted every 100 milliseconds. The designer may then save computation time by transmitting two copies of the same value for each computation. The bus specification is a design constraint that will be given to the designer separately from the requirements model; if the architecture model is being used, that is where it will be included.

Repetition rate is listed in the requirements dictionary as an attribute of external primitive signals, as we discuss in Chapter 8.

7.2 Input-to-Output Response Time

The second aspect of timing—input-to-output response time—consists of specifying the allowable range of response times (usually the maximum response time) from each event occurring at the system's input terminals, to each resulting event occurring at the system's output terminals. The incoming events occur in the world outside the system, and the outgoing events are actions performed by the system. Both are expressed in terms of signal values on the system's terminals—its inputs and outputs, as illustrated in Figure 7.1. In this way, the response time specification ties into the rest of the structure, since these signals and their allowed values are both specified in the requirements dictionary. No signal or value may appear in the response time specification that does not appear as an external signal in the dictionary; conversely, every external signal listed in the dictionary should appear somewhere in the response time specification (even if its timing is listed as noncritical).

Figure 7.1 shows some examples of response time specifications. For the sake of illustration, we have incorporated examples from different systems into one table. This would not be done in practice of course.

EXTERNAL INPUT SIGNAL(S)	EVENT	EXTERNAL OUTPUT SIGNAL(S)	EVENT	RESPONSE TIME
A/N_KSTRK	Any character	SCRTCHPD	Character appears	0.33 sec max
SHAFT ROTATION	Speed or acceleration changes	THROTTLE POSITION	Corresponding change	2.0 sec max
RESUME, BRAKING, TOP GEAR	RESUME turns on while not BRAKING and in TOP GEAR	THROTTLE POSITION	Starts returning to desired speed value	1.5 sec max

Figure 7.1. Response time specifications.

The first row is an example from a flight management system having an alphanumeric keyboard. When any character is entered through the keyboard, it is echoed on the bottom line of the display, known as the scratchpad, and is required to appear there within one third of a second of the keystroke signal.

The second row is taken from the Automobile Management System of Chapter 26, and, in effect, specifies the phase delay of one segment of a closed loop control system. The cruise control function of this system together with the engine and throttle controller form a control loop, with the car itself as the load that the loop drives. This kind of response time is critical to ensure that the loop will not go unstable, which in this case might result in violent accelerations and decelerations. It is understood in all timing specifications that they are to be read in conjunction with the string of processes linking the input signals with the output signals. In this example, it is necessary to discover what the "corresponding" change is.

The third row shows an event that is defined in terms of several signals. This is quite a usual situation, sometimes resulting in lengthy descriptions of the events.

These examples only illustrate the usual, simple case of a maximum response time. There are cases in which a minimum is also required, or in which multiple responses have complex time relationships with each other. In such cases, the response time specification is adapted to show these requirements, possibly being supplemented with timing diagrams, an example of which is shown in Figure 7.2.

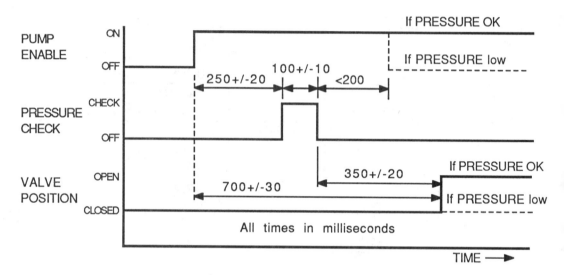

Figure 7.2. Timing diagram to supplement the response time specification.

In practice, the response time specification grows into a very long list, especially for large systems. It may be organized in any way that makes sense relative to the particular system being defined. Grouping the input events to correspond with the signal groups on the context diagrams is often a practical approach.

7.3 Summary

• Since users are only concerned with external timing, this is our only concern in the requirements model, too.

• Internal timing is deferred until the design phase.

- External timing has just two aspects: repetition rate and input-to-output response time.

- Repetition rate is specified, for external primitive signals only, in the requirements dictionary.

- Input-to-output response time is defined in tabular form, listing input events and their corresponding output events, and their required timing relationships.

Chapter 8

Requirements Dictionary

We have one more major component of the requirements model to describe, and although it has been left until last, it is in no sense less important than the others. On the contrary, it might well be considered the *most* important. We have described data flow diagrams, process specifications, control flow diagrams, control specifications, and timing specifications. The last component is the foundation on which all the data and control flows in all the diagrams and specifications are based. Our original composite diagram, Figure 3.1, shows the requirements dictionary off-line from the main structure, but it is a fundamental rule of the method that every data and control flow as well as every data and control store should be defined in it. This rule completes the goal of rigor we stated at the outset: We have already seen that processes are completely specified by their PSPECs and by their input and output flows, and that CSPECs each contain their own exact definitions. The dictionary provides an equally exact definition of every data and control flow, and of every store. Terminators are the only other component of the requirements model, and since they are by definition outside the scope of our system, we do not need exact definitions of them, only of the data flows the system shares with them.

Dictionary definitions describe two basic types of flows or signals: A primitive flow is an indivisible object or item of information that has its own intrinsic values and attributes; nonprimitives, or group flows, consist of groups of primitives. Primitive flows are either continuous or discrete, as discussed in Section 5.3. Examples of primitive continuous signals are shown in Figure 8.1, and of primitive discrete signals in Figure 8.2.

8.1 Primitive Attributes

Internal to the model, data signals need only Units as attributes, while control signals need only No. of Values and Value Names. The other attributes

NAME	DEFINITION	ATTRIBUTES			
		Units	Range	Reso-lution	Rate
BARO ALT	Barometric altitude	Feet	0–70,000	1	1 per 100 msec.
SHAFT ROTATION	Angular rotation of drive shaft	radians/ sec.	0–20,000	.1	On demand

Figure 8.1. Typical primitive continuous signal definitions.

NAME	DEFINITION	ATTRIBUTES		
		No. of Values	Value Names	Rate
IN AIR	Wheels off ground	2	On, Off	1 per 500 msec.
FLIGHT PHASE	Phase of vertical flight profile	4	Takeoff, Climb, Cruise, Descent	1 per 200 msec.

Figure 8.2. Typical primitive discrete signal definitions.

are usually assigned during design, that is, they are not a part of the requirements. For external signals, however (those contained in the context diagram flows), all of the above attributes usually must be specified, especially when the physical environment in which the system is to operate is known. In fact, in any given application, other attributes beyond those shown above might also need to be specified. External signals must conform to the constraints of the outside environment; other systems in that environment need to know the precise characteristics of those signals.

The Rate attribute has two possible interpretations. Standard data buses, such as the ARINC 429 bus in commercial aircraft, or the MIL-STD-1553 bus in military aircraft, have specific rates assigned to each signal they carry. System requirements (for stability, or for data-staleness reasons, for example) might demand a particular minimum recomputation rate for a signal, which might be slower than the bus rate. A recomputation rate slower than the bus rate means, for each recomputation, that the designer is free to transmit several copies of the same value. The recomputation rate is the one associated with functional requirements; the bus rate is often deferred to the design specification. The particular interpretation of Rate for any given application will be stated in the dictionary.

8.2   Group Structure

As we have seen in the context diagrams, flows leaving and arriving at the system are usually nonprimitives, representing large groups of signals. These groups decompose into smaller and smaller groups as they proceed down the DFD and CFD levels, until they reduce to their primitive components. The dictionary specifies the components and structure of each of these groups. It uses special symbols to do this, which are shown and described in Figure 8.3.

An example follows, which demonstrates how some of these symbols may be used:

```
VISUAL DISPLAYS = [ INIT/REF DSPLYS | ROUTE DSPLYS |
                    HOLD DSPLYS | PROGRESS DSPLYS |
                    CLIMB DSPLYS | CRUISE DSPLYS |
                    DESCENT DSPLYS | DES FRCST DSPLYS |
                    N1 LMTS DSPLYS ] + ( ALRTG/ADVSRY MSGS )
```

This sample dictionary entry indicates that the cockpit displays of a flight management system can be one of several types (initialization/reference, route, hold, and so forth), and any of them can have alerting/advisory messages superimposed. These messages bring to the crew's attention any unusual conditions, regardless of the particular current display. Of course, if there are no unusual conditions to report (hopefully, the normal case), no messages will be present.

Now let us look at a second sample entry:

$$\text{SELCTD NAVDS} = \{\text{NAVD CLASS} + \text{NAVD ID} + \text{NAVD FREQ}\}\,10$$

In this example, any number from zero to ten ground-based radio navigation beacons (navaids) is included in a selected group. Each navaid has a characteristic class, identification, and tuning frequency.

Each component of a definition is itself defined in the dictionary, and may decompose further into components of its own. Eventually, each component breaks down to primitives, which terminate the decomposition. Traditionally, dictionary entries are listed in alphabetical order of flow names, but modern data bases make this an arbitrary choice.

Symbol	Meaning	Description
=	composed of	This symbol indicates that the flow named on its left is composed of the flows named on its right.
+	together with	This symbol collects members into a group, but does not imply order. If ordering is required, it is specified by a comment in the dictionary or PSPEC.
{ }	iterations of	An expression enclosed within curly brackets may occur any number of times in a given instance of the flow. The brackets may be indexed: For example, $M\{\ \}N$ indicates any number of iterations from M to N. Thus:

$$\{\ \}2 \text{ implies } 0, 1, \text{ or } 2 \text{ iterations}$$
$$2\{\ \} \text{ implies } 2 \text{ or more iterations}$$
$$2\{\ \}2 \text{ implies exactly } 2 \text{ iterations}$$

Symbol	Meaning	Description
[|]	select one of	The square brackets contain two or more items separated by vertical bars. Any given instance of the flow will include exactly one of the items. [TARGET MACH | TARGET AIRSPEED] [SCREWS | NAILS | NUTS + BOLTS]
( )	optional	The expression enclosed within parentheses may or may not appear in a given instance of the flow.
" "	literal	Symbols enclosed within quotes literally constitute the data flow.

The following symbols are optional, and may not be needed if the dictionary is incorporated in a computerized data base.

Symbol	Meaning	Description
* *	comment	Asterisks enclose a statement that is not a formal part of the definition but that gives additional insight into its meaning.
\ \	primitive	In some dictionary formats, for identification purposes the backslash surrounds the definitions of primitives.

Figure 8.3. Requirements dictionary symbols.

8.3   Dictionary Data Bases

In the early days of structured analysis, the dictionary was kept in written or printed form, often using index cards. These days, the dictionary almost universally is stored in a computerized data base, from which any desired kind of reports can be extracted. This is particularly true if the whole method is automated, as is becoming more and more common. Interesting and useful reports become possible, such as a list of all flows appearing on a particular subset of the flow diagrams.

With each dictionary entry, considerably more information than the basic definition may be included for project management and control purposes. Entries such as the following are common:

- identification of originator of entry, and date entered

- identification of person making most recent change, and change date

- list of higher-level flows of which this flow is a member ("member of")

- list of flow diagrams on which this flow appears ("used in")

- comments—statements about the flow that are not part of the formal definition, but which aid the user in understanding it

Figure 8.4 shows a typical listing that could be found in a computerized dictionary. Figure 8.5 shows another useful dictionary output: an "indented explosion" of a large group flow, with several levels of decomposition. Here the structure defined by the dictionary definition is lost (together with, iterations of, and so on), but the composition of the flow is easy to see. Many other reports are possible, limited only by the capabilities of the data retrieval system.

8.4   Summary

- The dictionary defines all control and data flow in the flow diagrams.

- Flows, or signals, are either primitives or nonprimitives, the latter consisting of groups of the former.

- Definitions of primitives describe their physical form or information content, including a list of attributes. Several attributes are required for external primitives, few are required for internal ones.

Name	Definition	Data (D) or Control (C)
ACCELERATION =	\Measured vehicle acceleration\ Units: Miles per hour per second	D
ACTIVATE =	\Driver's cruise control activate command\ 2 Values: On, Off	C
AV SPEED =	\Calculated average trip speed\ Units: Miles per hour	D
AV SPEED RQST =	\Driver's request to display average trip speed\ 2 Values: On, Off	C
BRAKING =	\Input signal indicating brakes applied\ 2 Values: On, Off	C
CALIBRATE CMDS =	([START MEASURED MILE| STOP MEASURED MILE])	C
CALIBRATE PARAMETERS =	LOWER LIMIT + UPPER LIMIT + DEFAULT COUNT	D
CRUISE CMDS =	([ACTIVATE|DEACTIVATE]) + ([START ACCEL|STOP ACCEL])	C
CRUISE CTRL STATE =	\State of cruise control subsystem\ 3 Values: Inactive, Cruising, Accelerating	C
DEACTIVATE =	\Driver's cruise control deactivate command\ 2 Values: On, Off	C
DEFAULT COUNT =	\Constant = TBD; Default value of calibrated mile count\ Units: Dimensionless	D

Need to get this value from auto manufacturer

Figure 8.4. Dictionary listing.

```
FLT PLN
    CRNT FLT PLN LOCN
        ACT GO TO WPT
            ACT LATL GO TO WPT
            ALONG PATH DIST
            MOD ALONG PATH DIST
            MOD GO TO WPT
        LATERAL WPT DATA
            ENTRD WPT WIND
                ENTRD WPT WIND DIR
                ENTRD WPT WIND SPD
            FIX REFERENCE DATA
                REFERENCE POINT
                    ABEAM SELECTED
                    FIRST DISBEAR
                    FIRST DISBEAR TYPE
                    REFERENCE IDENT
                    REFERENCE LAT
                    REFERENCE LON
                    REFERENCE MAGVAR
                    SECOND DISBEAR
                    SECOND DISBEAR TYPE
                    THIRD DISBEAR
                    THIRD DISBEAR TYPE
            FLT PLN PRMTRS
                DEP ARPRT DATA
                    DEP ARPRT DATA-1
                        DEP ARPRT ELEV
                        DEP ARPRT IDENT
                        DEP ARPRT LAT
                        DEP ARPRT LON
                        DEP ARPRT MAGVAR
                        DEP ARPRT SPD REST ALT
                        DEP TRANS ALT
                        DEP TRANS DELTA
                    DEP ARPRT DATA-2
                        DEP ARPRT ILS FREQ
                        DEP ARPRT ILS FRONT CLS
                        DEP ARPRT ILS ID
                        DEP ARPRT ILS TYPE
                        DEP ARPRT REST SPD
                        DEP OFFSET ALT
                        DEP RWY ID
                        DEP RWY LEN
                DEST ARPRT DATA ...
```

Figure 8.5. Indented explosion of a large group flow.

- A special set of symbols is used to define the way primitives are structured into a group flow.

- Nowadays, most dictionaries are stored in computers, where much useful additional information can be recorded and special reports generated.

Chapter 9

Requirements Model Interpretation and Summary

9.1   The Requirements Model Interpreted

In Section 4.8, we described the properties of the process model represented by the basic structured analysis method, and illustrated the primitive network concept. We have now described the control structure that has been added to the basic method, and here we will discuss how this extension affects the model.

The idea of an idealized, infinitely fast model is still retained. In this respect, the control structure is very similar to the data structure: CSPECs and PSPECs both convert their inputs to their outputs the instant those inputs occur. Likewise, a process is active the instant the activator from its CSPEC goes from False to True.

The primitive network of Figure 4.11 becomes quite different, however. Figure 9.1 illustrates a primitive network with the control structure added. For the purposes of this figure only, process controls are identified with double-headed arrows. In the actual model, of course, they are not shown diagrammatically at all.

This rather complicated figure reveals a number of interesting facts. It should be looked at in conjunction with the feedback loop diagram of Figure 5.7. The two diagrams actually represent the same information, but in very different forms. You will notice in Figure 9.1 that control signals never flow into primitive processes, and from this diagram alone it is not clear why. Figure 5.7, however, makes it very clear that the role of control signals is to drive CSPECs that activate processes, and to provide control information to the outside world.

Some primitive processes *generate* control signals—the data conditions described in Section 5.4—which can be seen emanating from processes in Figure 9.1, and which close the loop from the processor to the controller in Figure 5.7.

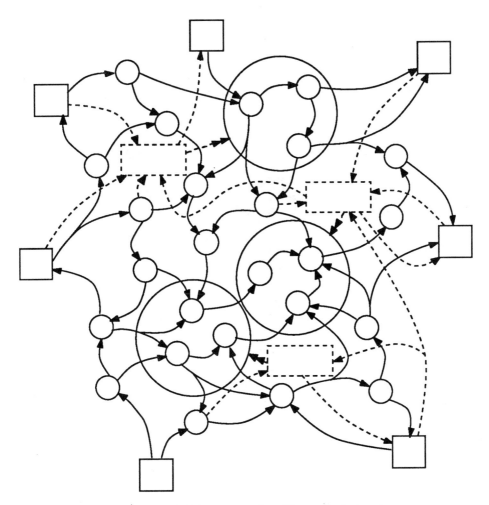

Figure 9.1. Primitive network with control structure.

Perhaps the most interesting fact revealed is that, whereas in the basic structured analysis model the primitive network completely discards the higher-level processes, in the extended method CSPECs are specifically associated with higher-level processes, so these processes become an integral part of the model. They are shown in the figure, surrounding the groups of primitives they contain. A process control from a CSPEC controls one of these groups: It turns on and off all the primitives in that group.

As was stated in Chapter 3, the requirements model appears to represent an actual machine, but this is not its intent. When interpreting the model, the internal partitioning into processes exists only for communication purposes; this partitioning does not necessarily have to be carried over to the design phase (although if the decision to do so is made based on design considerations, there is nothing wrong with it). The only property of the model that *must* be preserved in the design is the input-to-output functionality and timing. In other words, it is the overall transfer function from any given input(s) to the affected outputs, and the associated timing, which is required, not the details of how that transform happened to be expressed inside the model.

9.2   Requirements Model Summary

We have seen that the requirements model is based on information abstraction and decomposition, whereby we start with a very general statement of the system requirements and the communications it must have with the outside world. We then progressively decompose that general statement into more specific ones, until we arrive at a large network of primitive statements that are so small and concise that little room is left for ambiguity (Chapter 3).

This abstraction and decomposition procedure is carried out through leveling. Together with naming, numbering, and balancing, these conventions make the model self-consistent and self-indexing (Sections 4.3 and 4.4).

The model consists of a process structure, based on DeMarco's structured analysis, and a control structure, using finite state machine theory together with control flow diagrams, which are a variation on data flow diagrams (Figure 3.1). The leveling, naming, numbering, and balancing principles apply within the process structure, within the control structure, and in the interconnections between the two. Thus, the whole model provides a highly integrated structure, with simple, clear rules for navigating your way around it. In the large, complex systems for which the model was developed, this attribute is essential.

The set of DFDs models the data processing requirements of the system. They represent an idealized model that is not related to the system's implementation; in fact, this requirements model permits us to defer consideration of physical constraints until the design phase. The model may be thought of as a giant network of primitive processes interconnected through their data flows, a network in which each process is an arbitrarily fast, independent, data triggered processor (Section 4.8).

The set of CFDs parallels the DFDs, and represents the flow of control signals to CSPECs. They share the same names and numbers as the DFDs (Section 5.3). CSPECs provide the bridge from the control structure to the process structure; they contain the finite state machine aspects of the model; they are driven by control flows from the CFDs; and they activate and deactivate processes in the DFDs (Section 5.6). The bridge in the other direction is provided by data conditions: control signals flowing into the CFDs from primitive processes, where they are generated by tests on data signals (Section 5.4).

The whole model is analogous to a feedback control loop, with the data structure as the feed-forward transform, and the control structure as the feedback transform (Figure 5.7). In any given application, only part of this loop might be used. For example, we might have a simple information processor (basic structured analysis), or a pure finite state machine (control model only), or we might have an information processor that is controlled entirely by external signals (no data conditions). Any such variation is possible, depending entirely on the characteristics of the system being modeled.

Finite state machines are subdivided into combinational machines, whose behavior is determined entirely by current inputs (Section 6.1), and sequential machines, whose behavior is a function of both current and past inputs (Section 6.2). Combinational machines are represented by decision tables; sequential machines by state transition diagrams, tables, or matrices.

In practice, a given CSPEC might contain several decision tables, or state transition matrices, or both, and might extend over several pages of the specification. In such cases, the CSPEC is organized for ease of use through a users' guide, and a prescribed system of internal sheet numbering (Section 6.3).

From the requirements point of view, only the timing between events at the system inputs and outputs—the external timing—are of concern. Internal timing is entirely a design issue. External timing consists of rates at which inputs must be received and outputs recomputed, and response times between system inputs and system outputs. The timing rates are specified in the requirements dictionary; the response times are specified in a tabular timing specification, supplemented if necessary by timing diagrams.

All the data and control flows on the flow diagrams are specified in the requirements dictionary. Primitive flows have their physical attributes specified and group flows have their structure specified using a special notation.

All the components of the requirements model follow self-consistency rules through which every flow must have a specified source and destination, and the flow diagrams, PSPECs, CSPECs, timing specification, and requirements dictionary have strict simple relationships with each other. In addition, the components have a numbering scheme that makes the model self-indexing.

We have completed our description of the requirements model. Remember, this part of the book has described what the model consists of, and how to interpret it, once it is built. If you only intend to refer to existing requirements specifications, rather than prepare new ones, you may skip Part III. If you need to interpret architecture specifications, move on to Part IV, and if you intend to prepare them, you will also need to read Part V.

PART III

Building the
Requirements Model

Chapter 10

Overview

In Part II, we described the completed requirements model in detail, and it is necessary that you have read and understood that description before proceeding with the finer details of building the model. In Part III, we address the needs of those whose job it will be to define system requirements using the requirements model. In order to understand the role of the model, we must identify who will build it and who will use it.

10.1 Model Users and Builders

Who then are the users and the builders of the requirements model? What are their needs? Looking first at the users, they fall into two categories. In the first category are the system's end users, people who want to understand the functionality and performance of the system that is eventually to be built from the model. This category can often be divided further into subcategories, such as owners, operators, and maintainers of the system; each of these has its own special needs, which it may provide for the builder to include in the model. The main purpose of the model for these users is to verify that it interprets their requirements correctly.

The second category into which the users of the model fall comprises the designers and builders of the system, people who need a precise and correct requirements statement on which to base their work. They are as interested in the logical consistency of the model as they are in its operational functionality.

The end users are experts in the industry in which the system will be used and often know little about computers and software. The system designers and builders are experts in system and software development, and probably have only limited knowledge of the end users' industries. The problem is that these two groups rarely speak the same language, nor do they understand each other's needs. The requirements model provides a communication tool: a means to represent the requirements in a form both the end user and the designer can understand.

Who then are the model builders? To satisfy all the diverse user needs listed above, they must need the wisdom of Solomon, the patience of a saint, and a thick skin to boot! During the years that structured requirements analysis has been practiced, the role of those who carry it out has been progressively shifting. At first it was done mostly by programmers who had the vision to realize that they needed to get a better handle on the requirements of their software. As time went on, some people began to specialize in this phase of the development cycle, and became known as systems analysts. They concentrated more and more on user needs, and on understanding the user's business, and they devoted less and less time to the development of the software itself. In this book, we generally refer to systems analysts as model builders because, when working with the methods described in the book, they are building models.

The spread of the software boom into embedded, real-time systems, and the development of methods such as this one to handle the extreme complexity of these systems, has shifted the requirements definition process even further from the software developers. Today, model builders are quite likely to be from the user community itself, with little or no software background. They come from high-technology communities, such as avionics or chemical engineering. Because their industries are so complex and specialized, it is more important that they have a background in the specific high-technology field than in computer science.

The preceding paragraphs describe what is typical in industry today, but the situation at your site might be quite different: There are no rules as to who does the requirements analysis. For example, some corporations have their own people develop systems entirely for in-house use, in which case the user, analyst, and system builder may all be the same.

10.2   The Sources of Requirements

Most industries have grown up over many years, and have been doing very nicely, without computers or software. Not surprisingly, therefore, people in those industries tend to describe their specialties in ways that do not lend themselves to computing. Objects, actions, data processes, and control processes are intermingled with abandon, and specialized terms are used that may be meaningless, or even misleading, to the outsider.

In such environments, there is no chance that the analyst can just "pick up" the required technical knowledge in the course of the analysis. On the other hand, expressing the requirements in a structured form such as the requirements model provides will automatically make them more amenable to software design, even if the analyst who does that conversion is not conversant with software.

The task of building the requirements model is principally a process of interpreting the statements of needs from these various users, and constructing the model from their statements. This process will test whether the statements are self-consistent and complete, and will lead to further dialogue where they are not.

The user source statements will vary tremendously from one user to another, and from one project to another. They will vary from brief to voluminous, and from vague to specific. Some will be in informal memos, some in formal written specifications, some will be partly written and partly spoken, and some will be included in binding contract statements. Some of the more sophisticated users may even provide their requirements already in the form of a structured model, defined down to the level of detail of direct user concern. Your job as a requirements analyst is to take these statements in whatever form they come to you, interpret them, test them for consistency and completeness, resolve issues arising from these tests, deliver the eventual model to the designers, and continue to resolve all further issues that arise during the design and test process.

10.3   The Model Building Process

The steps to take in building the model are listed below. The order in which they are given should not be interpreted as the exact order in which they must be performed—only as a guide to the general flow. Typically, the model builder will work on several steps in parallel and will iterate back and forth between them several times over. Here then are the steps:

- Organize the customer/user requirements statements into major functional groups.

- Identify the external entities (such as other systems, operators, control panels) with which the system is required to communicate.

- Identify the major information groups that must flow between the system and the external entities.

- Start constructing a top-level flow diagram, by representing the major functional groups as processes, the external entities as terminators, and the major information groups as data flows between them.

- Study the resulting diagram and ask yourself such questions as the following:

- Is the scope of the model right? Should any of the terminators really be part of the system, or any of the processes be terminators?

- Do the processes relate well to the way the users view the system requirements? Would a repartitioning make the requirements clearer?

- Do the flows go to and from the right places? Can the processes reasonably produce their stated outputs with the given inputs? Would the picture be clearer if the flows were regrouped?

- Make any changes resulting from your answers to these questions.

- Draw a context diagram by collapsing the processes into a single process and, if appropriate, compressing the flows into fewer groups.

- Remove the terminators from the original top-level flow diagram, and form a level 1 diagram.

- Examine the major requirements, and decide if there are any modes or conditions of the system under which any of the top-level processes require deactivating. If so, identify the signals representing those modes or conditions, assign them as control signals, and construct a level 1 CSPEC. Before taking this step, be sure that the same effect would not be obtained through the inherent presence or absence of the appropriate data in these modes and conditions.

- Take each process in the current diagram, and decompose it to a child diagram (or PSPEC).

- Make the same control decision for each process in the new diagram as you did for the level 1 diagram; construct CSPECs and CFDs as needed.

- Each time you add a new data or control flow, add it to the requirements dictionary. If possible, add its definition to the dictionary as well.

- In parallel with your decomposition process, study the user requirements, divide them up into elementary requirements statements (usually a phrase-by-phrase division), and identify which process or CSPEC accommodates each one of them.

- Each time two or three levels have been done, review and revise them to improve their understandability and correctness; check for balancing errors and fix any you find. Resolve requirements ambiguities and omissions as you go along if you can; if you cannot fix them, note them for later resolution. Keep iterating frequently in this way; the longer you leave them, the more painful changes become!

- When you feel you can unambiguously express the function of a process in a few lines of text or equations, or with a simple diagram, write a PSPEC.

In the following chapters, we go over each of these steps in some detail, but we must warn from the outset that building a requirements model is not an exact science. In a sense, teaching the steps of model building is like teaching the steps for writing a novel: You can teach people some effective techniques, but you cannot teach them how to become great authors. Similarly, there is no single correct model for a given set of requirements: Different people will come up with different models, each of which might be equally effective. The model is a tool, and how it is used is partly a function of the system it is modeling. New users will very probably find new and ingenious ways to use it, and should be encouraged to do so.

In short, there is no way we could cover every possible application and every variation of effective and ineffective uses of the requirements model. Consequently, we have chosen to illustrate our points through a combination of concrete cases drawn from the Automobile Management System model, which is fully analyzed in Chapter 26, and a series of abstract examples where those serve the purpose best. In this latter case, we shamelessly use symbolic names for our signals, contrary to our own advice. Illustrating a point is very different from analyzing a system. Our goal is to point out the major variations, and to emphasize the important principles involved.

Chapter 11

Getting Started

In this chapter, we expand on the first four steps of the model building process that was presented in the previous chapter. Specifically, we will look at procedures for analyzing customer requirements, making the initial separation between data and control, establishing the system context, and partitioning the top levels.

11.1   User Requirements Statements

There is nothing standard about the form in which you, as the model builder, might receive a requirements statement from the customer or user. Some very large and costly systems have been developed from the briefest and vaguest of statements from the user. Other users, on the other hand, have a very detailed idea of what they need, and may provide you with a lengthy specification and want to be involved in every step of the development process.

If you receive few details, you will have to be very creative and put yourself in the user's role to decide what a reasonable system should do. It is very important in such cases to keep your users informed of the decisions you make; it usually turns out that they really do have opinions on what they want, but did not express them in their requirements statement. If the user gives you a very detailed specification, the difficulty might be to keep enough distance between the two of you to get the work done. Also, you might find that some of these detailed requirements are unreasonable, and have difficulty persuading the user to change them.

In either case, your job is to use the requirements model to create a statement that is agreeable to the user, that is correct and complete, and that provides a sound basis from which to start the design.

11.2 Separating Data and Control

In Part II, we showed the data and control structures of the requirements model already separated. Unfortunately, achieving this separation is one of the biggest hurdles to overcome in building the model. The two aspects will be totally intertwined in the customer requirements statement, and one of your first jobs is to separate them. You will have to decide for each statement whether it represents information flow or processing, and for each of these, whether it is data or control. Thus, you will partition the statements into data flows, control flows, data processes, and control processes. The control processes, of course, are finite state machines, which will eventually be contained in the CSPECs, and represented as decision tables, or state transition diagrams, tables, or matrices.

There are no cast-iron rules for making these categorizations, and some cases are arbitrary, but certain guidelines do apply, as follows:

- Continuous signals, and processes that act on them, are *always* categorized as data. This, of course, is because finite state machines, by definition, cannot handle such signals and processes.

- Discrete signals, and processes that act on them, are *usually* categorized as control, but there are exceptions.

- Terms like Activate, Turn On, Engage, and Execute are usually associated with control requirements.

The fundamental rule is to categorize according to the use to which the signal or process is put. Algebraic calculations and algorithms, and the signals that they use, should be categorized as data. Decision-making processes, and the signals *they* use—those whose purpose is to determine the operating mode of the system, or to decide which processes on the data side should be active—should be categorized as control. It sometimes happens that a given signal is used both ways in different parts of the system; in which case, it should be categorized as both, and appear in both the data and control flow diagrams. For example, a signal that controls a process and whose value appears on a display might be categorized both as data and control. Such a signal must have only one dictionary definition, however, where its dual role must be noted.

An important principle to bear in mind is that, in this model, CSPECs play their most valuable role at the higher levels. It is here that they control the activation of major system processes, something that basic structured analysis is not equipped to do. At the lower levels, many decisions of this type can be incorporated in the process specifications using conditional statements, and this is a very effective way to handle them. You should therefore be biased toward categorizing signals as *control* when they influence the system's major operating modes and high-level process activation, but toward *data* when they only involve low-level decisions. Some further guidelines are given in Figure 11.1.

In some cases, the choice is quite difficult to make, and people tend to agonize over these. Don't do that! In such cases, the choice is, in fact, usually quite arbitrary. In other words, in cases in which the choice is very difficult, it probably does not matter much which decision is made—a perfectly satisfactory model will result either way. This does not imply that the division into data and control is meaningless; in most cases, the choice will be quite clear and meaningful. It simply means that the two sets of data and control entities have a fuzzy boundary: Some members clearly belong to one set or the other, but other members might belong to either.

The processing and control requirements of the system can be defined entirely independently of each other. As an example, there is a complex algorithm for flying a commercial aircraft in the cruise phase of its flight. This algorithm is a function of the aircraft and engine characteristics, the current air data (barometric altitude, airspeed, temperature, and so forth), and operating cost data. Quite independently, there is a similarly complex control function that turns the algorithm on and off depending on whether cruise mode is appropriate. This function depends on the flight plan, air traffic control instructions, and other operational inputs. The cruise algorithm from the Automobile Management System does not contain any of the control function, and the control function contains none of the algorithm. They are *ex*trinsically related to each other, but not *intrinsically*.

Part of the strategy of keeping it simple is to make use of this independence, and, at each phase of building the model, to work on the data structure before the control structure. There are several reasons for choosing this sequence:

- It is the best way to find out if a control structure is simply not needed at that point. The data triggered, DFD-only approach is the simplest, and therefore should be used whenever possible. (Looked at another way, if we start building a control structure first, we might never realize it is not needed.)

- It is necessary to know what you are controlling before you can decide how to control it (just as in defining a control system for a plant or machine tool).

- Since the control structure is dependent on the data structure, the latter is needed to define the former. (This is essentially the same reason

Signal Type:	Categorize as:
Signal representing a continuous physical quantity *(airspeed, flow rate)*	Data signal
Many-valued discrete signal *(flight phase, model type)*	Depends on its use. If used to control (activate) process(es), assign as control. If used together with data signals in a calculation or algorithm, assign as data. Could be used as both in different parts of the system.
Binary signal *(air/ground switch, reaction enabled)*	Usually a control signal, but the same guidelines apply as for many-valued discrete signals. Alphanumeric keystrokes are an example of binary signals that might be treated as data.

Process Type:	Categorize as:
Process with continuous inputs and outputs, or with mixed continuous and discrete inputs or outputs.	Data process (FS machine has no way of handling continuous signals; process spec does)
Process with discrete inputs and outputs.	Usually control, but could be a data process if all its signals were assigned elsewhere as data, and if it does not control other processes.
Process with sequential states (i.e., response varies with past events).	Control process, using sequential machine representation—there is no other practical way to represent it.

Figure 11.1. Signal and process categories.

as the previous one—the method itself was designed that way based on the control system model.)

- Data processes should be "black-boxish"—defined independently of how, why, or when they are activated—the principles of minimum coupling (independence of processes) and maximum cohesion (strong functional connection between everything within a process) [12] are as applicable in this model as in all process models.

- The control structure is the area where it is most tempting to go beyond true requirements, and start getting into design. It is, for example, the area where the software implementation words "flag" and "bit" tend to creep in—sure signs that the author is thinking way beyond the level the user cares about.

An exception to the principle of minimizing the control structure occurs when a system, or part of a system, is control intensive—when there are few data processing requirements compared to the control requirements, and especially when the control functions are not used to activate processes, but to produce signals that are passed out of the system. In such cases, it may be desirable to allow the control structure to extend beyond the data structure. We discuss this further in Section 12.9.

The following passages from the Automobile Management System, analyzed in full in Chapter 26, illustrate some of the separation principles discussed above:

> *The system is to drive the actuator by means of an electrical signal having a linear relationship with throttle deflection, with 0 volts setting the throttle closed and 8 volts setting it fully open.*

> *The system is to measure speed by counting pulses it receives from a sensor on the drive shaft. Count rate from this sensor corresponds to vehicle miles per hour through a proportionality constant.*

There is no question that the signal driving the actuator is a data signal, since it is continuous. But what about the pulses from the drive shaft? Here we have a binary signal, which we might at first be inclined to designate as control, but look at what it represents, and more importantly, how it will be used in the model. The physical form of the signal is unimportant; it is a measure of a continuous variable—shaft rotation—and as such can only be designated as data. Avoid the temptation to describe the means by which the pulses might be converted to the measure of speed (triggering a counter, for example), as such a description becomes too implementation-oriented. The actual PSPEC for this process is shown in Figure 11.2. Notice that we leave

PSPEC 1.2; MEASURE SPEED

At least once per second, measure pulse rate of SHAFT ROTATION
in pulses per hour, and set:

$$\text{SPEED} = \frac{\text{pulse rate}}{\text{MILE COUNT}}$$

Figure 11.2. Typical PSPEC: a primitive requirements statement.

the designer to decide how to measure a pulse rate, but that, from another
part of the requirements statements, we insist that it be done, by whatever
means, at least once per second.

11.3   Establishing the System Context

Having made a start on categorizing the user requirements, our next task is
to decide which of those statements fall within the scope of the system we are
to define, and which describe the outside world with which the system is to
interface. It is quite usual and natural for both to be included in a narrative
system description: Often, the role of the system is only meaningful in the
context of the world in which it operates. In addition, the boundary between
the system and the world external to it is often not well-defined at the outset.
In many cases, it is necessary to discuss exactly what the user wants included in the system and what will be taken care of by other means. As a
simple illustration, consider this statement from the Automobile Management System:

> *The driver must be able to increase the speed at any time by depressing
> the accelerator pedal, or reduce the speed by depressing the brake.
> Thus, the driver may go faster than the cruise control setting simply by
> pressing the accelerator pedal far enough; when the pedal is released,
> the system will regain control.*

From this we see that the accelerator pedal can override the cruise control
system and vice versa, which leads us to conclude that neither one has a
direct mechanical linkage to the carburetor, and that therefore some kind of
parallel actuating device is required to make these override decisions. It is
certainly worth verifying whether we are expected to include this device in
our system. Our starting position should be to assume the worst, and include
within our scope everything that could conceivably be required in our system.
Later, we can eliminate items if it turns out they are covered elsewhere. In

this case, we would show the actuating device as a process within our system (Select Throttle Drive), and the accelerator and carburetor as terminators, as shown in Figure 11.3. It is better to make these assumptions and eliminate processes later, than to discover halfway through the development that there are items *no one* is covering! If, as expected, it turns out we are *not* required to include these items within our system, then the diagram reduces to the one shown in Figure 11.4, on the facing page.

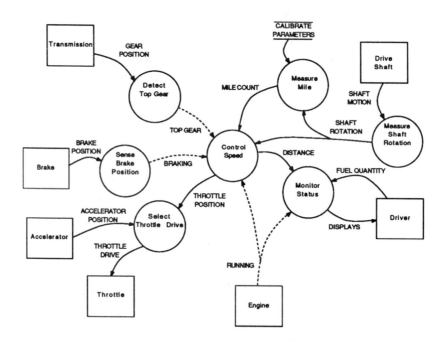

Figure 11.3. Assuming the worst: all conceivable functions included.

As suggested by these figures, during the early development of the model, it is often expedient to combine the context and level 1 diagrams into one. This greatly simplifies the task of determining the system boundary. The main system processes and the external entities all appear together, which makes it easier to decide whether a given process should be a terminator or vice versa. It is a simple matter later to separate the diagrams into their proper forms.

In constructing the data context and level 1 diagrams, work on the process model first, and set aside the statements you have categorized as control for inclusion in the control model when you are ready to build it. When that time comes, draw control flows to and from the terminators and processes that seem most appropriate. At this stage, this too can conveniently be done on the combined context/level 1 diagram.

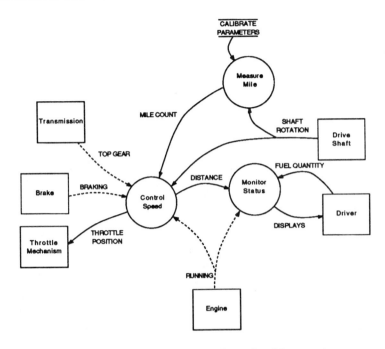

Figure 11.4. Functions reduced after checking system scope.

Returning to the Automobile Management System, another of the requirements statements is

> **Cruise Control:** *This function is to take over the task of maintaining a constant speed when commanded to do so by the driver. The driver must be able to enter several commands, including:* Activate, Deactivate, Start Accelerating, Stop Accelerating, *and* Resume.

These driver commands certainly have the appearance of control about them, so our first instinct would be to show them as control signals coming from a terminator called Driver and going to a process called Control Speed. We might also be inclined to group them together under the name CRUISE CMDS as shown in Figure 11.5, and make a corresponding dictionary entry, such as

$$\text{CRUISE CMDS} = ([\text{ACTIVATE} \,|\, \text{DEACTIVATE}]) + ([\text{START ACCEL} \,|\, \text{STOP ACCEL}])$$

Preferably, the Control Speed process will already exist in the data model, and our control flow will simply be added along with the existing data flows. This is consistent with our principle of working on the data side first.

Through these procedures, then, we will end up with a composite DCD/CCD/level 1 DFD/level 1 CFD diagram, which is a useful tool for assessing the overall scope of the system, determining what the system's major pro-

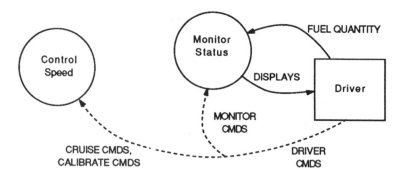

Figure 11.5. Diagram with a first-cut control flow.

cesses are, and showing the major data and control flows. When this level of analysis has been carried out, it is a routine matter to split the diagram into its four component parts.

11.4   Partitioning the Top Levels

The top-level diagrams are the ones that will determine how all the analysis from this point on is partitioned, and therefore, how the analysis tasks will be divided between the various analysts as we progress to the lower levels. In the model we are using for our illustrations, division of tasks is not a big issue because the system can readily be handled by one person, but in the large, complex systems to which the method is usually applied in practice, it can have far-reaching consequences. For example, different parts of the system might require different disciplines (flight control, communications, navigation, for example), so we would want to partition to make each high-level process specific to one discipline; in another case, we might attempt to choose the processes so as to divide the remaining effort evenly between them; a third possibility is that the user might want us to partition the model into functions with which he is familiar from past experience. Thus, because of the impact partitioning has on the remainder of the analysis, it is worth spending more time on it at this level than at lower ones.

A simple illustration of top-level partitioning is provided by the Automobile Management System, in which we might end up with a composite top-level diagram like Figure 11.6. A closer look at this diagram suggests that our earlier approach to include a level 1 process, Control Speed, might better be divided into two processes—Measure Motion and Control Throttle—since the former can then share its outputs with the Monitor Status process. This is shown in the level 1 diagram of Figure 11.7.

Our next task is to decide whether a control specification is needed at this level. The detailed criteria for doing this were discussed in Section 11.2, and will be discussed further in Chapter 14. Remember that it is preferable to

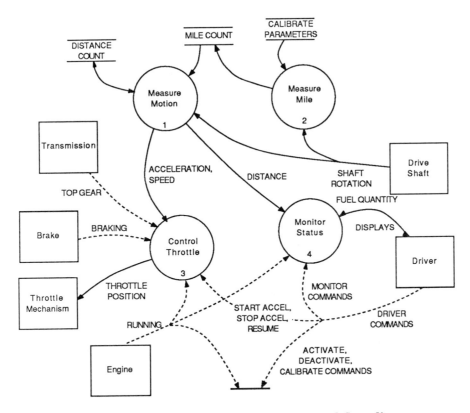

Figure 11.6. Composite top-level data and control flow diagram.

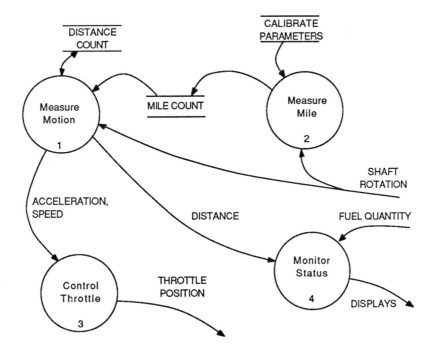

Figure 11.7. DFD 0: Control & Monitor Auto.

avoid a CSPEC if the conventional data driven model will do, but that where CSPECs *are* needed, they should be promoted to the highest possible level. There are two reasons for this: The first is that lower-level, local control can often be incorporated in PSPECs, and this should be done where possible to keep the model simple. The second reason is that *a control signal should never be used, directly or indirectly, to control an ancestor process of the PSPEC or CSPEC from which it was generated.* Doing so would create an ambiguous situation since, the moment such a signal caused its ancestor process to turn off, all the descendants of that process, including the signal's source PSPEC or CSPEC, would also turn off. The control signal would thus go to a null state, and the logic controlling the deactivation of the ancestor process would cease to depend on that signal. Unless some other control signal, not derived from within the ancestor process, is holding that process inactive, the activation will oscillate on and off. Promoting CSPECs to the highest possible level helps to ensure that control signals flow *down* the model's structure, and so cannot deactivate their own ancestors.

In the case of the Automobile Management System, two of the processes (Measure Motion and Monitor Status) can be left to respond to their input data as data triggered processes, but the other two must not run concurrently, so a CSPEC is included at this level as shown in Figure 11.8. It will deactivate one process while activating the other. Some of the control flows enter the CSPEC through the bar symbol; others continue down to lower levels for control purposes within those processes. Remember that the "unused" objects (Measure Motion, Measure Mile, MILE COUNT) in Figure 11.8 are simply there as reminders that they *are* used on the DFD in Figure 11.7.

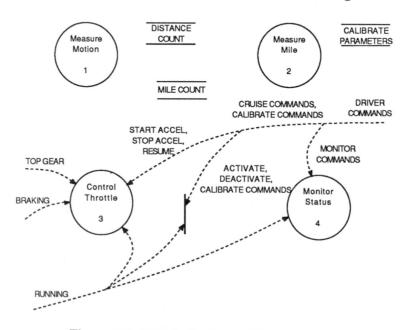

Figure 11.8. CFD 0: Control & Monitor Auto.

11.5 Summary

- User requirements statements come in every form imaginable. Your challenge is to take them in whatever form they come, and create a correct structured requirements model from them.

- Start by including everything you are given within the context, then repartition to exclude everything the customer/user agrees is outside the system's scope.

- Partition the top-level flows and processes in ways that are familiar to the user, and that will divide the later analysis into meaningful tasks.

- In any given area, try to build the data model before the control model, and try to minimize control.

- Keep the control structure at as high a level as possible as it is best suited for controlling the high-level modes of the system.

- Continuous flows and processes must be included in the process model; discrete flows usually are included in the control model, but may be in either.

- It is the *use* to which the flow is put rather than its form that determines which part of the model should include it.

Chapter 12

Developing the
Model's Structure

In this chapter, we continue our discussion of building the requirements model by considering the steps necessary to put together the whole structure of data and control flow diagrams. We cover issues of abstraction and decomposition in both processes and flows, naming processes and flows, use of stores, the role of the control model and restrictions on its use, and the proper place of the whole model in the development process. The flow diagram structure is the core of the model on which are based the process specifications, control specifications, timing specifications, and dictionary.

12.1   Abstraction and Decomposition

We first introduced the terms abstraction and decomposition in Part II, and will now take a closer look at their significance. Recall that they are based on the principles of information or data abstraction proposed by Parnas [13], whereby a system is first defined in a very general, abstract way, then this definition is progressively decomposed into finer and finer detail until a large set of small, simple definitions is obtained that exactly describes the original system.

The process in the context diagram, which we refer to as the context process, represents a very abstract statement of the system requirements—for example, Perform Flight Management and Control & Monitor Auto are expressions which, while they certainly embrace all the system requirements, give very little detail about what is to be done. Likewise, flows on the context diagram, such as AIR DATA and DRIVER COMMANDS, usually represent large groups of information while giving only a general idea of their individual components.

Level 1 diagrams express this same information, but in more detail, with the process decomposed into several subprocesses, and the flows divided into subgroups. The same procedure goes a step further in the level 2 diagrams, and so on. The idea is that the user of the model first gets a general idea of the requirements, and then can proceed to as much detail as desired by progressing down the levels. At each step of the way, the names of the processes and flows are chosen to convey as much meaning to the user as possible, consistent with the current level of abstraction.

The discussion so far has considered the model from the linguistic point of view—the point of view of the verbal descriptions on the diagrams—but there is an equally important mathematical point of view. The context process is not just a vague, general description of the total system requirements: It may equally well be thought of mathematically as the name of a set of subprocesses and their interconnections in its descendant diagrams. In this sense, it is very precise: The process consists of exactly those components shown on the descendant diagrams, and the flows consist of exactly what the dictionary says. Moreover, the leveled subsets of processes have the very special property of being mutually exclusive—not two processes share a subprocess. This is the means by which ambiguity is avoided: It translates into the property that a particular requirements statement at a given level of detail is only included at one point in the model. The *relationships* between these statements are precisely shown by the flows between them. Thus, we can see that the guidelines in the following sections, whose thrust is to minimize the flows and simplify the diagrams, are not just artistic niceties, but translate into grouping together related requirements statements as closely as possible, and expressing them as simply as possible.

These linguistic and mathematical aspects of the model finally come together in the process specifications, which consist of short narrative, but precise, statements. (For the purposes of this discussion, equations are considered to be narrative statements.)

12.2 The Seven-Plus-or-Minus-Two Principle

In starting the decomposition process, the first issue that arises is how much to decompose at each level. Fortunately, we are assisted here by one of the most frequently quoted principles in structured methods, described more than twenty years ago by G. A. Miller [10]. It shows that in a remarkably diverse range of human activities, our abilities are at their best when we deal with a number of facts, objects, or whatever, in the range from five to nine. Beyond that range, our performance falls off dramatically (it does not merely level off, it actually decreases), while below that range, we are not really challenged.

This principle has been widely applied in structured analysis as a guideline for deciding on the optimal number of processes when decomposing down to a new DFD. While this is good advice for DFDs that have fairly simple flow patterns, it breaks down in cases in which there are many flows with complex patterns. A diagram with just five processes but with flows weaving and branching between them all may be too complex to be useful. In such a case, it may be quite appropriate to have only three processes. Miller's principle still applies, but when flow patterns are complex, you should judge the total complexity of the diagram rather than merely counting the number of processes. In a similar way, a diagram whose structure is very simple, such as that of a transaction center, may have many more than nine processes without taxing our capabilities.

12.3   Grouping and Decomposing Processes

The end result of the abstraction/decomposition procedure is a nicely structured, top-down representation of the requirements. However, the *construction* of the requirements model cannot usually be done entirely top-down. Recent papers by Parnas [14], and by Swartout and Balzer [17], have pointed out that in reaching the final model, there will be iterations between all levels from the highest to the lowest, as well as between requirements and design. The important thing is that the end result presents the requirements to the users in a top-down fashion, whereby they can choose the amount of detail of interest simply by selecting the corresponding level in the model.

User requirements tend to consist of many, quite detailed, statements, and much of the time you will find yourself working from these upward to the more abstract levels. The procedure is in many ways quite arbitrary. You can start at any point, and work upward or downward or both, but the important thing is repeatedly to iterate and refine what you have, until a clear, simple model results. Here are some of the principles and guidelines to follow in constructing a leveled set of processes:

- Minimize the total number of flows, both the total number on the diagram, and the number associated with a given process ("starve your bubbles," is a popular saying in SA circles). This can be done by grouping flows together under a single name, or by grouping processes together to push some flows down to a lower level.

- Try to distribute the flows evenly between the processes. A process with many more flows than others in its diagram is a candidate for splitting into component processes ("bubbling up"). Possibly some of these components can then be grouped with other processes on the diagram.

- Don't sit thinking about how to start your diagram—get something down on paper (or on your interactive, graphic screen), and start refining it: The mind is better at improving on things than creating them.

- A flow or a process for which you cannot think of an appropriate name is a candidate for repartitioning because it probably consists of unrelated elements.

- As far as possible, concentrate all the processing of one input, or group of inputs, in one region of the model so as to avoid half-processed data.

It frequently happens that the effects of modifying a given diagram will cause several levels of its ancestors to be revised. This can be a frustrating process, but the quality and clarity of the end result makes it well worth the effort. Good interactive automated tools make this process of iterating over multiple levels enormously easier.

Figure 12.1 illustrates a process with many flows and its partitioning and regrouping. Figure 12.2 shows a "busy" group of processes, having many mutual interactions, that are relegated to a lower level.

Throughout the process of building a leveled set of diagrams, continuously check that the rules of balancing, stated in Section 4.3, are observed, and add new data flows and their definitions to the dictionary. Balancing and dictionary entries will be much harder to do later when your initial thought process is lost.

12.4   Grouping and Decomposing Flows

As described in Section 4.5, data flows are abstracted in much the same way as processes. Primitive signals are grouped together and given names descriptive of the group. Looked at from the opposite direction, the groups are decomposed as they progress down the diagram levels until they are reduced to primitive signals. Every group, subgroup, and primitive is defined in the dictionary.

Consistent with the fact that PSPECs are assumed to have universal access to time, there should not normally be any flows representing time. Since time is a parameter used by a very high percentage of process specifications, explicitly flowing it to all those PSPECs would quickly get out of hand. We will discuss this further in Section 13.3.

Splitting and merging flows

The conventions for splitting and merging flows, which were introduced in Figure 4.7 and further illustrated in Figures 12.3 through 12.10, are worth careful attention. Figure 12.3 shows the simplest kind, in which a flow splits

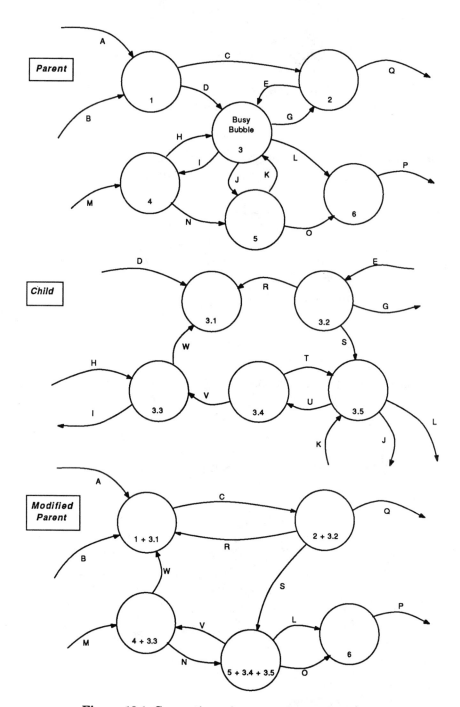

Figure 12.1. Correction of uneven flow distribution.

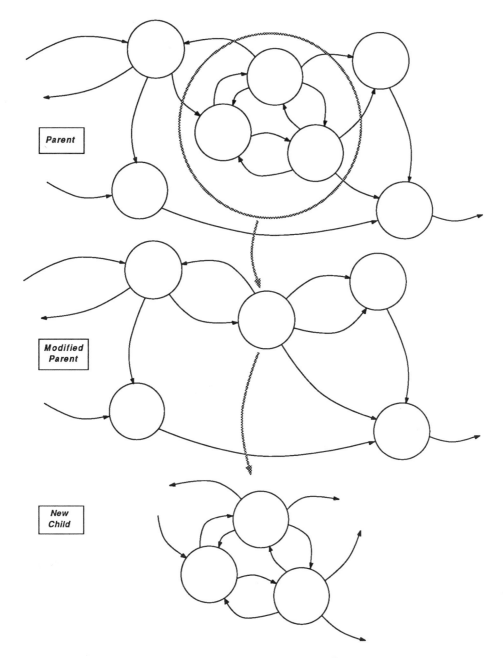

Figure 12.2. Correction of clustered processes.

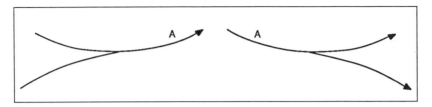

Figure 12.3. Splitting and merging data flows.

or merges, and the entire flow on the trunk is replicated on the branches. This is usually represented by labeling the trunk with the flow name, but *not* labeling the branches—implying that the branches "inherit" the name of the trunk. In this figure the whole flow goes to, or is derived from, both branches.

In Figure 12.4, a split or merge is accompanied by a decomposition or grouping. In this case, one or more of the branches is labeled with a subgroup name. An unlabeled branch indicates that the whole flow passes along it.

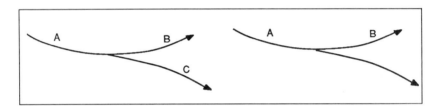

Figure 12.4. Decomposing data flows.

Splitting and merging flows must balance in the same way as flow diagrams. It is essential that every member of a flow is accounted for. If a flow splits into subgroups, it is necessary that all the members of the subgroups are also members of the parent group, and that every member of the parent group appears at least once among the subgroups, all as defined in the dictionary.

It sometimes happens that a particular group flow is used in a certain part of the system, while in another part of the system that same group is used with the exception of just a few of its members. The new group can be made into a separate flow with its own name, but this can lead to many flows with only slightly different compositions. Another alternative is to use the original flow only, but where it enters the part of the system that does not use all of its members, show those unused members flowing into a branch labeled "not used," as illustrated in Figure 12.5. Proper balancing ensures that every member of a group appears at least once in the descendants of the process it enters, or on a "not used" branch.

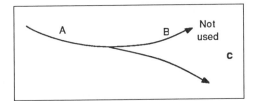

Figure 12.5. Splitting off unused flows.

Unlike processes, the children of data flows are not necessarily mutually exclusive. In other words, the subgroups of a parent group may share some members. Consider, for example, three flows whose dictionary definitions are

$$X = A + B + C + D + E + F + G + H$$
$$Y = A + B + C + D + E$$
$$Z = D + E + F + G + H$$

Figure 12.6 shows Y and Z branching from X, which might at first sight lead us to believe that the dictionary definition of X is

$$X = Y + Z$$

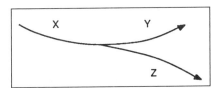

Figure 12.6. Flows with common members.

Substituting the definitions of Y and Z into this expression would lead to a definition of X different from the one above—the terms D and E would be duplicated, indicating that a given instance of X would contain two instances of D and E. The apparent definition of X is therefore wrong: The branching flow indicates that D and E are replicated at the branch, while the other members of X separate from each other. It is necessary to refer to the dictionary definitions as well as the flow diagram to reach this conclusion. The flow diagram is correct, however, because Y and Z are indeed subsets of X. (Notice the distinction between *replication*, which is the copying of a single instance of a flow onto two branches, and *duplication*, which is the inclusion of two instances of a member of a flow within the flow's definition.)

An important message here is that the exact definitions of data flows are contained in the dictionary, not on the flow diagrams. From the flow diagram alone, the definition of X might be not only the two given above, but also

$$X = [Y|Z]$$

or,

$$X = (Y) + (Z)$$

or many others. The ambiguity is resolved *only* through the dictionary.

Multiple flows

The convention of showing multiple flows on a single arc, shown in Figure 12.7, may be used in several different situations. The flows may not form a cohesive group such that a good descriptive name can be found for them, such as SHAFT ROTATION, MILE COUNT, or FUEL QUANTITY. Or the convention might be used where the group is only flowing to a nearby process, so grouping them under a single name would not provide the benefit of decluttering several diagrams. Or it might be used to list all the component members of Y and Z on their respective branches in Figure 12.6. In this case, there would be more clutter on the diagram, but less ambiguity in the flow definitions. You must use your judgment in each particular case to decide which is more appropriate.

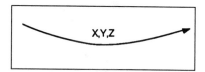

Figure 12.7. Multiple flows.

It is always possible to show separate flows on separate arcs passing to or from the same bubbles; in fact, showing them on a single arc could be considered cheating on the principle of starving your bubbles. Listing many flows on one arc conceals the fact that there *are* many flows. But inevitably, large, complex systems *do* involve many flows, and techniques for reducing the resulting clutter are needed. Don't abuse this convention, however: If the number of flows can be reduced, then do it, whether or not they are shown on a single arc.

The two-way flow shown in Figure 12.8 is used to indicate that the same flow or flows pass in both directions between the same two places. It is fre-

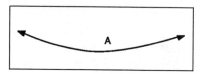

Figure 12.8. Two-way flows.

quently used, for example, between a process and a store, where the process sometimes updates the store's contents, and at other times uses the previously stored values.

The half-arrow convention in Figure 12.9 has a similar role. It reduces the clutter on a diagram when several flows pass in opposite directions between the same two points. This convention should only be used with simple arcs: Do not attempt to use it in combination with splitting and merging flows. Too much ambiguity will result.

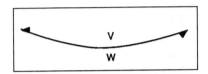

Figure 12.9. The half-arrow convention.

Flow trees

Finally, the splitting and merging conventions are frequently extended to multiple splits and merges in a single structure, as illustrated in Figure 12.10.

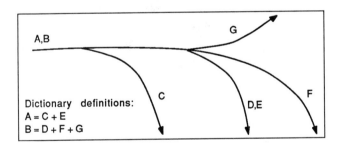

Figure 12.10. A flow tree.

The important principle to bear in mind when using such structures is that conservation of flows applies; or, to put this concept in the colloquial, "what goes in must come out." All incoming flows (explicitly named or implied through dictionary definitions) must be matched by those same flows, possibly grouped in different ways, leaving the structure. A further constraint is that the implied directions of the branches must be correct—it must be possible to trace a flow from its source to its destination without doubling

back at an intersection. Intermediate branches of the flow tree do not have to
be labeled, but they may be if you decide it improves the clarity.

12.5 Naming Processes and Flows

Choosing concise, meaningful names for processes and flows is central to
building a good model. It is true that from a purely technical point of view
meaningless, symbolic names are quite sufficient, for example, DFLOW 3574,
CFLOW 14 215, or PROCESS SIGNAL GROUP 73. The flows are precisely defined
in the dictionary, and the processes rigorously decomposed down to their
primitives, so why do we need meaningful names? The reason is that we are
trying to describe a set of system requirements so that a human reader can
clearly understand them, preferably with minimum reference to the dictionary. To achieve this, both the process and the flow names must be as descriptive as possible.

First, there are two inviolable naming rules that relate to the division of
the model into objects (flows) and actions (processes). Flows, being objects,
have names that must not contain verbs. Processes, being actions on those
objects, have names that must start with a verb, followed by an object.

Beyond these rules, the goal in choosing names is to have them describe
the exact scope of the process or flow, nothing more and nothing less. With
the limitations of natural language, and the diverse structure of modern systems, this goal cannot usually be achieved completely, but part of the skill
you must develop is to approach it as closely as possible. The principle is the
same as if we were trying to write clear narrative text: We must choose the
most appropriate words and combine them together in the most effective way.
The difference here is that the way the words are combined together is
heavily constrained.

As an illustration, consider the flows in the Automobile Management System, fully described in Chapter 26:

$$
\begin{aligned}
\text{DRIVER CMDS} &= \text{CRUISE CMDS} + \text{MONITOR CMDS} + \\
                  &\quad \text{CALIBRATE CMDS} \\
\text{CRUISE CMDS} &= (\,[\,\text{ACTIVATE}\,|\,\text{DEACTIVATE}\,]\,) + \\
                   &\quad (\,[\,\text{START ACCEL}\,|\,\text{STOP ACCEL}\,]\,) \\
\text{MONITOR CMDS} &= (\text{START TRIP}) + (\text{MAINT COMPLETE}) + \\
                    &\quad (\text{AV SPEED RQST}) \\
\text{CALIBRATE CMDS} &= (\,[\,\text{START MEASURED MILE}\,| \\
                      &\quad \text{STOP MEASURED MILE}\,]\,)
\end{aligned}
$$

Within the scope of the given system, the names of these flows describe their
purpose quite well. In contrast, DRIVER CMDS might, for example, have been

called just COMMANDS; CRUISE CMDS called CMD SET 1; MONITOR CMDS called CMD SET 2; and CALIBRATE CMDS called CMD SET 3; with much less value to the user.

Abbreviations

As you will have noticed, abbreviations are used frequently in our examples, including those above. On large systems, there is a conflict between using meaningful names and keeping the diagrams decluttered. Inevitably, as we get deeper into the system, the names become longer and contain more words. Abbreviations are used to keep the total length of these names within reasonable bounds, but they should be chosen so as to be understandable without reference to a definition. It is important to use the same abbreviation for a given word throughout one project, and for that purpose, a project dictionary of abbreviations is very useful. To reiterate: The purpose of the project dictionary is not to define the meanings of the abbreviations, but to ensure that everyone on the project is consistent. Note that this dictionary should not be considered to be a deliverable item to the customer; if the abbreviations have been properly chosen so that their meanings are clear, the customer will not need the project abbreviations dictionary.

Try to avoid abbreviations whenever you can. The best way to do this is to choose short words. The following examples have been taken from real projects: The first word is the one originally used; the second is the word we used to replace it, usually with improved understandability. As you see, the word pairs are not synonyms, but, in the contexts in which they were used, the shorter words conveyed the intended meanings more effectively, and did not require abbreviating.

executable	ready
generate	make
determine	find
activate	start
gradient	slope
discontinuity	jump
restriction	limit, bound
power interruption	glitch

The above discussion of abbreviations refers principally to flow names. There is usually enough space within process bubbles to make abbreviations unnecessary; furthermore, process names are local, and are always read in the context of their inputs and outputs, so they rarely need to be as long as flow names.

12.6   Use of Stores

Data and control stores save the results of a data or control process after the process inputs have disappeared. As we described in Section 4.6, their contents remain until replaced with something new, and can be used any number of times by any number of processes; that is, they have nondestructive readout. The structured analysis method often is used with the convention of destructive readout, whereby the contents of stores remain only until they are read, then they disappear. We have found the nondestructive readout convention to be more useful, because in practice stored information is frequently needed several times. If for some reason destructive readout is needed, the receiving process can write "0" or "null" back into the store.

In every other respect, stores are treated exactly the same as flows:

- Like group flows, the names of stores are the names of their total contents, and must be defined in the dictionary.

- Flows leaving stores are exactly analogous to branch points in a flow. An unlabeled flow inherits the name of the store, and all the store's contents flow along it. A labeled flow must be a subset of the stored information. All the store's contents must leave it and be accounted for at some destination.

- Flows entering stores follow the same rules as those leaving, except when some of the store's contents are read-only; in which case, input flows must be labeled with the subset of the store's contents they carry.

Stores may be used quite liberally in the requirements model, wherever you feel they will clarify the meaning. For example, in an iterative loop, a store is appropriate at the point in the loop at which the results of its processing are read out to the outside world. In computerized systems, they never imply artificial requirements, for all the data and control flows are stored in some memory device or medium anyway. In the event driven model of McMenamin and Palmer [9], stores serve the central role of coordinating the results of processing asynchronous external events.

In Sections 4.6 and 5.5, we discussed stores just containing data that appear on a DFD only, stores just containing control that appear on a CFD only, and stores containing both data and control that appear on both diagrams. Review these sections to remind yourself of the implications of these different configurations.

12.7   Functionally Identical Processes

The statement we made in Section 12.1 that two (or more) processes never share a subprocess is always true, but it is also true that two different subprocesses may be functionally identical. Whether such subprocesses in fact eventually share a common software function is entirely a design decision, but if the subprocesses are large, it is expedient to define their common functionality only once. This can be done by expanding one of the processes to fully define its function, but not expanding the other. The unexpanded process is given its own name and number in the usual way, but it also contains the number of the expanded process, in parentheses, as a reference. The unexpanded process is then treated as a primitive, but its PSPEC just gives the equivalence of its inputs with those of the expanded process. Figure 12.11 illustrates this.

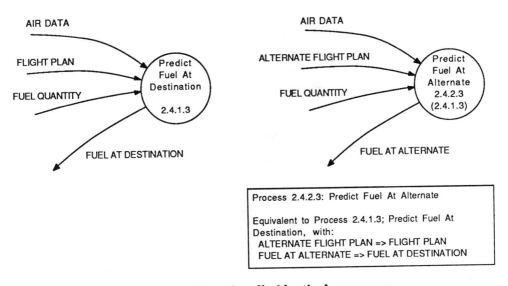

Figure 12.11. Functionally identical processes.

Be sure only to do this with large, high-level processes. With small, low-level "utility" functions, cross-references to remote parts of the model will only lead to confusion. Remember again, we are not concerned here with design optimization, only with expressing the requirements in a clear and unambiguous way. The designer might well be interested in finding common modules at all levels, but they might not correspond to the processes in our model.

12.8   De-emphasizing the Control Model

There is a tendency when building the requirements and architecture models to overspecify control. This tendency is much less among those whose background is in the application of the system, rather than in its implementation.

The reason for this bias is clear. Those whose education, training, and inclination are to put the actual systems together and get them working will naturally be inclined to specify implementation details such as flags, counters, calls, and interrupts that are so much a part of their work. The idea of an abstract model of a set of requirements is alien to people with this background.

Unfortunately, the control model lends itself to the introduction of implementation details, even though they have nothing to do with the system requirements. The control model should be used to describe the logic that controls major, high-level system states, not to describe detailed interactions among primitive processes. The latter almost always can be expressed using the basic data driven process model, that is, when the data arrives at the process inputs, the process will perform its tasks immediately and instantaneously. Because this is not the way the system will, in fact, be implemented, many analysts feel compelled to send a flag along with the data for no purpose other than to turn the process on when the data arrives. This is not necessary, and should not be done.

The control model was devised to take care of situations that the existing process model could not readily handle, and should only be used in such situations. As you proceed through the analysis, your order of preference at any given point should be to use, first, no control, that is, the process model only; second, combinational control, which is the simpler form of control; or third, sequential control when there is absolutely no other choice. Approaching the task in this way, you will use the basic process model as much as possible, and minimize the amount of control. Remember that in the combined model, processes do not *have* to have an activator: They can and preferably should be left as data triggered processes, as in the basic process model.

A common example of overspecification of control is the case in which a number of processes generate alternative system outputs, only one of which is needed at any given time. In practice, it is very likely that only the one process will be operating and that the other processes will be turned off, but this is *not* a system requirement. From the requirements point of view, all these processes can run simultaneously all the time, and another process can select which one to use. This could well be the simplest way to express the requirements. The designer remains free to implement it either way, as long as the transform from system input to system output is preserved.

12.9 Control Intensive Systems

The guidelines expressed in the previous section apply universally: Avoid implementation details in the requirements model, and beware of the temptation to use the control model to describe them.

The requirements model was developed principally for use in systems that have significant amounts of both processing and control. In such systems, it makes sense to treat the whole system as a feedback control loop in which the feed-forward part consists of the processing, which is modeled first, and the feedback part consists of control, which is structured around, or "slaved" to, the processing structure.

There are, however, some systems that are inherently control intensive—systems having mostly finite state machine properties with very little, or no, data processing. Many manufacturing process control systems are of this type, for example. They are characterized, of course, by inputs and outputs that are almost all discrete-valued. To describe the requirements of such a system using the control model only does not constitute overuse of control; rather, it is the only way to do it.

With such systems, it may be necessary to use the model in a somewhat different way. Up to this point, and as illustrated in Figure 3.1, we have slaved the control structure to the data structure. With control intensive systems this does not make sense. Two alternatives are possible: The first alternative is that a standalone control structure can be developed, dividing the requirements into separate combinational and sequential machines, embedding these machines into CSPECs, and linking the CSPEC inputs and outputs through CFDs. These CSPECs will, of course, not contain process activators as there will be nothing to activate. The composite chart of the model becomes that shown in Figure 12.12.

The result will be a model much like a leveled set of DFDs and PSPECs, but instead, consisting of CFDs and CSPECs. At the lowest levels, then, we will have flow diagrams all of whose flows go into CSPEC bars and none into bubbles, resulting in the idea of a primitive CSPEC.

The second alternative is to follow the basic principle of the method, to have the control structure slaved to the process structure, and to embed all the control processing in a few large, multi-sheet CSPECs, following the guidelines given in Sections 6.3 and 14.4. This approach greatly increases the importance of the users' guide, discussed in the above sections, which describes the internal structure of a CSPEC. The users' guide becomes the *only* means for the user to find his or her way around most of the specification, as the overall structure of the model does not help inside CSPECs.

12.10 The Dilemma of Detail: Requirements Versus Design

Perhaps the biggest single difficulty in constructing a requirements model is knowing where to stop. Unfortunately, there is nothing inherent in the method to help you; it is entirely possible that the analyst will go into more detail than the designer needs, and put design in the requirements model.

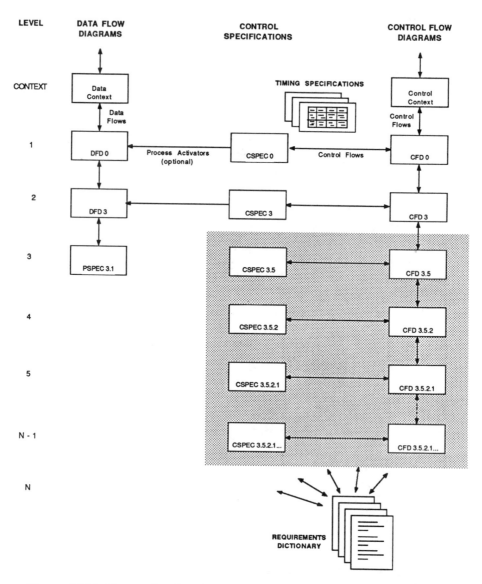

Figure 12.12. Composite chart of the model for control intensive system.

This difficulty is magnified by the truism that "one man's requirements are another man's design." On large, high-technology projects, this is especially significant. For example, the development of a commercial jet transport starts with an analysis of the general size and capability goals. Then, studies of the technologies needed to achieve these goals will be performed. Next, various overall aircraft configurations will be compared, and the project will be divided into the different technology areas for further analysis. At this point, the overall capabilities of the avionics systems will be established, and candidate configurations studied. The major avionics systems will be identified, and possibly subcontracted out to separate vendors for design studies. Within each vendor company, the requirements for each system might be divided into subsystems, and the requirements for each of these specified. Eventually, possibly after more levels of subdivision and refinement, actual hardware and software designs will be performed.

Different people are involved in each step of this lengthy procedure; each considers the task definition he or she passes on to the next step as requirements, and everything beyond that as design. It follows that *there is no absolute measure of what are requirements and what is design.* The only measure is a relative one: What do the people who will be taking the next step need to know to do their job (their requirements), and what is within their expertise to do on their own (their design)? Thus, you must know the organization you are working in, and the particular function and expertise of the group to which your requirements definition is addressed, to decide where to cut off that definition and where to extend it further.

Your task is to take the problem statement as it is presented to you, analyze it in accordance with your own expertise, and extend it just far enough to satisfy the needs of the group responsible for the next step, without encroaching on their territory.

12.11 The Final Product

After you have been through all the iterations and refinements we have described above, there is still one more thing to take care of—the style and layout of the diagrams. Remember that one of the prime goals of the method is human understandability, and this can often be enhanced greatly by choosing an "expressive" layout for your diagrams. By this we mean that if there are some special symmetries or asymmetries, or if there is some principal direction of flow, or any other property that can be expressed graphically, then the diagrams should be laid out to illustrate this. These expressive features cannot be quantified, but can contribute significantly toward giving the reader a quick intuitive feeling for the general form of the system. We have tried to apply these principles of style and layout to the diagrams in the examples of Part VI, and we suggest you look at them to see how well they express the essential form of the systems.

If you conscientiously follow the guidelines we give here, iterate until you're blue in the face, starve your bubbles, minimize the control structure, cut the model off just at the point at which the designer takes over, and make the layouts descriptive, you will have a beautifully simple and expressive requirements statement. You will proudly march into your boss's office and present the fruits of your efforts. And the boss will say: "You took *how* long to do this?"

The trouble is, the better the job you do, the simpler the end result looks, and the less people will be impressed with the effort you put into it. Only those who have been through the agony of leveling and re-leveling and refining and minimizing will really appreciate what it takes. We have no answers for this difficulty; we can only warn you not to be surprised when it happens to you, and suggest you keep copies of all those intermediate diagrams (or of earlier versions in your automated tool) as evidence.

12.12 Summary

- The goals of building a leveled set of diagrams are to make a clear, concise requirements statement at each level of detail, and to partition the requirements into mutually exclusive subsets with precisely defined relationships.

- Normally, include from five to nine processes on a diagram, but reduce this number when the flow patterns are very complex, and increase it when they are very simple.

- Strive to make the diagrams simple with an even distribution of activity. Iterate up and down the levels to achieve this goal.

- Decompose flows in parallel with processes. This may be done between parent and child diagrams, or through branching and merging flows on a diagram.

- Choose clear, concise process and flow names in order to create understandable diagrams. Abbreviations may be used only if the meaning is not lost.

- Use data or control stores anywhere that they help clarify the meaning. They must follow exactly the same rules of naming and decomposition as flows.

- Define high-level, functionally identical processes only once, with the other instances simply referencing the defined one. At the detailed levels, identification of common processes should be deferred to the design phase.

- Use the simplest form of the model that you can: the process model alone wherever possible; otherwise, try the combinational machine; and only as a last resort use the sequential machine.

- Use a control structure independent of the process structure only if the system is by nature control intensive.

- Clearly define the division between requirements and design at the outset based on consideration of the functions of the organization and the roles of the people in it.

- Choose a layout and style for the diagrams that makes them clear and understandable, and illustrates the structure of the system.

Chapter 13

Preparing Process Specifications

13.1 The Role of Process Specifications

Ultimately, it is the PSPECs and their interconnections that define the processing requirements. All the data flow diagrams could, in principle, be thrown away and no information would be lost. Removing the DFDs would take Figure 4.11 one further decomposition step, and would replace all the primitive bubbles with their PSPECs, which is not a very useful representation but which would provide all the information you could possibly need.

It is at the PSPEC level that we finally remove the last trace of abstraction, and get completely specific. The reader of the PSPEC can see precisely what the transform from input to output is to be. The primary role of the process specification, therefore, is *to describe how its outputs are generated from its inputs; it must do nothing more and nothing less.* In other words, an input that is not used in any statement in the specification, an output whose generation is not described, or a flow mentioned in the specification but not appearing as an input or output of the bubble are all errors.

Somewhere, every user requirement statement must be reflected as one or more statements in the PSPECs. The additional information that they might include is subject to your judgment, as discussed in Section 12.10. How much information you put into one PSPEC is also a matter of judgment. Each PSPEC should be short enough to avoid ambiguity and confusion, but long enough to be nontrivial. The constraints imposed by the control structure sometimes will dictate a PSPEC size smaller than you would otherwise have chosen. Since our adherence to the structure of Figure 5.7 demands that control signals do not flow into primitive processes, we sometimes will have situations in which a process has to be split into parts small enough so that each part can be activated or deactivated by a process activator.

The actual size of a PSPEC, however, is much less important than its content. A long PSPEC that does not contain all the user requirements it should is as bad as a short PSPEC that contains design details. The trick is to include all the requirements and nothing but the requirements.

13.2   The Different Types of PSPECs

PSPECs come in several different flavors: They can consist of text, equations, tables, or diagrams, or any combination of these. They should *not*, repeat *not*, contain code, or even pseudocode. We hope the reasons for this are clear by now.

The following paragraphs detail some of the more common types of PSPECs, but do not restrict yourself to conforming precisely to the format of the examples given here. It would be impossible to cover in this book every eventuality that might arise in real use. Keep the fundamentals of balancing, understandability, and lack of ambiguity in mind, and within those bounds, do whatever suits your project best.

Textual PSPECs

Textual (narrative) PSPECs are used where the process being specified is procedural. They are especially appropriate when used to describe manual operations, as follows:

> Select LABEL with destination matching DESTINATION.
> Create LABELED BAGGAGE by attaching selected LABEL to BAGGAGE.
> Then issue LABELED BAGGAGE.

Textual PSPECs are almost universally used in the business application areas to which traditional structured analysis is usually applied; they are much less usual in the engineering-oriented applications to which these extended methods are applied. In engineering applications, the equation form described below is much more common. As discussed in Section 4.7, structured English is used where narrative PSPECs do occur, and will be covered further in Section 13.4.

Equations in PSPECs

Where the outputs of a PSPEC are derived from the inputs via some mathematical process, equations are the appropriate means of representing that process. Consider, for example, the cruise control specification of Figure 13.1 taken from Chapter 26. Here, the output voltage controlling throttle position is defined as a function of speed error, with a restriction on positive rate of change of throttle opening to avoid jerky operation. The mathematical presentation is very effective here (although, of course, it *could* all be said in

Set:

$$V_{Th} = \begin{cases} 0; & (S_D - S_A) > 2 \\ 2(S_D - S_A + 2); & -2 \leq (S_D - S_A) \leq 2 \\ 8; & -2 > (S_D - S_A) \end{cases}$$

subject to:

$$\frac{dV_{Th}}{dt} \leq .8V/sec.$$

where:

$$V_{Th} = \text{THROTTLE POSITION}$$
$$S_D = \text{DESIRED SPEED}$$
$$S_A = \text{SPEED}$$

Varies throttle opening from closed to fully open as speed varies from 2 mph above desired speed, to 2 mph below it. Restricts rate of opening to .8V/sec.

Figure 13.1. A PSPEC with equations.

words), but the less formal descriptive comment at the end is helpful for the reader as a quick summary.

It often happens that the process to be described is in the form of a very large set of complex equations that already exist in standard engineering or mathematical texts. The Kalman-filter equations, used for making optimal estimates from multiple stochastic inputs, are an example of this. One of their applications is to make the best estimate of aircraft position from a variety of noisy navigation inputs. Their direct mathematical form is much too large to put in one PSPEC (it would more likely fill a hundred or so), but to split it in accordance with the traditional structured analysis guidelines would simply obscure its meaning: Each PSPEC would contain one tiny part of the algorithm that would be quite incomprehensible on its own.

The way to deal with this situation is to retain the equation set in its complete form, include it as an appendix to the requirements model, and reference it from multiple PSPECs. In this way, we keep the advantages of both the efficient mathematical representation of the equations, and the functional decomposition of the method.

Great care must be taken, when using this approach, to preserve the balancing principles. Make sure that there is a one-to-one correspondence between the variables used in the equations in the appendix, and the flows going in and out of the PSPECs. It is usually expedient to list the equivalences between the variable names and the flow names, as illustrated on a small scale in the cruise control example of Figure 13.1; in practice, these equivalence lists can get very long.

Tables in PSPECs

Tables may be used quite freely in PSPECs wherever they are the most expressive way to convey the message. One particularly convenient use is where a number of alternatives exist for the generation of the output. For example, in Figure 13.2 the outputs X and Y are generated from inputs A and B through different equations depending on the values of A and B. This example is similar to the CASE construct familiar to programmers, but it must not be represented in this way; remember, we are avoiding implementation details.

INPUTS		OUTPUTS	
A	B	X	Y
< 0		$A^2 + B^2$	$A^2 - B^2$
≥ 0	$< A$	$2AB \cos \Theta$	$2AB \sin \Theta$
	$\geq A$	$2AB \sin \Theta$	$2AB \cos \Theta$

Figure 13.2. A tabular PSPEC.

Be creative in the use of tables. There are surely tabular forms peculiar to your own applications of which we are not aware, and you should use them wherever appropriate. The tabular decision tables and state transition matrices, which we describe in Chapters 6 and 14 for use in control specifications, may equally well be used in PSPECs if their function within the model is local, not global. The only form of table that is illegal in PSPECs is the process activation table, which may only be used in CSPECs.

Diagrams in PSPECs

It has been our experience that when analysts are presented with a diagrammatic method, they tend to conclude that the diagrams of the method are sufficient and that other kinds of diagrams are unnecessary. Nothing could be further from the truth! When we say that "a picture is worth a thousand words," we mean *any* picture, not just a DFD or CFD. This point is especially important in engineering applications in which diagrams of all kinds historically have played a central role in all descriptive material, including requirements specifications. We have seen engineers get tied up in excruciating knots while trying to describe a subsystem in text or equations in their

PSPECs, when a simple diagram would have done the job exquisitely. The sad part is that, if they had been writing a traditional narrative specification instead, they would have included the diagram without a moment's hesitation. The guideline to follow is: *If you would have included a figure, diagram, or table in a traditional narrative specification, then you should include it in your structured specification.*

Figures 13.3 and 13.4 are examples of the kinds of diagrams that should be used in PSPECs. Figure 13.3 depicts the lateral flight profile of an aircraft in traversing three waypoints, and Figure 13.4 defines a coordinate system to be used in some associated equations. These are typical engineering applications: Imagine trying to describe them in words; you would probably fill several paragraphs, and still not end up with as effective a description.

13.3   Some Important Signal Conventions

Time-continuous and transient signals

In Section 5.3, we discussed the distinction, in the information domain, between continuous and discrete signals. Both of these types of signals can be

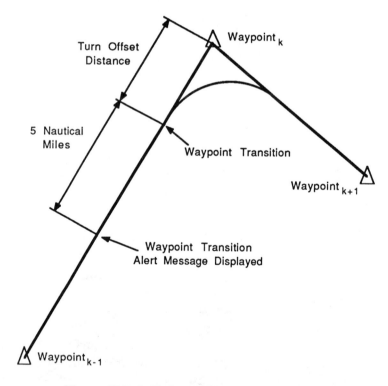

Figure 13.3. A flight profile used in a PSPEC.

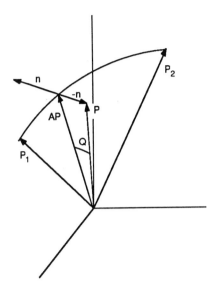

Figure 13.4. Geometrical relationships used in a PSPEC.

either continuous or transient in the time domain. Generally in the requirements model, signals are considered to be present continuously in time. In
other words, when a process generates a particular value of a signal, it is
considered to remain until it is changed or turned off. Thus, a process receiving that signal may reread it any number of times before it changes.

In some cases, however, we need a signal that is transient in time; that is,
a signal that is normally in a null state, but that assumes its desired value
momentarily, and then returns to the null state. When this characteristic is
required, it is indicated in the PSPEC by the word "issue." A specific example
of this occurs in the Automobile Management System, in which we need to
sample average speed on demand and store the sample. The PSPEC that carries out this sampling is

PSPEC 4.1.3; ISSUE AVERAGE SPEED

Issue:

$$\text{AVERAGE SPEED} = \frac{\text{DISTANCE} - \text{START DISTANCE}}{\text{TRIP TIME}}$$

If we had used such words as "calculate" or "output," we would have intended
the more usual time-continuous case, whereby AVERAGE SPEED would continuously vary in time as the parameters on the right-hand side of the equation
varied.

Signals that are continuous and discrete in the information domain, and
continuous and transient in the time domain, are illustrated in Figure 13.5.

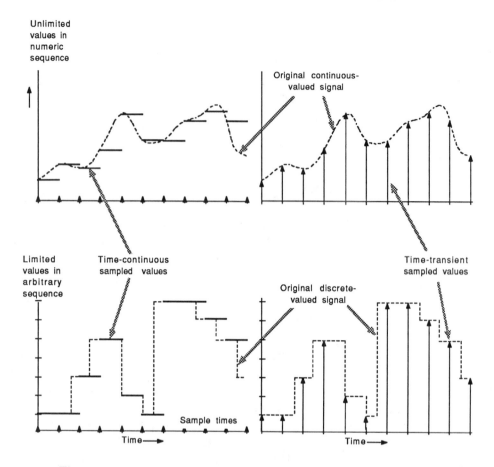

Figure 13.5. Continuous, discrete-valued, and time-discrete signals.

Universal access to time

Since time is such a universal parameter, typically needed by many processes throughout a system, we have adopted the convention that it is universally available to all PSPECs and CSPECs without appearing in the form of signal flows. Thus, it is always acceptable to reference either absolute time (that is, Greenwich Mean Time or whatever local standard you are using) or relative time (that is, time that has passed since an event known to the process occurred).

Since time does *not* appear as a flow, and therefore is not defined in the dictionary, you should be careful to fully specify exactly what time reference and units you are using. If time is needed relative to some event *not* known to the process, then that particular measure of time *should* be included as a flow, emanating from a process that has the necessary time reference.

13.4 Structured English

The goals of structured English are twofold: It is intended primarily to eliminate the characteristic vagueness and ambiguity of standard text, and secondarily to keep the specifications understandable to nontechnical readers. It is essential to meet the first goal, but, since most modern systems are of interest to technical people only, the second goal is less important. Nevertheless, structured English remains a useful tool to have available, and it is a good idea to become proficient at using it to write narrative PSPECs. The types of words and the constructs allowed in structured English were listed in Section 4.7.

How, then, should structured English be written? A good approach is to write the requirements as short, independent phrases, then connect those that must be related with the appropriate connecting words. If a number of statements are to be connected, avoid the temptation to write a long, compound sentence; instead, write them as an itemized list, with their relationships stated at the beginning.

As an example, look at the following compound statement:

> Select the BEST NAVAID COUNT NAVAID DATAs, whose NAVAID POSITION is closest to BEST POSITION, which satisfy the in-range criteria in the table below, and which are not in UNUSABLE DME.

which would be better written as

> Select NAVAID DATAs subject to the following:
>
> > select BEST NAVAID COUNT of them,
> >
> > those selected have their NAVAID POSITION closest to BEST POSITION,
> >
> > they satisfy the in-range criteria in the table below,
> >
> > they are not in UNUSABLE DME.

(DME stands for distance measuring equipment, a ground-based transmitting device used in aircraft navigation.) In this relatively brief example, the original statement can be correctly interpreted with care, but longer compound sentences can easily contain irreconcilable ambiguities. On the other hand, the itemized list can be arbitrarily long without this same difficulty.

As the examples illustrate, capitalizing the flow names, and using lower case letters for the rest of the text is helpful in separating the two. The flow names must be exactly identical to those on the diagrams and in the dictionary; otherwise, they do not balance. A good automated tool will verify this.

One of the most common words used to show conditional actions is "if." The conditional construct is allowed, as long as its argument is one of the PSPEC's inputs, but if there are several conditions involved, or several levels of indentation, it is usually better to use a decision table. Decision tables were introduced in Section 5.6 and are described further in Chapter 14.

It is sometimes advocated that a dictionary of allowed words be maintained for any given project, listing those words that may be used in that project's PSPECs. We have not found this to be very useful as the number of words inevitably becomes very large. Using the list of allowed word *types* given in Section 4.7, coupled with the judgment of the analysts, seems to work well.

13.5   Annotating with Comments

With all the attention to rigor and conciseness, PSPECs tend to be very terse. It is frequently a very good idea to add comments to aid the reader in understanding the reason the PSPEC is there, where it was derived from, a summary of the meaning of a set of equations, or any other information you feel might be helpful in understanding it. They can also be useful, during the development of the model, to carry temporary reminders of things that need to be done, or additional information that needs to be obtained.

Comments should be clearly identified as such, either by surrounding them with a symbol (we use asterisks), or having a "Comments" field labeled as such. Remember, however, that comments are not a part of the formal specification, so they must not describe any functionality of the PSPEC that is not already defined in the body. Remember, too, that comments should be updated to reflect changes in the requirements. For this reason (if for no other), do not be tempted to write a whole parallel narrative specification in the form of PSPEC comments! That would defeat the purpose of the structured approach, and return us to an unmaintainable requirements specification. No automated tool will help you in updating the comments.

Many of the PSPECs in the examples of Part VI include comments. Look at them and see how they complement the formal part of the PSPECs.

13.6   Summary

- PSPECs embody the ultimate level of detail in the decomposition process. They must define precisely and exclusively how their outputs are generated from their inputs.

- PSPECs may contain concise text, equations, tables, or diagrams, or a combination of them, depending on whichever is most appropriate.

- The default convention is that PSPEC outputs are time-continuous; if a time-transient output is required, it is signified by the word issue.

- By convention, PSPECs have universal access to time, both absolute and relative.

- Textual PSPECs should be written using the allowed words and constructs of structured English.

- Comments should be used to provide useful background on the rationale behind the PSPEC, but not to repeat what it says nor to add further requirements.

Chapter 14

Preparing Control Specifications

14.1 Avoiding Control Specifications

In Sections 11.2 and 12.8, we have described the benefits of de-emphasizing the control model. Although this chapter addresses the preparation of CSPECs, it is worth reminding ourselves that we will put a CSPEC together only when we have thoroughly satisfied ourselves that it is really needed. In other words, we will put a CSPEC together only when we have satisfied ourselves that the requirement cannot be represented using the simple data triggered structured analysis model; that the decisions involved cannot easily be incorporated into one or more PSPECs, using simple IF statements; and that the requirement involves decisions affecting relatively major operating modes of the system, and will thus activate and deactivate higher-level processes.

If all of the above are true, then we can proceed with confidence that a CSPEC is truly needed, but we still have another decision to make. Our first attempt will be to represent the requirement using the simpler, combinational machine, in the form of decision tables or Boolean equations. We can do this if the control function we need is dependent only on the current values of our available control signals. If the function is at any time dependent on past values of those signals, then we must use a sequential machine, and record those past values in the form of states.

But before we decide to use a sequential machine, we must further satisfy ourselves that the states we need have not already been created elsewhere in the model. If they have appeared elsewhere, then we can represent them as control signals, route them into the CSPEC we are now building, and use them as inputs to a combinational machine.

Only if none of these possibilities exists will we proceed with the sequential machine, which is the most complex type of CSPEC and requires state transition diagrams or their equivalent tables or matrices. These CSPECs

160

often will end up being composite ones with combinational event and action logic in addition to the intrinsic sequential machine. By carrying out this procedure throughout the building of the model, we will achieve our goal of minimizing the control stucture, and constraining the sequential parts of that structure to a few high-level areas that drive the rest of the model.

Thus, when interpreting a narrative specification, the analyst must decide whether a combinational or a sequential representation is needed. If he sees requirements that are based on ongoing present conditions versus transitional or past events, he should use a combinational representation. The following illustrates this point:

> *The system shall provide outputs to the autopilot only when activated from the mode control panel, and when all status conditions are normal.*

This suggests that some existing signals can be logically combined to decide whether outputs should be sent to the autopilot. Thus, simple combinational logic can probably be used.

Conversely, a statement such as,

> *If the aircraft has passed top of climb, then engine cruise parameters shall be selected.*

would lead us to conclude that the system will switch between two states (from CLIMBING to CRUISING) at the top of the aircraft's climb, thus requiring a sequential representation.

In the following two sections, we will look closer at the details of combinational and sequential control, and how to construct the various diagrams, tables, and matrices they entail.

14.2 Combinational Control

Let us assume that the particular part of the system we are working in can be represented with combinational logic. Our first goal should be (as always) to find the simplest way to represent it. In the very simplest case, there may be a one-to-one relationship between our CSPEC inputs and the processes to be activated. This is true of CSPEC 4.1 of Chapter 26:

CSPEC 4.1; MONITOR AVERAGE SPEED

START TRIP	activates	process 4.1.1; Start Trip
RUNNING	activates	process 4.1.2; Clock Trip Time
AV SPEED RQST	activates	process 4.1.3; Issue Average Speed

No tables or equations are needed here: It is necessary only to state the relationships.

If all the inputs and outputs of the process are binary, then expressing the requirement in Boolean-equation form might be best:

$$A = B \cdot C + \overline{(D \cdot \bar{E} + \bar{C} \cdot F)}$$
$$W = (\bar{B} + X) \cdot \overline{(Y + Z)}$$

In the usual case, however, the inputs, and/or outputs will be multi-valued, and they will have complex relationships with each other. List all the inputs and their values, and lay them out as a complete decision table, in which every combination is included. Then, for each combination, decide on the values of the outputs. For example, if

INPUT 1 has values A, B, and C;

INPUT 2 has values On and Off;

INPUT 3 has values X, Y, and Z;

OUTPUT 1 has values α, β, γ, and δ; and

OUTPUT 2 has values ϵ, ζ, η, and θ.

you will end up with something like Figure 14.1. (Note that the row numbers on the right are included only for future reference.)

The complete tabular form shown in the figure ensures that every possible combination of input values is evaluated. You will find that in many cases only a few combinations are of interest, and that you are tempted to bypass this step. Do so with caution: It is very easy to overlook a combination if you do not, at least once, force yourself to consider every one of them.

Having constructed a complete table, study it to find ways to simplify it. Often, there are combinations that have identical outputs (the "don't care" output is usually one of these), which might be grouped together. In our figure we see that many combinations produce OUTPUT 1 = δ and OUTPUT 2 = θ, so these are the first candidates for grouping. Since each of the two outputs has four values, there are $4 \times 4 = 16$ total possible output combinations; we have just accounted for one of them, so there are a possible fifteen remaining. In fact, those that are left in the figure form just five other groups of the possible fifteen, and by rearrangement of the rows in the table, we can reduce it to the table shown in Figure 14.2. In this restructuring, the numbers on the right indicate the corresponding rows in Figure 14.1. Notice that when INPUT 1 = C, the value of INPUT 2 does not affect the output—the "don't care" state. This is indicated by leaving that INPUT 2 cell blank.

INPUT 1	INPUT 2	INPUT 3	OUTPUT 1	OUTPUT 2	
A	On	X	α	ϵ	1
		Y	α	ϵ	2
		Z	δ	θ	3
	Off	X	δ	θ	4
		Y	β	ϵ	5
		Z	β	ζ	6
B	On	X	δ	θ	7
		Y	δ	θ	8
		Z	δ	θ	9
	Off	X	β	ζ	10
		Y	δ	θ	11
		Z	γ	ζ	12
C	On	X	δ	θ	13
		Y	δ	θ	14
		Z	γ	η	15
	off	X	δ	θ	16
		Y	δ	θ	17
		Z	γ	η	18

Figure 14.1. A full decision table.

The last entry in the table has "Other" under all three input columns, meaning this row accounts for all input combinations that have not already been included. Any of the rows could be moved to the bottom and labeled "Other," in which case, the one now there would have to be moved up in the table and expanded to explicitly list each of its input combinations. We chose to put this particular one at the end because it has the largest group of outputs associated with it, and putting this group into a single row minimizes the size of the table.

For simply binary systems, there are formal procedures described in the literature [2,7] for carrying out this minimization. They consist of combining pairs of rows that have identical inputs and outputs except for one column, which becomes a "don't care" in the combined row. This is repeated for all such pairs, then repeated again for pairs of already combined rows, and so on, until no more matching pairs can be found.

INPUT 1	INPUT 2	INPUT 3	OUTPUT 1	OUTPUT 2	
A	On	X	α	ε	1
		Y			2
	Off				5
		Z	β	ζ	6
B		X			10
					12
C		Z	γ	η	15, 18
Other			δ	θ	3, 4, 7, 8, 9, 11, 13, 14, 16, 17

Figure 14.2. A reduced decision table.

In most practical cases, however, many of the signals are multi-valued rather than binary, so the above procedure does not apply. Although in principle the procedure could be extended to cover the multi-valued case, an informal procedure of looking for obvious commonalities in the inputs and the outputs has been found effective.

Be very careful when reducing decision tables by the informal approach to ensure that all the rows remain mutually exclusive. This is a necessary attribute for an unambiguous table. It is possible, especially as the result of incorrect use of the "don't care" entries, to have input combinations duplicated in more than one part of the table. If these duplicate entries have different output values, then the table is ambiguous. Consider, for example, Figure 14.3, in which the same three inputs given in the previous tables are combined differently. The row numbers from Figure 14.1 are shown on the right, and we see that rows 14 and 17 (boldface) have been duplicated. If the output values corresponding to those duplicate entries are different, then the table is ambiguous.

We have seen people use a single control signal both as an input and an output of a decision table. The idea is that the combinational machine will

INPUT 1	INPUT 2	INPUT 3	
A	On	X	1
		Y	2, 5, 8, 11, **14**, **17**
B	Off	Z	12
C			13, **14**, 15, 16, **17**, 18
Other			3, 4, 6, 7, 9, 10

Figure 14.3. An ambiguous set of input combinations.

act as a one-shot device such that, when the signal turns on, the machine will immediately turn it off again. This practice should be avoided: It is prone to ambiguous interpretation, and if the one-shot action is needed, it can be provided unambiguously by a sequential machine.

Process activation tables

Process activation tables are simply decision tables, some or all of whose outputs happen to activate processes. Their construction is exactly the same as that of any other decision table. The process activation outputs are, of course, always binary, and by convention are marked "1" for conditions that activate the process, and "0" for those that deactivate it.

The extended use of PATs, introduced in Section 6.3, in which a sequence of activation is indicated by a corresponding sequence of numbers should be used sparingly. Usually, the flows on the DFD are sufficient to show any sequence in which the processes operate, and the process activators can all come on at once. A sequence *is* needed in cases in which two processes communicate through a store, and in which the receiving process must use the new data entered by the sending process rather than the old data. In such cases, the activation sequence will signify that the first process loads new data into the store before the second one reads it. This is a subtle point, because our ideal model is assumed to operate "instantaneously." For practical purposes, we can say that instantaneous means faster than is detectable by our system; that is, if the system responds in microseconds, then our model works in nanoseconds, and so on.

Controlling transaction centers

A special variation in the use of decision tables occurs in controlling transaction centers. Transaction centers and their control were introduced in Sections 4.2 and 5.7. They are a fairly common type of DFD structure, reflecting the fact that quite often our systems have to choose between many similar options. These options may be as minor as choosing one of several values for a single variable, or as major as choosing one of several alternate high-level processes, such as engine thrust calculations for takeoff, climb, cruise, or descent, for example.

The special variation in the use of decision tables occurs with the optional representation for control of a transaction center introduced in Section 5.7, in which a CSPEC directly references branches in a PSPEC. This optional representation is *only* allowed for transaction centers whose processes are primitives. At higher levels, the processes must be kept separate, and if activators are needed at all, each process must have its own.

This optional representation is really a deviation from the method's fundamental principle of conforming with Figure 5.7, and keeping data and control separate since the CSPEC references the "inside" of a PSPEC. The option was allowed, because the alternative is worse! A wide transaction center with small, primitive processes produces many small, similar PSPECs, each of

PSPEC 1.3.1.1; Issue Target Speeds

Set SPEED SCHEDULE to value selected from
PERFORMANCE DATA in accordance with CSPEC 1.3.1

CSPEC 1.3.1; Manage Performance

DISPLAY PAGE	ROUTE STATUS	PSPEC 1.3.1.1 SPEED SCHEDULE value
Climb	Active	Active Climb Speed
	Modified	Modified Climb Speed
Descent	Active	Active Descent Speed
	Modified	Modified Descent Speed
Cruise Climb	Active	Active Cruise Climb Speed
	Modified	Modified Cruise Climb Speed
Cruise Descent	Active	Active Cruise Descent Speed
	Modified	Modified Cruise Descent Speed
Cruise	Active	Active Cruise Speed
	Modified	Modified Cruise Speed
Hold	Active	Hold Speed
	Modified	Hold Speed

Figure 14.4. Alternative representation of transaction center control.

which would have its own activator. It is much more concise and understandable (and therefore more consistent with the fundamental goals of the method) to collapse all these PSPECs into one, with many internal branches, and to reference these branches in the CSPEC.

Figure 14.4 shows an example derived from a commercial flight management system. This highly repetitive structure is typical of transaction centers. Sticking strictly to the principle of separation of data and control would require each line of the CSPEC table to control a separate PSPEC.

14.3   Sequential Control

If the processing requirement cannot be represented by the simple data triggered model, nor by reference only to its current inputs, then the only choice we have left is to represent it using one of the sequential machine constructs.

We introduced sequential machines in Section 6.2. In the following paragraphs, we discuss how to identify states, events, and actions, and how to decide which form of representation to use.

As always, we start by going back to the basics, and refer to the fundamental goals of the requirements method. The structure and rules of the method take care of the goals of rigor, completeness, changeability, and maintainability. The goal over which we have the most control is understandability. The requirements method provides the means to meet this goal, but it does not actually meet it for us; there are many ways in which we can produce incomprehensible models.

Choosing states

In choosing the states, events, and actions, we must do two things: Choose those that are familiar to the users, so that they will relate to them; and use names that the users normally use. Thus, for the vertical mode in a flight management system, we would choose the states Takeoff, Climb, Cruise, Descent, and Hold, for the corresponding phases of flight, and we would use those actual names for them, rather than, say, Flt Phase A, Flt Phase B, or worse yet, State L473, State L474, and so on. Many engineers are fond of this last kind, which are entirely useless for conveying information to anything but a machine.

We could also choose states that, instead of corresponding to these actual, well-understood phases of flight, might extend, perhaps, from lift-off to halfway through climb, from there to ten miles into cruise, and so on. There might be reasons why these would be convenient for building the model, but they would not be a good choice because of the confusion they would cause the user.

Choosing the representation

The state transition diagram is the most graphically descriptive choice of representation, and should be used whenever practical. It is practical as long as the number of states and transitions is small enough to allow a readable diagram on a single sheet. Where this point is reached is a matter of judgment and personal preference, but the seven-plus-or-minus-two rule can be applied here just as it can in DFDs. If the total number of chunks of information is within that range, then an STD can be used; beyond this, use one of the two types of state transition matrix or a state transition table. These diagrams, matrices, and tables were illustrated in Figures 6.4 through 6.7.

The choice between the two types of STM and the STT is also a matter of judgment. Both types of STM have some built-in completeness checking, and they are perhaps a little more descriptive, but they can use up a lot of space. It is a good idea for each project to decide which one to use and then stick with it. The worst choice of all is to have a random mix of representations.

The state-to-state form of the STM has some interesting properties that might occasionally be useful. For example,

- The entries in the body of the matrix have the same event/action form as appears on the STD transitions, so cross-checking is easier than with the state/event STM.

- The form makes it easy to trace allowable state sequences. This can be useful for testing and system failure analysis.

- The state-to-state STM can be turned into a binary matrix by entering a 1 wherever a transition is allowed and a 0 otherwise. Raising this matrix to increasing powers through binary matrix multiplication should eventually result in an all-1s matrix. If it does not, then there is at least one inaccessible state.

Special conventions of the method

Mathematically, a sequential machine is represented as a 5-tuple. This 5-tuple consists of a set of input symbols (the input vector); a set of states (the state vector); a set of output symbols (the output vector); a next-state function, which maps the input vector and the current-state vector onto the next-state vector; and an output function, which maps the input vector and the current-state vector onto the output vector.

In terms of our model, each event is an input symbol, which may be any discrete function of the machine's input signals in terms of their values. Each action is an output symbol, which may be any discrete function of the machine's output signals in terms of their values. States in the model and in the mathematical representation have a one-to-one correspondence. The collection of transition arcs between the states represents the next-state function. Finally, the associations between the transition arcs and the actions represent the output function.

We introduced the Mealy and Moore models in Section 6.2. It is useful to understand their relative merits when preparing control specifications. The Mealy model is a direct model of the mathematical representation—the output function is related both to the current input and the state. The Moore model, however, restricts the mathematical representation to a form in which the output function is related only to the state, not to the input. It would seem at first sight that the Moore model is somehow less general than the Mealy model, but it can be proved [2,7] that a machine represented in either one of these forms always has an equivalent in the other. The price that is paid for the greater simplicity of the Moore model is that, for a given machine, it will usually require more states. It is also less flexible in practice.

In fact, in the requirements method, we use a hybrid approach that takes best advantage of both models. While the basic approach is to associate the actions to the transitions (the Mealy approach), where convenient the states themselves may be associated with actions (the Moore approach). This is very convenient in the frequent case in which the response of the machine is independent of the transition path it took to get to its current state. The alternative would be to attach the same action to all arcs going to that state.

Another convention of the requirements method is that actions associated with a transition *continue in effect until the next transition occurs*. This, too, is very convenient in that we can always assume that if the output of a sequential machine activates a process (as they often do), then that process will remain activated after the transition has occurred. This is a necessary feature for processes that are required to continually process new data after they are first activated. Processes that perform a one-shot activity do so each time they are activated, then wait for the next activation. The fact that they *are* one-shot must be stated in their PSPEC(s), as discussed in Chapter 13.

Our purpose here is not to write a detailed text on finite state machine theory, but to describe how some of the common techniques from that theory can be used within the requirements model. There are many other useful techniques in finite state machine theory, however, that might be worth examining when you come to build a requirements model. Some of these are

- determining whether two automata are equivalent,

- developing an event sequence that will force the machine into its start state from any unknown state, and

- developing an event sequence that will force the machine to return to its current state.

Building a sequential machine

Now we will walk through the derivation of one of the sequential machines in the Automobile Management System of Chapter 26. The statement from the customer (in this case, the automobile manufacturer) is

> *The driver will be provided with* Activate, Deactivate, Start Accelerating, Stop Accelerating, *and* Resume *controls. The system can be operated any time that the engine is running and the transmission is in top gear. When the driver presses* Activate, *the system selects the current speed, and holds the car at that speed.* Deactivate *returns control to the driver regardless of any other commands.* Start Accelerating *causes the system to accelerate the car at a comfortable rate until* Stop Accelerating *occurs, when the system will hold the car at this new speed.* Resume *causes the system to return the car to the speed selected prior to braking or gear shifting.*

Following our own advice, we will assume that the processing part of the model, or at least that a first iteration of it, has already been worked. The resulting DFD is shown in Figure 14.5, derived from other parts of the requirements statement.

The inputs to the machine certainly include the ones explicitly listed—Activate, Deactivate, Start Accelerating, Stop Accelerating, and Resume. We can also deduce that the machine will need inputs representing Running,

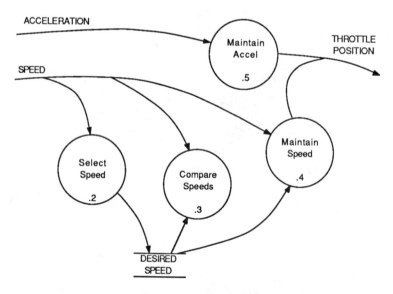

Figure 14.5. Data flow diagram showing throttle control.

Braking, and Top Gear. Its outputs must cause the system to perform the following actions: "selects the current speed," "holds the . . . speed," "accelerate the car," "return . . . to the speed selected."

Two likely candidates for states are Cruising and Accelerating. Another would seem to be Inactive, but a closer look reveals that the inactive condition is not quite that simple. If speed control is interrupted by braking or gear shifting, then we can return from the inactive condition to the previously selected speed; if the system has just started, or if it went inactive due to the Deactivate command, then we have to reselect a speed. It is possible, then, that we need two states for the inactive condition. As a start, we will call them Inactive, for the "reselect a speed" case, and Pausing, for the "return to speed" case.

By tracing through typical sequences of events, we can construct an STD from the above signals and states. The Inactive state will also be the Start state, and when Running turns on, that is the state to which we will go. The driver will reach the desired speed and press Activate, causing the system to select the current speed and switch to the Cruising state. At some later time, the driver might want to accelerate to a higher speed, and will press the Start Accelerating control. The system will switch to the Accelerating state, and will cause the car to accelerate until the Stop Accelerating control is pressed, when it will return to Cruising. Any time we are Cruising and the brakes are applied, or the transmission shifts out of top gear, the system will go to the Pause state, and stop maintaining speed. It will remain in this state until either Resume or Deactivate is pressed, when it will return to Cruising or Inactive, respectively.

These and some other sequences give rise to the STD of Figure 14.6. At this point, it is a good idea to use the model to investigate possible combinations of states and events that might not have been covered in the requirements statement. To this end, two checks should be made: One is to examine what would or should happen if each of the specified events occurs when the machine is in states with which that event is not currently associated; the other is to consider all possible state transitions that do not already exist.

Carrying out this "what if" exercise with Figure 14.6 raises the question of what to do if the driver presses Start Accelerating while the system is in the Inactive or Pausing states. The requirements statement only addresses this driver action when we are already in Cruising. It seems reasonable that this transition should be allowed, but this is exactly the kind of issue that should not be taken for granted one way or the other. The issue should be raised with the customer and resolved before completing the model. This is a small illustration of the ability of the method to reveal omissions or alternatives in the requirements statement.

This Automobile Management System is completely modeled in Chapter 26, and you should study that chapter carefully to see how the STD is integrated with the rest of the model.

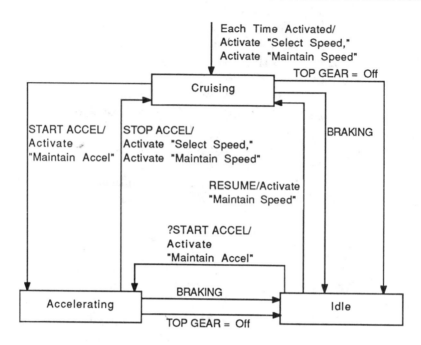

Figure 14.6. Control specification showing throttle control.

14.4 Multi-Sheet CSPECs

The reasons we need to allow for multi-sheet CSPECs were given in Section 6.3. In some actual engineering applications, we have seen CSPECs that have been as long as fifteen to twenty sheets. We do not encourage their use, but sometimes they are unavoidable.

Such long, multi-sheet CSPECs most commonly occur where a large sequential machine is required, usually with many transition events relative to the number of states. The state transition matrix, which has states on the vertical axis and events on the horizontal, is the most useful representation in this case, because the matrix can extend over any number of sheets, with the states repeated on the left-hand side of each sheet, and the events listed consecutively from one sheet to the next. This is illustrated in Figure 14.7.

If the machine has both a large number of states *and* many transition events, then a matrix representation may not be the best choice. Neither axis could be repeated on each sheet, and we would end up with a matrix of *sheets* to find our way around, not a very practical arrangement. It would be better to revert to the state transition table illustrated in Figure 6.5, where each current state is listed once with a list of the transitions from it. This list can obviously extend over many sheets. When using this representation, you should independently check all combinations of current state with next state,

State \ Event	Event 1	Event 2	Event 3	Event 4	Event 5	Event 6
State 1						
State 2						
State 3						
State 4						

Sheet m of n.

State \ Event	Event 7	Event 8	Event 9	Event 10	Event 11	Event 12
State 1						
State 2						
State 3						
State 4						

Sheet (m+1) of n.

Figure 14.7. A multi-sheet state transition matrix.

and state with event, to be sure none has been overlooked. The STT itself will not be of much help to you in doing this.

As implied in Section 6.3, sequential machines are often preceded and followed by combinational logic converting the actual CSPEC inputs to the events required by the sequential machine, and its actions to the signals needed by the rest of the system. This logic is carried out in decision tables, in the usual way. The convention of arranging the CSPEC in the sequence of event logic, sequential machine, and action logic is a logical one, and helps the users find their way around. It was illustrated in Figure 6.10, and is repeated here for convenience in Figure 14.8. Each of the elements in this figure may occupy a single sheet or more than one sheet, depending on the size of the logic.

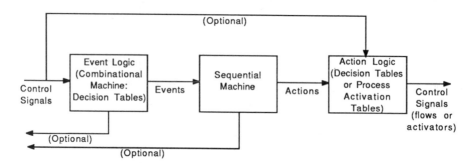

Figure 14.8. Organization of a composite CSPEC.

Although any size and complexity of combinational or sequential CSPECs is allowed, we must point out that in most instances large CSPECs are not necessary. Insisting that all the control logic for a single DFD must go in a single CSPEC forces us to allow CSPECs to be of any size. In practice, though, our experience has been that the opposite effect occurs: The fact that the *system's* control logic is partitioned into DFD-sized chunks results in CSPECs being generally quite small, and easily accommodated on single sheets. Furthermore, if the analyst conscientiously minimizes the amount of control logic included in the analysis (which is often synonymous with keeping design considerations out of it), then this too leads to small CSPECs.

One caveat we must make here is, do not confuse the relationships between CSPEC bars (on the CFD), CSPECs, CSPEC objects (DTs, PATs, STDs, and so forth), and CSPEC sheets. The following statements summarize these relationships:

- There may be any number of CSPEC bars on a CFD, but they all reference the whole associated CSPEC (that is, none of them is associated with any specific CSPEC object or sheet).

- There is no more than one CSPEC per CFD.

- A single CSPEC may contain any number of objects, and may be spread over any number of sheets.

- CSPEC sheets are components of the printed specification but have no special correspondence with the CSPEC objects. There may be one or several objects on a sheet, or one object (such as an STM) may spread over several sheets.

- Flows between objects are internal to the CSPEC, and if there are many of them they should be summarized in a users' guide within the CSPEC. They should not appear on the CFD as this would violate the principle of information hiding, and cause clutter and confusion.

Little more needs to be said. There is nothing fundamentally different about a long CSPEC as opposed to a short one. Just follow the organization described in Section 6.3, number the sheets "sheet m of n," and include a guide at the beginning of any CSPEC that is more than about three sheets long. The guide should include an overview of the CSPEC, a description of its organization, and a list of the sheet numbers on which each input, output, and internal signal appears.

14.5   Fitting CSPECs In

Usually, there is no difficulty knowing where a given CSPEC belongs in the structure: It goes with the DFD it controls. It might well be that not all the control signals you need are available on the corresponding CFD, but that should not be difficult to remedy because control signals flow up and down the levels of the CFDs just as data signals do in the DFDs. Bring the signals you need to that CFD and terminate them in bars showing they go to the CSPEC.

Now, to get you thinking about the structure of the method, we will prove that the apparent constraint of insisting that a DFD should be controlled only from its own CSPEC is actually no constraint at all. The proof is very simple. Take any complete requirements model, with any number of CSPECs. Take all those CSPECs, and incorporate them into, say, CSPEC 0, the top-level CSPEC. Treat as binary control signals all the outputs that previously were process activators. Take each of these new control signals, and route them back to the locations of their previous CSPECs. Now create new CSPECs, with these binary signals as inputs, and include in them trivial process activation tables, which convert the binary control signals back into the process activators they originally were.

This procedure results in a model that has all its control logic in one huge central CSPEC, and in which trivial local CSPECs provide the process activation where needed.

Now we certainly *don't* recommend that you do anything like this in practice; the point of this exercise is to illustrate the fact that we actually have complete freedom to put the logic for any function anywhere in the system. Of course, exercising this freedom at random would produce terrible results, but used with discretion, it can be very helpful. For example, if you know that several DFDs are controlled by the same or similar logic, then it might make sense to express that logic in just one CSPEC, generate outputs from that CSPEC corresponding to all the process activators, and route them to the other DFDs through trivial CSPECs like those described above. An exercise such as this one illustrates the great flexibility the requirements method provides.

In general, any logic that is common to a number of processes, whether used directly for process activation or not, can be expressed in just one CSPEC and routed to its other destinations through the CFDs. This is a very common practice, with the result that many CSPECs generate control flows as well as process activators. The extreme example of this use of a CSPEC is one that produces control flows, but no process activators at all.

Floating CSPECs

When using CSPECs without process activators, as with everything else, do it so as to elucidate the requirements, not obscure them. We cannot repeat this too often.

Why would such a CSPEC be needed? Two situations are common. The first is one in which a process needs an activator derived from several control signals, and these signals are in a part of the structure remote from that process. Then it makes sense to create a CSPEC where most of the source signals already exist, and flow just the one signal to its destination, rather than flow all the source signals there. Figure 14.9 illustrates such a floating CSPEC.

In the second situation, the CSPEC's output signals are needed as outputs from the system, and their generation is not associated with any process activation.

Of course, in either case, the logic could be moved into some other CSPEC in which there *is* process activation (in the manner of our proof above), but if the two sets of logic are not related, this is an artificial and confusing construction. The principles are the same as the ones we use for the process model: Partition to minimize flows (or interfaces), and avoid partially processed information and cascading logic.

Time in CSPECs

One last special case needs discussing: As in PSPECs, *time,* both relative and absolute, is assumed to be available in all CSPECs. It should be used with discretion, however: It is another feature fraught with the risk of getting into design. It should never be used to define the internal timing of the eventual implementation, for example, such things as calling rate. Remember also that repetition rates of external signals are already defined in the dictionary.

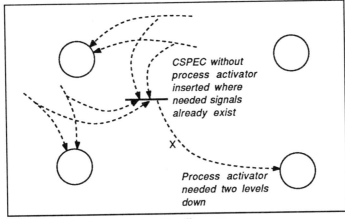

Parent diagram

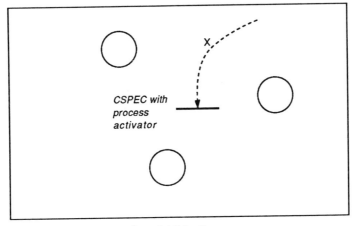

Grandchild diagram

Figure 14.9. A floating CSPEC.

One legitimate use of time in a CSPEC is that in which repetition rate *is* a necessary parameter of an algorithm the system is to perform. This is true, for example, in the Kalman filter, and in fact in digital filtering in general.

The use of time as a universally available signal leads to the interesting possibility, that has occasionally occurred in practice, of a CSPEC with no inputs (at least, none that appear on the CFD). This happens when the *only* purpose of the CSPEC is to specify the repetition rates of its processes.

CSPECs in the total structure

At the beginning of this chapter, we advised you to avoid using CSPECs wherever possible. Now that we have been through the details of putting them together when they *are* needed, it is worth taking another look at where they fit in the total structure.

CSPECs are the central part of the extensions to the basic structured analysis method: They are the means for integrating finite state machines with flow diagrams. In spite of their importance, they should not be over-used. The reason we need them is to perform functions that basic structured analysis cannot perform, and these are the tasks to which they should be applied. These tasks are characterized by changes of major operating mode of the system, which translates into CSPECs controlling high-level processes. Thus, in putting together the whole structure of the requirements model, you should concentrate your application of CSPECs at the higher levels, and bias yourself more and more against using them as you progress down the levels. At the lowest levels, logical decisions that might be made using CSPECs can often just as well be made using PSPECs, and doing so will simplify the structure.

14.6 Summary

- Avoid using CSPECs wherever possible. If unavoidable, try to keep them at high levels. Choose combinational machines over sequential machines.

- Minimize decision tables and process activation tables by combining similar rows, and using "don't care" conditions.

- Collapse wide, primitive transaction centers into a single process, and control its internal branches from within the CSPEC.

- Use the same principles in naming states, events, and actions as you use in naming processes and flows: Make them meaningful and user-oriented.

- Use the STD if the model is fairly simple; otherwise, use one of the STM types, if possible. Only the largest and most complex machines should require the STT.

- Organize multi-sheet CSPECs in a logical way that is easy to follow; number the sheets "*m* of *n*," and include a users' guide at the front if the CSPEC is longer than three sheets.

- Include a given CSPEC at a place in the model where most of its outputs are to be used, or where most of its inputs already exist.

Chapter 15

Defining Timing

15.1 Timing Overview

Although the primary purpose of this chapter is to discuss preparing response time specifications, it is worth first reviewing all the aspects of timing covered so far, in order to put them in perspective with each other and with the role of the requirements model.

First, recall our discussion in Chapter 7 explaining that only external response times should be specified in a requirements model; all internal response times are entirely a design consideration, and must be left to that phase. This makes the response time specification relatively simple, but it is vital nevertheless, for it specifies the times to which the sums of the internal responses in the eventual system must conform.

Second, external inputs must be received at a certain rate, and external outputs produced at a certain rate. This parameter of external primitives is specified in the dictionary. The rate for the outputs is the required recomputation rate, which may be different from the data bus rate. The latter is a design constraint obtained from the standard specification for the bus. Again, repetition rates of internal signals should be left to the designer's discretion.

Finally, we stated in Sections 13.3 and 14.5 the convention that all PSPECs and CSPECs have access to absolute and relative time. This convention should be used with great discretion, making sure not to violate any of the no-design caveats in the above paragraphs. There are two specific cases where use of the convention is justified. One is the case in which an external primitive signal is being generated, and its rate or time relationship with another signal is an important requirement; the other occurs where repetition rate of a process is an essential part of that process, as in the case of a digital filter. Other cases may occur in practice, but scrutinize them carefully for design contamination before proceeding.

Figure 15.1 illustrates the various parts of the timing requirements picture. It illustrates external primitive flows shown on the data context dia-

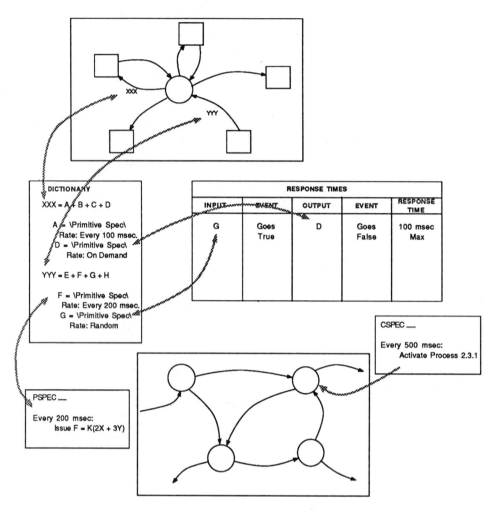

**Figure 15.1. Dictionary, response time,
PSPEC, and CSPEC timing specifications.**

gram and defined, with their repetition rates, in the dictionary. The figure
shows an entry in the response time specification linked to the rest of the
model through definitions of its input and output flows in the dictionary. Finally, the figure shows time invoked in a PSPEC, linked to the rest of the
model through the dictionary, and in a CSPEC, linked through the process
activated.

15.2   Response Time Specification

The response time specification is the only part of the requirements method
dealing exclusively with timing. Working on it can be a useful exercise early

in the program. Since it relates to events at the system boundary, it is a good vehicle for thinking of the system as an event driven model.

If you have been provided with (or have written) an operational requirements specification, this will be a good starting point for the timing specification. It will be written in terms of operations external to the system, and without reference to specific interface signals. It is these operations that are important to the user, and that should be focused on when specifying the timing. You will have to translate these operations into the specific signal values that represent them at the system boundary, but when writing the timing specification, always retain the original operational terms as well as the signal values, so the user understands your meaning.

The timing specification is particularly likely to involve iterations during the design phase. Obviously, we would like our systems to respond instantaneously to everything, but, sadly, the physical reality cannot support this ideal. We are thus faced with the question, How far from this ideal can I go without compromising the usefulness of the system? In some cases, there is a quantitative answer to this question, but in many others, the answer is only qualitative. It is very likely we will pick some response times that turn out to be very difficult to achieve in practice, and compromises will have to be made. It is therefore important to involve the designers in this activity as early in the development as possible.

Response time to the interactive human interface (for example, individual keystroke responses) is generally required to be less than half a second, and it should be consistent. There are usually some interactions in which this guideline is impossible, notably, those involving large amounts of processing. For example, in a flight management system, echoing the crew's keyboard inputs, and displaying current status information can readily be done in less than half a second; assembling a whole new flight plan might take tens of seconds, and this is quite acceptable—the crew will not want to see all the flight plan data immediately. Other response times will be determined by stability or performance criteria, and it will not be acceptable to compromise these.

In any given system, there will typically be a large group of interactions whose response times are not very critical, but that must, nevertheless, be constrained to *some* extent. The assembly of a new flight plan, mentioned above, is an example. When design tradeoffs are to be made, these are the response times for which compromises are most likely to be acceptable.

In highly critical systems, in which system reliability and safety are prime requirements, automatic built-in testing is a required function, and the repetition rate within which it cycles through a complete system test is critical. For example, if a memory location goes bad, it is important that corrective action be taken before dangerous errors result. This kind of response time should be included in the response time specification. The worst kind of error in such a system is the noncatastrophic kind, in which the data is reasonable but wrong. In such cases, the built-in test might be the only means of alerting the operator.

It is important that the timing specification should balance with the requirements model. This means that every external primitive signal should appear at least once in the timing specification, and that no other signals should appear there.

The importance of the response time specification cannot be overemphasized. It is one of the three major inputs to the software designers; the other two being the requirements model and the hardware characteristics (including the hardware/software interface).

15.3 Summary

- Timing requirements relate only to external timing. Internal timing is a design issue.

- Three types of timing are specified: external response times; reception rates and recomputation rates of external inputs and outputs respectively; and timing required as part of the functionality of a user-required process.

- Starting the response time specification early will help you better understand the system as an event driven model.

- The response time specification is likely to be subject to re-examination during the design phase.

- Response times can be critical for stability and safety considerations, as well as for operator interactions.

- The response time specification must balance with the dictionary: All its input and output signals must be defined in the dictionary.

Chapter 16

Managing the Dictionary

The purpose, form, and symbols of the dictionary were described first in Chapter 8, and illustrations of dictionary listings were given in Figures 8.4 and 8.5. As mentioned there, it would be unthinkable these days to implement the dictionary in anything other than a computerized data base, either separately or as part of a comprehensive automated tool. This book is not the place to discuss data base management in detail—there are many excellent texts on the subject, such as references [3,8]. What we will do here is define the fields the data base should contain, and some of the useful reports it should produce.

16.1 Flow Types

Figure 16.1 shows all possible combinations of flow types, and their attributes. To read the table, find on the left the combination of type parameters you want; on the right, opposite that combination, are all the attributes that type should have. In the type fields, blank entries indicate the "don't care" case; attributes shown in parentheses are optional.

Now we will focus on each one of these types and attributes to define them precisely.

TYPE:

Group/Primitive
Group flows are collections of other group and/or primitive flows. Think of them as separate flows traveling together down the same pipeline. Their members are not combined together in any way, and may be separated at any point. *Primitives* are single, indivisible information flows.

183

TYPE				ATTRIBUTES		
Group/Primitive	Internal/External	Control/Data	Discrete/Continuous			
Primitive		Control		*Invalid—control signals may not be continuous*		
	Internal	Data	Continuous	(Range) (Resolution)	(Rate)	Name (Used In) (Member Of) (Comments)
				Units		
	External			Range Resolution	Rate	
			Discrete	Value Names (No. of Values)		
	Internal				(Rate)	
Group				Backus-Naur Definition		

Figure 16.1. Flow types and their attributes.

Internal/External

Internal flows exist only inside the system: They are not themselves, nor are they members of, any flows on the context diagrams.

External flows are those through which the system communicates with the outside world, and are always context diagram flows, or parts of them.

Note that the difference between an internal and external flow may be as little, for example, as the fact that one is a validated version of the other; if they have different names, they are different flows as far as the model is concerned.

Control/Data

Control flows are those whose principal purpose is to modify the operating mode of the system; they are always discrete, and are shown on the CFDs with broken lines.

Data flows are used in calculations and algorithms within processes; they are shown on the DFDs with solid lines.

Discrete/Continuous

Discrete signals have a finite number of unique values. All values are equally significant, hence any change in value is likely to have significant effect on the system.

Continuous signals have an unlimited number of ordered numerical values; small changes in signal value usually have insignificant effect on the system. For the purposes of the model, any digital quantization performed by the implemented system is ignored.

ATTRIBUTES:

Name

This is the principal identifier of flows, and is their *only* identification on the diagrams. All names must be unique, and are intended to be descriptive. Mandatory.

Backus-Naur Form Definition

Other than the name, the *only* attribute of group flows. The structure of the group is expressed using symbols in a modification of BNF described in Figure 8.3. Mandatory for groups.

Units

Physical units (pounds, feet, or joules, for example). Mandatory for continuous primitives.

Range

The limits within which a continuous primitive signal exists (−1000 to +60,000 ft., ±300°C, and so on). Usually required for External signals, should rarely be used for Internals—leave to the designer.

Resolution

The smallest magnitude increment the signal is required to represent (.01kg., .5gal, for example). Same comment as for Range.

Rate

The rate at which a signal is to be updated. Not necessarily the same as the data bus repetition rate. Same comment as for Range.

Value Names

List of the names of the values of a primitive discrete signal. Mandatory for these signals.

No. of Values

The number of values of a discrete primitive. Strictly speaking, it is unnecessary because this information is available from the previous item, but it provides a very valuable cross-check, especially during development.

Used In

A list of the DFDs, CFDs, PSPECs, and CSPECs in which a flow appears. Can be further enhanced by identifying the source and destination points. Only recommended as an automatic entry from an automated tool—manual maintenance of this field would be impractical.

Member Of

A list of other dictionary entries of which this entry is a member in the BNF definition. Same comment as for Used In.

Comments

Include any additional information that might help the user to understand the purpose, origin, and so forth, of the entry. Optional, but highly recommended.

A good dictionary data base will include fields for all of these items, and will prompt the user for required items. It may well contain other fields as needed by the application or the tool with which it works.

Resolution can alternatively be called *Precision,* but note that it is *not* the same as *Accuracy;* nor is it the same as *Repeatability.* Accuracy is a measure of how close a signal is to its correct value, while repeatability indicates how much variation there will be from one calculation to another of the intended same value. A signal could have a resolution of .01cm. and be in error by .5cm. Accuracy and repeatability should be specified in PSPECs where needed.

16.2 Dictionary Symbols

The symbols defined in Figure 8.3 are based on (but do not strictly conform to) the Backus-Naur Form. It is best to get used to referring to the symbols by their names in the "meaning" column of that figure: In that way, you will avoid confusing them with their usual algebraic meanings.

The BNF definitions of a flow cover all possible forms of that flow; at any given instant, a particular *instance* of that flow will occur in the model. Thus, a flow with the definition

$$Z = A + [B|C + D] + 1\{E + (F)\}10$$

might have a particular instance consisting of

$$A, C, D, E_1, F_1, E_3, D_{17}, E_{17}$$

or another instance consisting of

$$A, B, E_{10}, F_{10}, E_{21}$$

The subscripts identify particular instances of the terms to which they are attached; each of these instances will have a particular value. For example, E might represent a pressure measurement from any of thirty pressure sensors. The definition requires that, in any instance, measurements from any one to ten of these sensors is needed. In the first instance given, two measurements are included, which happen to come from the third and seventeenth sensors. Each of these measurements will have a particular value.

Some important thoughts to keep in mind when using these symbols are

+ (together with) does not imply ordering, nor does it imply any kind of operation on the individual members of the group. It simply collects them together in a set.

{} (iterations of) allows any number, within the stated range, of objects from the named class within a single instance of the flow. A typical case would be {NAVAIDS} 10 in a FLIGHT PLAN. NAVAIDS are radio navigation beacons distributed around the world; a number of them will be selected according to some complex criteria for use in a given FLIGHT PLAN.

[|] (select one of) is the *exclusive* OR function, expressed in Boolean notation as $\oplus$. It applies where exactly one of a set of objects is to be selected in any given instance.

( ) (optional) is actually redundant as it can be expressed as { }1. It occurs so frequently, however, that the simpler version is very useful.

All the above symbols may be nested at will, but may not overlap each other's range: The range of one must be completely contained within the range of the other. Thus,

$$\{A + (B\} + C)$$
$$[A + \{B| + C\} + D]$$

would be meaningless.

" " (literal) encloses the actual data that appears in the flow, as opposed to the name of a variable that can contain that data. It is often used, for example, to represent actual messages that will appear on a display.

As stated earlier in this chapter, the Used In and Member Of fields are dependent fields, which should be derived from other parts of the data base. They are extremely useful for tracing flows throughout the model, but in systems of any significant size, they are impossible to maintain by hand.

A useful inconsistency check that can be performed by an automated tool is to find "circular definitions," like

$$A = B + C$$
$$B = D + E$$
$$D = F + A$$

which produces an infinite loop, and is illegal.

The "multiple overlapping subsets" of flows, discussed in Section 12.4, and repeated below for convenience, should be supported by logic that balances the flow diagrams with the dictionary. In other words, the flows Y and Z in that section should be recognized as members of X, even though they do not explicitly appear in its definition.

$$X = A + B + C + D + E + F + G + H$$
$$Y = A + B + C + D + E$$
$$Z = D + E + F + G + H$$

16.3 Summary

- The attributes assigned to the various flow types must conform with Figure 16.1.

- The definitions, expressed in modified BNF, must cover all possible instances of the flow.

- When a particular instance occurs, each of its components takes on one of its specified values.

- Nowadays, dictionaries are almost universally implemented in a digital computer. Choose one that supports all the dictionary constructs and relationships, and that has flexible access and reporting capability.

PART IV

The Architecture Model

Chapter 17

Overview

The architecture model is created to model the system's design—to show the configuration of physical modules that perform all the required data and control processing. The requirements are mapped into an architecture model taking all the design constraints into account. These constraints include performance requirements, growth and expansion capability, testability, safety and availability requirements, the implementation technology, the software programming language, maintainability requirements, and the user interface. Which of these considerations play the critical or deciding role depends on the system being designed.

In arriving at a system's architecture, we must take into account the overall objectives for that system, how it is embedded in the larger framework of a higher-level system, and how it relates to other systems that are part of the product line and either complement or overlap with it. We must also consider the feasibility, both in terms of resources available and whether the technology is cost-effective within the marketplace. The end product models the system in terms of its physical components, its physical processes, the information that flows between them, and how that information flows between them. The process is iterative because the constraints on a system's architecture are often in conflict with each other.

The architecture model is equally applicable to any level of system architecture definition. The upper levels show partitioning of the system into architecture modules regardless of hardware and software allocation. Lower levels show the hardware and software modules derived from that system partitioning (described in depth in Part V). The model uses the components shown in Figure 17.1: architecture context diagrams, architecture flow diagrams, architecture interconnect diagrams, architecture module specifications, architecture interconnect specifications, and the architecture dictionary.

In Part IV of the book, we describe the components of the architecture model, and in Part V, the development of the architecture model and its use.

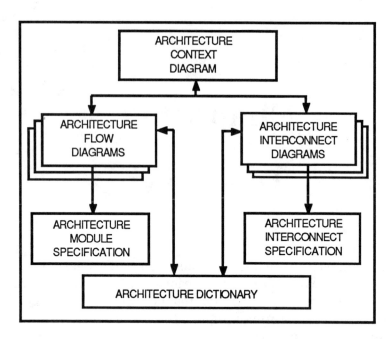

Figure 17.1. Architecture model components.

17.1   Requirements-to-Architecture Template

The requirements model was the first iteration of system definition in which the system's data and control aspects were modeled. The model could be thought of as a template, as illustrated in Figure 17.2. The architecture model for the system shows the physical allocation of the requirements model's data and control processing and flows into the physical entities (subsystems) that will perform the allocated tasks. In addition, it shows allocation of the inputs and outputs, maintenance processing, and the user interface.

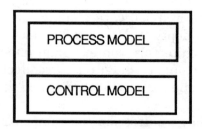

Figure 17.2. Requirements template.

The architecture model assigns the processes of the requirements model to physical modules that constitute the system and establishes the relationships between them.

The definition of the physical modules adds four more perspectives to the two (functional and control processing) addressed by the requirements model. These four are input processing, output processing, user interface processing, and maintenance or self-test processing, as illustrated in Figure 17.3, which shows the data and control model as the central core around which the architecture model is built. The four added perspectives take us closer to the specification of a physical system.

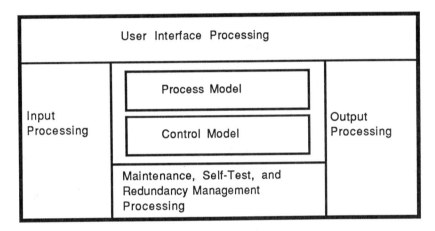

Figure 17.3. Architecture template.

The creation of the architecture definition is akin to the concentric rings that are seen on a slice through a tree trunk; the concentric rings reveal the age of the tree. In the system specification process, those rings would reveal the perspectives that need to be added to completely specify the system. The number of tree rings grows with age; in that same sense, the viewpoints we add to the specification grow with iterations of the systems development process.

The input and output processing blocks represent the additional processing, beyond that of the requirements model, needed for each architecture module to communicate with the other modules and to transform the information to and from an internally usable form.

The user interface block is a special case of the input and output processing blocks. It needs to be separated from the input and output blocks because there are many special considerations, such as human factors, that affect the definition of the user interface. These considerations do not apply to the definition of the interfaces between two architecture modules or between the system under development and other entities (systems) in the environment. The maintenance and self-test block represents any modules required to perform the self-monitoring, redundancy management, and data collection for maintenance purposes.

Consider as an example the requirements model for the Automobile Management System that was introduced in Parts II and III. The DFD for the Automobile Management System shows several required processes, but does not take into account architectural considerations. For example, what processor will do the actual computations needed to determine speed of the vehicle? How will the automobile's shaft rotations be converted to recognizable signals inside the system? How will the Automobile Management System interface with the throttle? How will the driver of the automobile interface with the Automobile Management System? How will the system monitor itself?

The architecture template shown in Figure 17.3 helps in answering such questions, which are important in defining the architecture. In Figure 17.4, the architecture template is adapted for the Automobile Management System.

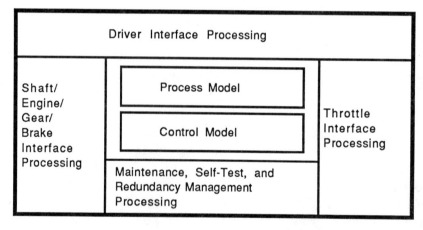

Figure 17.4. Architecture template for the Automobile Management System.

While allocating certain processes from the requirements model to the architecture model, it will be necessary to repartition the existing requirements, and more requirements will be illuminated—their resolution taking the system closer to an implementation. The architecture model is a hierarchical layering of modules that are defined by successive application of the architecture template to each of the blocks in the model, as illustrated in Figure 17.5. The top level of the model represents the major subsystems and each successive layer represents components of these subsystems.

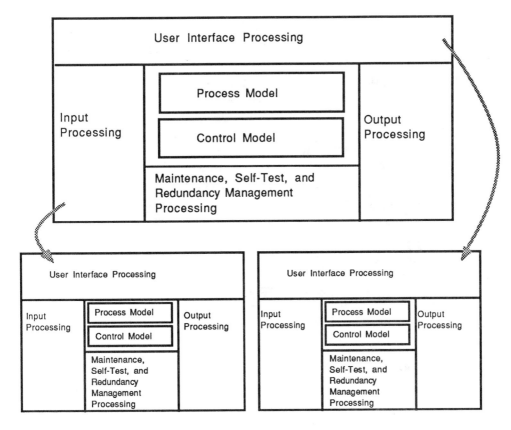

Figure 17.5. Architecture model layering.

17.2 Architecture Model Symbols

The architecture model requires the addition of three symbols to represent, respectively, the architecture modules or the physical processes, the information that these physical processes communicate, and the channels by which this communication takes place.

Architecture module

An architecture module is either a fundamental entity or a grouping. Groupings of functional processes (bubbles and PSPECs) and control processes (CSPECs) and their associated flows are allocated to the architecture module from the requirements model. A fundamental entity corresponds to an individual physical module; a grouping of fundamental entities represents a subsystem that contains several physical modules. This is analogous to the requirements model in which a process bubble was used to represent either a primitive process or a higher-level grouping of processes.

The mapping between the architecture modules and the bubbles in the requirements model can be one-to-one or one-to-many in either direction. The reason for the latter is that several hardware and software technology decisions might have to be made in defining an architecture module. The mapping can also depend on where a functional partitioning was stopped during requirements modeling. What may have been a primitive process from a requirements perspective may turn out to be a nonprimitive from the architecture, hardware, or software design viewpoint.

The symbol for an architecture module is shown in Figure 17.6. It is a rectangle with rounded corners containing the name of the architecture module and a number. Unlike process names in the requirements model, an architecture module is named using a noun with no verbs.

CRUISE CONTROL
SYSTEM
3

Figure 17.6. Architecture module symbol.

The above shape and naming conventions ensure a visible difference between the architecture and requirements models. As well as avoiding confusion, these conventions reinforce the fact that architecture modules represent actual physical entities and cannot be viewed as abstract functional processes in the sense that the requirements model can.

Information flow vector

An information flow vector represents all the information that flows between any two architecture modules. These flows may be either single elements or groupings of elements, and may contain data flows, control flows, or both. The symbol for the vector is shown in Figure 17.7, and consists of straight solid or dashed lines with only right-angled bends, unlike the data flows on a DFD, or the control flows on a CFD.

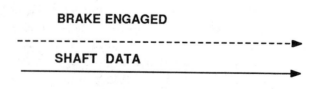

Figure 17.7. Information flow vector symbol.

The name of an information flow vector is an abstraction of all the data or control flows contained within it. It contains no verbs, since processing can only take place inside architecture modules, not inside flow vectors.

Information flow channel

An information flow channel is the physical means by which information flows from one architecture module to another. Such channels represent the physical communication path over which architecture modules communicate. It may be constructed of any material or energy carrier, such as an electrical, mechanical, or optical channel.

There can be many different types of channels, each requiring different symbols. Figure 17.8 shows three such symbols for an electrical bus, a mechanical linkage, and an optical link.

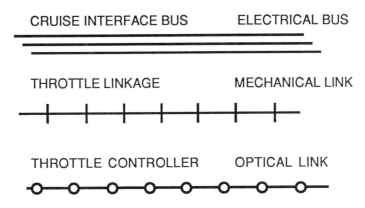

CRUISE INTERFACE BUS   ELECTRICAL BUS

THROTTLE LINKAGE   MECHANICAL LINK

THROTTLE CONTROLLER   OPTICAL LINK

Figure 17.8. Information flow channel symbols.

The name of an information flow channel represents its communication medium. If types of linkages are used between architectural modules other than those indicated in Figure 17.8, additional symbols may be added to the group, but they are chosen so that all linkage types are distinct.

The remainder of Part IV describes the components and structure of the architecture model in detail. After reading it, you will be in a position to interpret a completed architecture model and to use it as a basis for understanding the structure of the resulting system, or implementing that system. Part V describes how to construct the architecture model.

Chapter 18

Architecture Diagrams

18.1 Architecture Context Diagrams

The architecture context diagram (ACD) establishes the information boundary between the system being implemented and the environment in which the system has to operate. The ACD is the highest-level diagram for any system. It represents the system as a source for information flowing out to entities in the environment and as a sink for information that it receives from these entities.

The elements that make up the ACD are: one architecture module, representing the system; terminators that represent entities in the environment with which the system communicates; and information flow vectors that represent the communications that take place between the system and those entities. An ACD may only contain one architecture module representing the system, but there can be any number of information flow vectors and environmental entities with which the system communicates.

Can there be a difference between the context established in the requirements model by the data and control context diagrams? In most cases the answer is no, but there are exceptions, which we will discuss in Part V.

The ACD is drawn using the architecture template shown in Figure 17.3, the system whose architecture we are trying to define being the one architecture module in the center. The ACD uses the architecture template to categorize the external entities in the environment, and helps in identifying their type. Figure 18.1 shows an ACD using the architecture template.

An ACD is not only the context diagram for the system whose architectural definition is taking place, but it also establishes the place of the system in a higher-level system. All systems are embedded in some larger system. By identifying and categorizing the environmental entities and placing our system in this higher-level framework, we can "Think Globally and Act Locally." We often tend to forget the purposes and reasons for the system we are working on, and this higher-level perspective allows us to view the bigger picture. The ACD establishes the place of the Automobile Management System in a higher-level system, the automobile system.

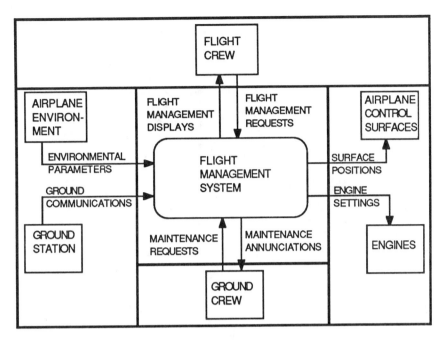

Figure 18.1. ACD for a flight management system.

The ACD shown in Figure 18.1 identifies some entities in the input/
output, user interface, and maintenance processing blocks. Notice that the
Flight Crew and Ground Crew interfaces communicate with the system in
both directions: They are both sources and sinks of information. This is a
very common situation: The net flow between the system and a given entity
may be very large in either or both directions. As a result of this two-way
flow, an entity may appear in both the input and output processing blocks in
an ACD. For example, in Figure 18.2, the ACD for the Automobile Management System, if there were some communication in both directions between
the system and the throttle, such as monitoring the current throttle position
in addition to driving the throttle, the throttle would appear in both the input and output processing blocks.

18.2 Flows and Interconnects

The architectural representation scheme shows two aspects of the architecture: the information flow between the various architecture modules that
constitute the system, and the means by which the architecture modules communicate with each other. In other words, it shows the information and the
channels on which it travels.

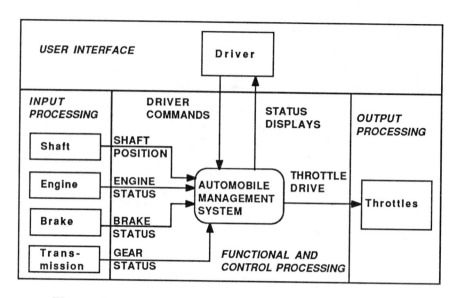

Figure 18.2. ACD for the Automobile Management System.

The two aspects of the architecture may be shown on the same diagram or on two separate diagrams, depending on the needs of the system. The choice depends on which is the best means for showing the system architecture. For large and complex systems, two diagrams are used: the architecture flow diagram showing the information flow between the architecture modules, and the architecture interconnect diagram showing the channels by which the information flows from one architecture module to another. For simpler systems, the two diagrams are combined into one.

18.3   Architecture Flow Diagrams

An architecture flow diagram is a network representation of a system's physical configuration; it documents the information flow between all the architecture modules, of which there can be any number in the system. The AFD also represents the allocation of processes and flows from the data and control flow diagrams into architecture modules. Architecture modules have their own symbol, and communication between them is represented using the information flow vector symbol, expressed as a solid line for data and a dashed line for control.

The relationship between the bubbles in the requirements model and the modules in the architecture module depends on the depth of the decomposition in the requirements model and the criteria for doing the allocation. An AFD may have any number of architecture modules and information flow vectors. In the requirements model, the limit for human understandability and comprehension suggested a 7 ± 2 limit on the number of processes on a single data flow diagram, but the number of architecture modules on an AFD depends on the number of physical entities that have to communicate at the same level of system definition.

An AFD can be drawn using the architecture template shown in Figure 17.3. This is best understood by looking at actual illustrations: Figures 18.3 and 18.4 show two AFDs, and Figures 18.5 and 18.6 show the architecture template adapted for these AFDs. As these figures show, using the architecture template helps in allocating processes and in assigning implementation tasks.

As a further illustration, one allocation of the Automobile Management System might result in the AFD shown in Figure 18.7, where the processes and flows from the requirements model result in seven architecture modules: four for input processing and one each for output processing, user interface processing, and the central functional and control processing. There is no architecture module identified for maintenance or self-test processing. This could mean that the system being defined has had no processing for allocation to that block or that the processing required for that block might be simple enough to allocate to one (or all) of the other architecture modules.

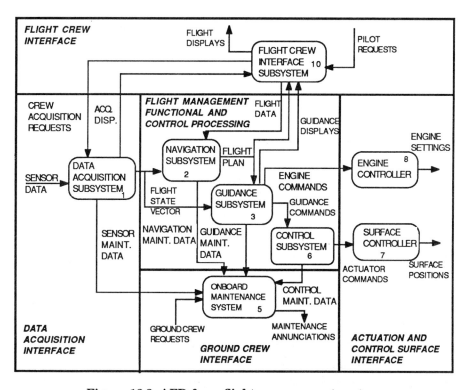

Figure 18.3. AFD for a flight management system.

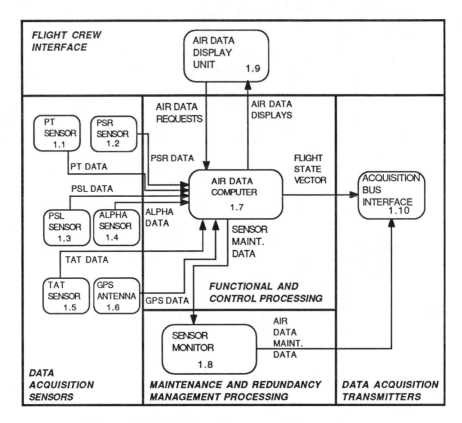

Figure 18.4. AFD for a data acquisition subsystem.

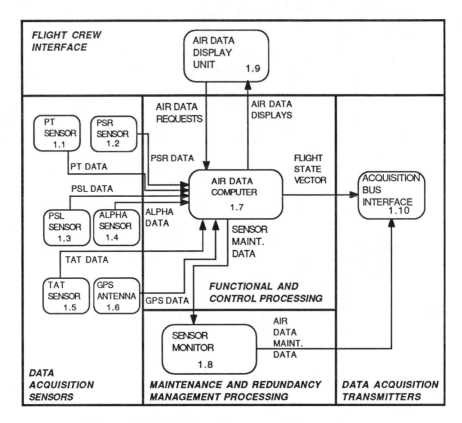

Figure 18.5. Architecture template for a flight management system.

The allocation process for the Automobile Management System has established several different relationships between the processes in the requirements model and those in the architecture model. Compute Speed, for exam-

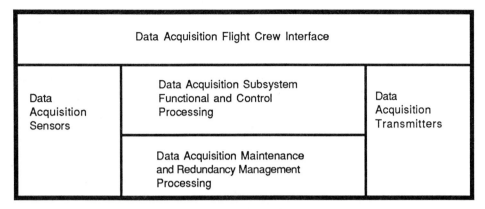

Figure 18.6. Architecture template for a data acquisition subsystem.

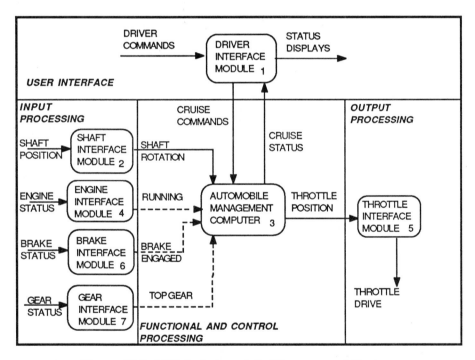

Figure 18.7. AFD 0: Automobile Management System.

ple, is partially allocated to different architecture modules, illustrating that an entire process from the requirements model need not be allocated to just one architecture module: It may be split between several.

The reverse is true of several other processes on the top-level DFD for the Automobile Management System. For example, the processes for calibration, controlling speed, and monitoring the automobile for maintenance purposes are all allocated to the automobile management computer module. Thus, there is no predetermined relationship between the processes in the requirements model and their eventual place in the system architecture, but it is essential that there be traceability from one to the other. This is achieved through the architecture module specification.

Decomposition of architecture flow diagrams

The AFD is decomposed to show the next level of system architecture definition, as shown in Figure 18.8, in which AM is used to signify an architecture module, and IF to represent information flow. What we are really decomposing are the architecture modules; hence, it is not important whether the decomposition takes place from the architecture flow diagram or the architecture interconnect diagram.

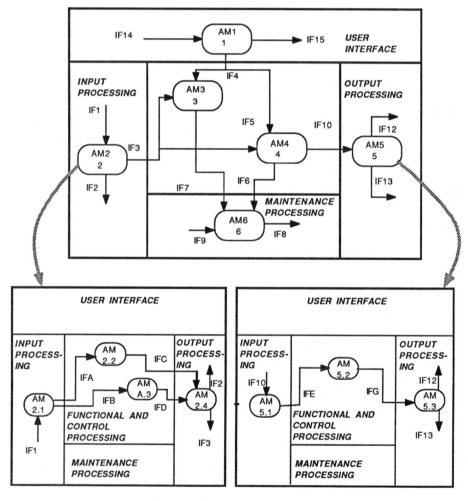

Figure 18.8. AFD layering.

The decomposition of the architecture model is not the same as the functional decomposition of the system. It is a decomposition in the sense that the architecture template is applied successively to each of the modules in the parent AFD to create the next level of AFDs. This process then continues to be applied to successive layers until the system is completely structured.

The architecture template is used as an allocation guide at each level of system definition, but recall there is no requirement that every level of the system have modules in every block of the template.

The modules on the top-level AFD for the Automobile Management System have been decomposed to further define their component physical entities. The architecture template was applied to the shaft interface module and the throttle interface module, shown in the top-level diagram, Figure 18.8, to produce decompositions resulting in the AFDs of Figures 18.9 and 18.10, respectively.

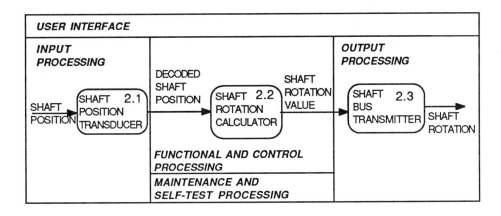

Figure 18.9. AFD 2: Shaft Interface Module.

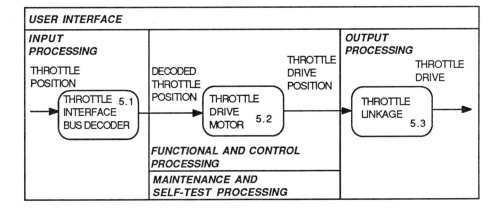

Figure 18.10. AFD 5: Throttle Interface Module.

This hierarchical layering of the architecture flow diagram, along with the specification written for each architecture module, allows architectures ranging from a pure hierarchy to a completely distributed network ("tangled hierarchies," in the words of Hofstadter [6]), or anything between. This range includes very complex systems whose architectures may be partially networks and partially hierarchies.

Redundancy

For various reasons, including reliability or safety, systems may have redundant modules or redundant processing, which are shown in the architecture model. We have adopted the convention with respect to redundant modules that, if they are *totally* redundant, they may be shown as a single module on the AFD, even though their multiple occurrences will appear on the architecture interconnect diagram (as discussed in the next section). However, if two modules are *not* totally redundant—that is, they have some functional difference, however small—then they are considered not redundant at all, and appear as unique modules in the architecture model.

18.4   Architecture Interconnect Diagrams

An architecture interconnect diagram is a representation of the communication channels that exist between the architecture modules; it shows the physical means by which the modules communicate. Architecture modules may communicate by any type of channel and any type of energy or material medium. A radio signal, an electrical bus, a mechanical link, or an optical link are all examples of communication channels.

An AID always corresponds to an AFD; there may be an AID for every AFD in the system definition. The AID shows the same architecture modules as its AFD, but, unlike the AFD, it shows redundant units if they exist. Both architecture modules and communication channels may include redundancy, which may occur in varying levels (dual, triple, or quadruple, for example). As noted earlier, redundant units are completely identical, including any redundancy management processing; otherwise, they would be shown as separate architectural modules or channels. A sample AID is shown in Figure 18.11.

The components of an AID are architecture modules and communications channels, both of which can include redundancy. Redundant modules and communication channels are labeled to show how many of each exist. The multiple channels or modules may be referred to as "lanes" or "units." The main purpose is to show the different modules as illustrated in Figure 18.12A, which shows the labeling for a dual-redundant set, and 18.12B, which shows the labeling for a triple-redundant set.

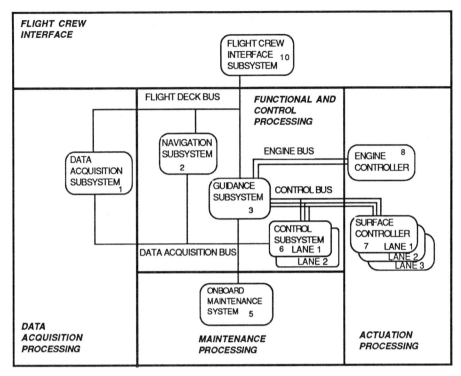

Figure 18.11. AID for a flight management system.

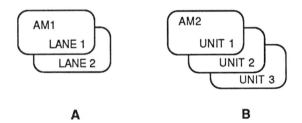

A   B

Figure 18.12. Redundancy of architecture modules.

Consider a dual-redundant architecture module and a dual-redundant communication channel. There are several ways in which these redundancy requirements could manifest themselves. They can be shown graphically on an AID, as in the three parts of Figure 18.13. Figure 18.13A shows the case where module A, unit 1 communicates with module B, unit 1. Figure 18.13B shows the case where module A, unit 1 communicates with both units of mod-

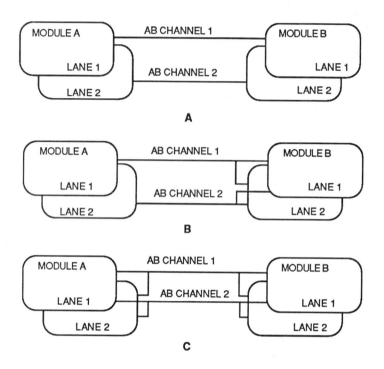

Figure 18.13. Redundancy of architecture channels.

ule B. Figure 18.13C shows the case in which both units of module A communicate with both of the units in module B.

Architecture interconnect diagrams copy their architecture flow diagram
in that they show the same architecture modules and follow the same layering rules. Successive layers of the AID and of the AFD are created in the
same way, by application of the architecture template. The names and numbers of an AID are the same as those of its AFD.

The top-level and shaft interface module AFDs for the Automobile Management System are shown in Figures 18.14 and 18.15. In these diagrams,
some redundancy in the shaft interface module has been assumed for illustra-
tive purposes. Redundancy in systems may be required for many reasons and
may come from a number of different sources. One common reason is that the
available technology will not provide the required reliability with just one
module. Other examples are the need for a high Mean Time Between Un-
scheduled Removal (MTBUR), or Mean Time Between Failure (MTBF), or
safety requirements, any of which may necessitate some critical functions to
be duplicated. Regardless of its origin, the redundancy of a system is shown
as part of the interconnection of the modules on the AID.

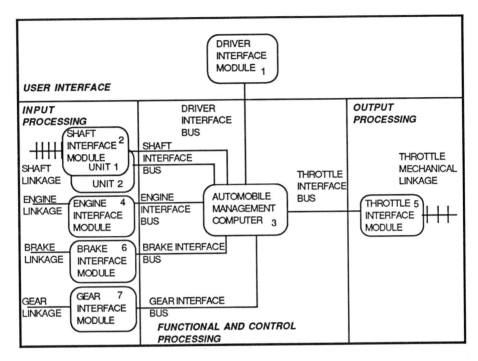

Figure 18.14. AID 0: Automobile Management System.

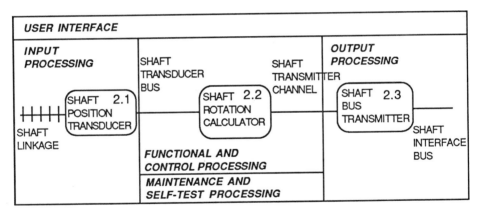

Figure 18.15. AID 2: Shaft Interface Module.

18.5 Summary

- The architecture context diagram gives an overview of how the system physically fits in its environment.

- The architecture flow diagram shows the physical modules of the system at each level of detail, and the information flow between them. It is prepared using an architecture template.

- The architecture interconnect diagram shows the physical communication channels on which the AFD information flows. In simple cases, it may be combined with the AFD.

- Redundancy of modules or channels may be required for reliability, safety, or other reasons, and is illustrated on the AID by showing all the redundant items.

Chapter 19

Architecture Dictionary and Module Specifications

The architecture model graphical components are supported by components that document allocation of the requirements model components to architecture model entities. These components are illustrated in Figure 19.1.

Each architecture module and channel in the system has an architecture module specification that might be textual, graphical, or a combination of the two, and which specifies the processing and flow allocation to that module. For each architecture communication channel, an architecture interconnect

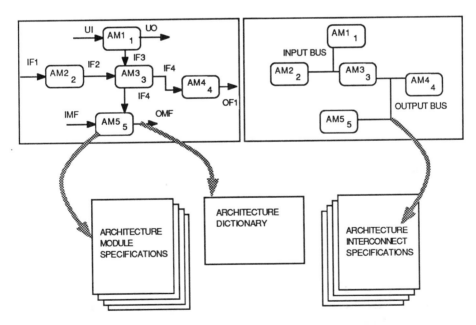

Figure 19.1. Architecture model support components.

213

specification is written to specify the characteristics of that channel. Further, the requirements dictionary is enhanced to show the allocation of the flows to architecture modules. The following sections describe the architecture module specification, the architecture interconnect specification, and the architecture dictionary.

19.1   Architecture Module Specification

As indicated above in Figure 19.1, an architecture module specification is written for every module in the architecture model to state the allocation of data flow, control flow, and processing to be performed by that module. The AMS can be written in a variety of ways; at the very least, it identifies requirements model components to show their allocation. This can be done in the form of a listing of requirements model components or a traceability matrix. The components listed include DFDs (or processes from DFDs), CFDs, PSPECs, and CSPECs, as appropriate.

The reasons for the particular allocation of the requirements model may be listed in the AMS. For example, in the Automobile Management System the architectural requirements might dictate that the shaft rotation computation be allocated to the shaft interface module. The requirement might be that that computation must have a certain reliability as dictated by the National Transportation Safety Board. The AMS might state that architectural tradeoffs showed it was not possible to attain this reliability within the technological constraints of the automobile management computer module, so the shaft rotation computation was partitioned off to the shaft interface module. Other factors that might be stated include market or vendor preferences. For example, suitable state-of-the-art components might be available, but their use may be unacceptable from a cost or risk standpoint.

An AMS consists of three parts: First is a brief narrative specification of what the module is required to do; second, a listing of any architectural requirements for the system; and third, a statement of the allocation of the requirements model components to the architecture module. Figure 19.2 shows the AMS for the automobile management computer module from AFD 0 of the Automobile Management System. When a process is allocated to an architecture module, all the data and control flows into or out of that process and all the children of that process are allocated along with it.

In Figure 19.2, the entire contents of process 2, from the top-level DFD for the Automobile Management System, have been allocated to the automobile management computer module, whereas process 8 from the DFD is only allocated partially to that module, the remainder being allocated to the shaft interface module. The AMS for the automobile management computer module lists only those processes that have been allocated to it in their entirety.

AMS : AUTOMOBILE MANAGEMENT COMPUTER MODULE

DESCRIPTION: The AMC has been allocated all the software
in the system because only one processor could be used.

ARCHITECTURE REQUIREMENTS: The system shall be built
using M68020 microprocessor chips.

ALLOCATION: The AMC has been allocated DFD/CFD
processes: 1, 2, 3, 4, 8.6, and CSPEC 0.

Figure 19.2. Architecture module specification.

The rule is, the AMS lists the highest-level process from the requirements model whose entire set of descendants is allocated to that particular architecture module. The same rule applies for the allocation of CSPECs, which may also be split among architecture modules. For example, Figure 19.3 shows a DFD with its corresponding CFD and CSPEC.

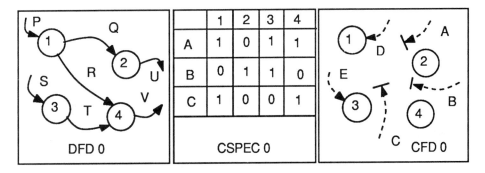

Figure 19.3. A DFD, CFD, and their CSPEC to be allocated.

If the allocation process resulted in allocating processes 1 and 2 to architecture module P, for example, and processes 3 and 4 to architecture module Q, then the decision would have to be made about how to split the corresponding CFD and CSPEC. The way this is done depends entirely on the needs of the particular system and its architecture. If the decision is to split the activation to correspond with the modules, then module P will contain the control flows and activation that go along with processes 1 and 2 and module Q will contain those that go along with processes 3 and 4. Activation tables split in this way are shown in Figure 19.4.

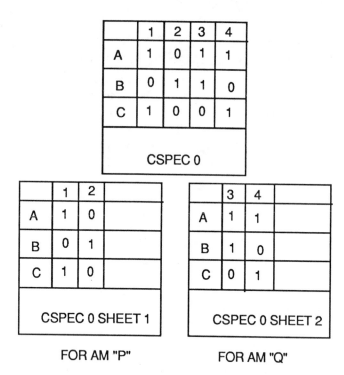

Figure 19.4. Splitting CSPECs for allocation.

In the original control specification, there were three signals controlling processes 1, 2, and 3. The two activation tables are now placed on separate sheets in the control specification and the respective sheets are listed in the appropriate architecture module specifications. Thus, the activation table for processes 1 and 2 would be listed in the AMS for module P and the activation table for processes 3 and 4 in the AMS for module Q.

This same sort of splitting and allocation to separate AMSs is also done for the other entities in a control specification, such as decision tables and state transition diagrams. An important role of the AMS is to list the specific components from the requirements model: process name or number, or CSPEC number, or specific sheets from a CSPEC.

The AMS example we have just seen shows a listing of the requirements model components; alternatively, this allocation can be specified using a traceability matrix, as shown for the Automobile Management System in Figure 19.5. The traceability matrix can also be used to show the allocation of CSPECs or their individual sheets.

The timing specification from the requirements model is inherited by each architecture module affected by those requirements. In coming up with an allocation for a system, it is not only important for the system modules to satisfy just the process and control requirements but the desired architecture

TRACEABILITY MATRIX AFD 0 : AUTOMOBILE MANAGEMENT SYSTEM

ARCHITECTURE MODEL COMPONENTS / REQUIREMENTS MODEL COMPONENTS	SHAFT INTERFACE MODULE	AUTO-MOBILE MANAGE-MENT COMPUTER	THROTTLE INTERFACE MODULE	DRIVER INTERFACE MODULE	GEAR INTERFACE MODULE	BRAKE INTERFACE MODULE	ENGINE INTERFACE MODULE
MEASURE MOTION 1		X					
MEASURE MILE 2		X					
CONTROL THROTTLE 3		X					
MONITOR STATUS 4		X					
DETERMINE ENGINE STATUS 9							X
DETERMINE GEAR STATUS 10					X		
DETERMINE BRAKE STATUS 7						X	
COUNT SHAFT ROTATIONS 6	X						
INTERFACE WITH DRIVER 8.1 8.2 8.3 8.4 8.5				X			
VALIDATE DRIVER REQUEST 8.6		X					
MOVE THROTTLES			X				

Figure 19.5. Traceability matrix for the Automobile Management System.

must also meet the system's timing requirements. This is a consideration of the tradeoff process by which the system's implementation architecture is developed. The timing requirements therefore have to be satisfied along with all the other requirements.

The purpose of defining an AMS is to clearly, unambiguously, and completely state the design allocation of the requirements model to architecture modules. Any of the schemes shown in this section might be used for that purpose as long as the AMS fully records the allocation of the components from the requirements to that AMS's architecture module.

19.2 Architecture Interconnect Specification

The architecture interconnect specification establishes the characteristics of the communication channels on which information travels between architectural modules. It describes the transmission medium and the information formats.

A communication channel can consist of any energy or material medium that carries information. Examples are: a twisted pair of wires carrying electrical signals, an optical link that transmits information via light intensity, or a mechanical or radio signal. The AIS captures these characteristics, so, for example, if two architecture modules communicate via an optical link, as shown in Figure 19.6, the corresponding AIS would specify that link. If the communication channel between the automobile management computer module and the driver interface module is a serial digital bus consisting of a twisted pair of wires carrying electrical pulses, then that fact would be recorded in the AIS. This is shown in Figure 19.7 for the driver interface bus, which defines the serial data format and the signal characteristics for that bus.

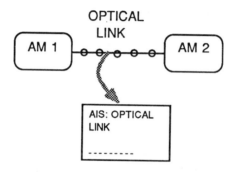

Figure 19.6. Interconnect channel and corresponding AIS.

An AIS is written for every communication channel on an architecture interconnect diagram, as illustrated in Figure 19.1, but they may be simplified when there are many channels that have the same characteristics. Often, the channels in a system either are standardized or are designed to use the same technology to minimize recurring manufacturing and maintenance costs.

For example, in AID 0 for the Automobile Management System, if the shaft interface module, the driver interface module, and the throttle interface module were all to communicate on separate channels but with identical characteristics, then the AISs for these channels could refer to a common document that outlined the channel specification. This could either be a separate document or an appendix.

Both for the AIS and the AMS, the content of the specification is paramount, while the particular format or layout is of little consequence. All that matters is that the end objective of obtaining a clear and unambiguous specification is attained.

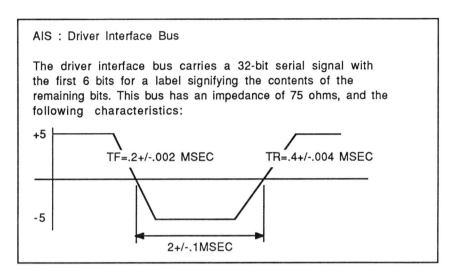

Figure 19.7. A typical AIS.

19.3   Timing Requirements

The requirements model timing specification must be allocated to architecture modules, information flow vectors, and information flow channels in the same way as the other requirements model components are allocated. But the timing specifications do not just get allocated; they play a pivotal role in selecting the implementation technology. They are a determining factor in the tradeoff between different hardware technologies, and in the tradeoff between hardware and software. Only after these tradeoffs have been made are the requirements model timing specifications allocated to the resulting architecture components.

Unlike the requirements model timing, which is only applied to the external signals, allocation of the timing requirements to the architecture model results in specific timing constraints on the internal architecture modules. For example, if there were a 500 msec maximum timing requirement from input flow A to output flow B, and if the processes that transform A into B were allocated to three different architecture modules, X, Y, and Z, then the decision would have to be made as to how much time to allocate to each of these modules. The 500 msec might be assigned as 200 msec, 100 msec, and 200 msec respectively to the three modules. These timing requirements would be imposed on the processes allocated to those three modules: The hardware or software allocated to module X, for example, would have to meet the 200 msec constraint. This might translate into the imposition of a specific rate at which the output of module X must be transmitted to modules Y or Z, and this attribute would be added to the architecture dictionary as the minimum required update rate at which that output must be transmitted to achieve the desired timing performance. Alternatively, the 200 msec constraint might simply be included in a response time specification for module X, constructed in just the same way as the requirements model response time specification.

Every timing constraint from the requirements model is used in the architecture tradeoff process, and allocated to the resulting modules in the above manner. This procedure is repeated through the architecture layers until each hardware and software module has a specific part of the overall timing constraints allocated to it. In this manner all the requirements model timing constraints are involved in the evaluation and selection of the implementation technology and structure.

19.4   Architecture Dictionary

The architecture dictionary consists of a listing of all the data and control elements that flow between the architecture modules as well as between architecture modules and external entities. The architecture dictionary is an enhancement of the requirements dictionary from the requirements model with the appropriate architectural information added. It shows the allocation of data and control flows to architecture modules and indicates the communication channel on which the signal flows. To establish traceability between the requirements model and the architecture model, there is total allocation of flows from the requirements dictionary to the architecture model. Figure 19.8 shows part of the architecture dictionary for the Automobile Management System.

The additions beyond the requirements dictionary information are the names of the architecture modules between which the information flows, and the names of the communication channels on which this information travels. This additional information is provided for every primitive data and control element in the requirements dictionary. Groupings of flow elements may also have this information as long as they flow in their entirety along the same channel and information flow vectors.

The architecture dictionary contains at least the attributes indicated above, but may have more. For example, the driver interface bus in the Automobile Management System carries several pieces of information, such as the driver's requests for controlling speed and average trip speed. The AIS for this bus shows that it also carries a label giving information about the contents of the flow so that the receiving module can interpret the data it sees. This label would be included in the architecture dictionary.

The actual information included in the architecture dictionary depends on the needs of the specific system. Any additional information beyond that identified in Figure 19.8 has two purposes: to uniquely define the architecture of the system, and to provide traceability between the requirements and architecture models. If it meets these objectives, it is acceptable.

Name	Composed of	Type	Origin Module	Destination Module	Channel
Activate	\Driver's cruise control activate command\ 2 Values: On, Off	C	Driver Interface	Automobile Management Computer	Driver Interface Bus
Braking	\Input signal indicating brakes applied\ 2 values: On, Off	C	Brake Interface	Automobile Management Computer	Brake Bus
Desired Speed	\Desired speed cruise control is to maintain\ Units: Miles per hour	D	Automobile Management Computer		
Fuel Quantity	\Entered value of fill-up fuel quantity\ Units: Gallons Range: 0-18 gallons	D	Driver Interface	Automobile Management Computer	Driver Interface Bus
Throttle Position	\Output signal driving throttle position\ Units: Volts Range: 0-8 volts	D	Automobile Management Computer	Throttle Interface	Throttle Bus

Figure 19.8. Partial architecture dictionary
for the Automobile Management System.

19.5 Summary

- All the objects in the architecture model are supported by detailed specifications and by the dictionary.

- The architecture module specification defines the allocation to a module of data flows, control flows, and processing.

- The architecture interconnect specification defines the characteristics of the communication channels between the modules.

- The architecture dictionary lists all the data and control elements that flow on the channels, and adds physical information beyond that given in the requirements dictionary.

Chapter 20

Completing the
Architecture Model

The architecture model components covered so far show the partitioning of the system requirements into physical components that will be used to implement the system. The architecture modules contain requirements that are components from the system requirements model: Each AFD/AID module contains allocated DFDs, CFDs, PSPECs, CSPECs, and flows. In Part V, we show this allocation for the Automobile Management System.

20.1   Allocation to Hardware and Software

Now that we have seen how the requirements model components are allocated to architecture modules, it is time to see how these architecture modules will accomplish their allocated tasks. Each module will be implemented in either hardware, software, or some combination of the two. The system-level partitioning provides a context for allocating the system functions to hardware and software components, and identifies the requirements for these components. To carry out this allocation, we use the same components that we used to map the system requirements: DFDs, CFDs, PSPECs, CSPECs, and a dictionary.

As an illustration, we use one of the modules from the Automobile Management System: the automobile management computer module. This module has been allocated all the flows and processes associated with controlling speed and the maintenance supervisory and monitoring functions. It could be designed such that either all the allocated processing is performed in hardware, or all of it in software (still, of course, requiring a hardware host). In either of these cases, the requirements allocation to the architecture module would be identical with the allocation to hardware or to software.

Another option would be to divide this allocation between hardware and software. If, for example, from the top-level DFD, the calibration process were to be allocated to hardware and the remaining processes to software, then the hardware and software partitioning would divide the DFD in two, as shown in Figure 20.1. One division represents the hardware requirements, and the other, the software requirements.

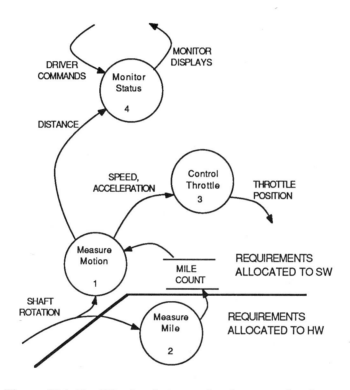

Figure 20.1. Partitioning between hardware and software.

Each piece of the requirements model for the whole system is partitioned in this way between hardware and software. Every system requirement is allocated to the architecture model first, and then mapped into hardware or software. This step establishes requirements for the lower-level system.

20.2 The Hardware and Software Architectures

The completed architecture model with the hardware and software partitioning brings the system specification one step closer to implementation. Figure

20.2 shows the deliverables that have been produced thus far by the modeling process.

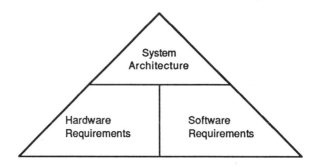

Figure 20.2. System, hardware, and software requirements hierarchy.

Beyond this, what remains to be done is to define the separate software and hardware architecture and implementation. The architecture model components can be used to perform these tasks as well.

At the end of the specification process, both the requirements model and the architecture model will have been used to successively define first the system and then its components, which are the hardware and the software. Figure 20.3 shows the deliverables at the end of this system, hardware, and software definition process.

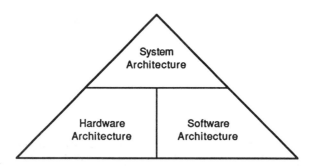

Figure 20.3. System, hardware, and software architecture hierarchy.

We would like to clarify our use of triangles to illustrate the requirements and the architecture models. They are useful for showing hierarchical relationships between various elements of the models, but we are aware that this symbol might give the impression that the models are symmetrical, with equal numbers of decomposition levels on all branches. This impression is wrong! The models are normally asymmetrical, with widely differing levels of decomposition. We chose to use the triangles anyway, for the sake of simplicity and to avoid diagrams that look like abstract art.

We will discuss and illustrate in greater detail hardware and software partitioning and architecture development in Part V.

20.3   The Complete Architecture Model

The architecture model represents the system as a hierarchically layered set of networks. At each level of system definition, the architecture template is used as a guide to help the allocation process. The hierarchy starts out by establishing the place of the system in the environment, using the architecture context diagram. Thereafter, each successive layer defines the system as a network of modules. The definition of each level is viewed from two perspectives: one to establish the information flow between the architecture modules, and the other to show the physical interconnections between them.

For each level of system definition, there are two types of specifications: First are the architecture module specifications, which specify the processing and flows allocated to the architecture modules; second are the architecture interconnect diagrams, which specify the communication channel characteristics. The AMS shows the allocation of the requirements model processes and flows; the AID shows the physical communication channel characteristics. These specifications are written for every module and every communication channel in the system. The architecture module specifications must balance with each other and must provide traceability between the requirements model and the architecture model.

The diagrams and specifications are supported by the architecture dictionary to show the allocation of flows. The architecture dictionary also helps establish traceability between the requirements model and the architecture model.

We shall now see how all the components of the architecture model fit together, what their roles are in the model and what relationships exist between them. For this purpose, Figure 20.4 shows a vertical slice through the model.

The very top level of the model is the architecture context diagram that establishes the boundary between the system and the environment in which it has to operate. In the case of the Automobile Management System, for example, this environment would be the total automobile system, which includes the vehicle and the driver, and through the ACD we would see how the Automobile Management System interacts with the rest of this larger system. The set of diagrams depicted below the architecture context diagram are the level 0 diagrams, labeled AFD 0 and AID 0; they identify the physical entities that constitute the system.

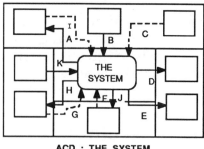

ACD : THE SYSTEM

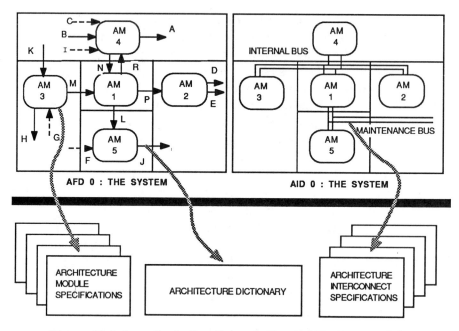

Figure 20.4. A vertical slice through the architecture model.

The information flows on AFD 0 and on the architecture context diagram match exactly: All flows shown coming into or going out of the system at the context level map exactly into the modules on AFD 0. The diagram labeled AID 0 establishes the communication channels that exist between the modules in the system and the channels by which the system communicates with external entities. Successive layers of the model then show the physical decomposition of the upper-level modules in the system.

The architecture model, then, as viewed in Figure 20.4, defines the modules that constitute the system, the communications between the modules, the processing performed by them, and the flows and their location in the model. The components of this model integrate with each other and with the requirements model in well-defined ways. We shall look at the development of this model in Part V.

PART V
Building the Architecture Model

Chapter 21

Overview

The architecture model described in Part IV is the end deliverable representing the system in terms of its physical modules. The process by which this model is developed varies according to the many different criteria that must be taken into account beyond the functional and control requirements captured by the requirements model. Some of the more common of these criteria are listed below.

The purpose of the architecture definition process is to take into account all the architectural requirements and help in the design tradeoff and decision process. This will result in an acceptable system design.

There are many ways to configure a system to meet a given set of requirements. There is no one architecture that will always result from the procedures outlined here. For the development of a system's architecture, the design factors that can play critical roles could include

Reliability: The design must result in a system that is available for use (has no faults) more than a specified percentage of the time.

Safety: The design must be "fail-safe"—that is, when its performance degrades, it must do so gracefully so that safety is not jeopardized.

Maintainability: The system needs to be checked for correct operation in service and must collect data for error isolation.

Testability: The system must be designed so that its requirements can be verified and validated.

Cost: The design must result in a system that can be built within a specified total dollar amount.

Technology: Decisions have to be researched to determine the technology that will best meet the system's cost constraints.

Performance: The system must meet some particular timing or behavioral constraints, such as overall response time to certain critical operations, or calculating flight paths to achieve a desired fuel economy.

Growth and Expansion Capability: The design must allow for future functional expansion.

21.1 Architecture Development Process

Here in Part V, we show how to transform from the requirements model, described in Parts II and III, to the architecture model, whose end result was described in Part IV.

The system architecture is developed in several iterative stages, first using the architecture template to enhance the requirements model and then allocating these requirements. The steps to create the complete system specification are

1. Generate the requirements model to capture the system's functional and control requirements.

2. Enhance the requirements model by adding input and output processing using the architecture template.

3. Allocate the enhanced requirements model to physical entities in accordance with the chosen technology, to produce the architecture model.

The requirements model is a technology-*independent* statement of the essential functions the system is to perform. The architecture model is a technology-*dependent* statement of the system's design. The implementation of the intermediate, enhanced requirements model will depend on the technology selected, but this selection has not yet been made, so we refer to this intermediate stage as the *technology-nonspecific model*. It is discussed in detail in Chapter 23.

The first step in the architecture development process, then, is to identify and arrange in order of priority those factors that are critical to the needs of the specific system. Some factors may be in direct conflict with each other: For example, the most maintainable and testable system may have so much processing overhead that functional performance is affected.

Safety is another example of a critical design criterion: We would want the Automobile Management System to be fail-safe, to minimize the probability of failures that could jeopardize human safety. What could potentially go wrong with the Automobile Management System that could cause safety problems? From the architecture model in the previous chapters, we can see two possibilities: One possible problem would be obstruction of the drive shaft by the shaft interface module, impeding normal operation of the vehicle; the other might be inadvertent movement of the throttle by the throttle interface module, causing unexpected acceleration. Either of these would be a safety hazard.

Another factor that can play a role in development of the architecture model is the system's performance. The total input-to-output reaction time might have to meet some timing constraints such as the amount of time the system is allowed to respond to a "disengage" input. This type of performance requirement might place computational and speed constraints on the architecture modules.

Taking all such factors into account, we must determine all the possible architecture requirements and constraints for the system and trade off the various possible architectures to identify that which is most acceptable. The resulting architecture may take several iterations to develop.

We have seen how safety and other nonfunctional requirements could require additional processing, but none of these requirements appeared in the requirements model. This is because the requirements model was built to identify what the system has to do regardless of how it does it; that is, safety requirements are not part of the logical statement of what the system has to do. The architecture template, on the other hand, specifically identifies nonfunctional requirements for the system. Only at this point, when we try to decide on the system's architecture, do we discover the safety limitations of the technology.

In the following chapters, we look at this architecture development, or physicalization, process. The requirements model created a technology-independent statement of what the system has to do. Now we shall see how we can use the requirements model and the architecture model iteratively to effectively create a complete system specification.

21.2 Systems Come in Hierarchies

Before we look at the details of architecture development, we want to highlight an important property of the model and of the world it represents: Both natural and manmade systems come in hierarchies, and the architecture model is no exception. The broadest illustration of this hierarchical structure is the very universe we live in, as illustrated in Figure 21.1. One of the smallest structures is the atom; at the next level is the molecule, which is a

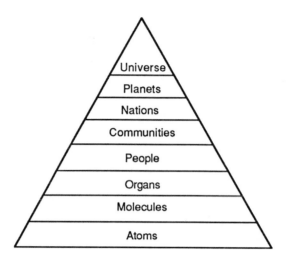

Figure 21.1. Hierarchical nature of natural systems.

systematic grouping of atoms; at a higher level are living cells, consisting of molecules; at still higher levels we have organs, then people, social organizations, communities, countries, the planets, and the universe. Each level in the hierarchy is composed of some organized grouping of the elements in the level below.

Manmade systems have similar properties. In an automobile, for example, we have mechanical and electrical components grouped together into subassemblies, which are further grouped into subsystems, such as the Automobile Management System. These subsystems form the whole automobile system, which is a part of the transportation system, and so on. The significance of this is that, at each level, the architecture model naturally reflects this hierarchical structure, and at each level of the hierarchy, it applies the same set of guidelines for representing the structure. It thus allows us to simplify a complex system structure into a series of similar iterative steps, which follow the natural form of the system. It supports the concept that one person's requirements are another person's design in that each of these iterative steps incorporates one requirements-to-design transition.

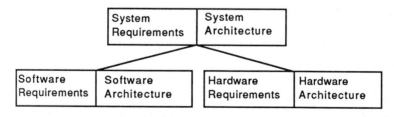

Figure 21.2. Hierarchical nature of systems development.

What we shall be doing in the following chapters to create the system's architecture is to apply the architecture template to every layer of the system, stabilizing the upper levels as we proceed to the lower levels, as illustrated above in Figure 21.2.

We first want to determine the system's top-level requirements and architecture. At the level below that, we want to divide the architecture into the hardware and software requirements and architecture. The benefits of using this approach are

- We view the system *as* a system, not as a mere collection of hardware and software components that come together to do some portion of the total task.

- We can see how the system integrates. The hardware and software are tied together by the higher-level specification, providing us with traceability, and a clear system partitioning.

- As we work with each particular specification, we can address the issues concerning that level of definition without having to worry about lower-level details or unstable upper levels.

When we view the system as a hierarchy, we reduce the complexity of the development process into manageable chunks. In doing so, we ensure that integration between models and between levels is well-defined. This will result in developing a more testable and maintainable system that meets the customer's requirements. The requirements and architecture models together allow us to concentrate on one aspect of the system and one level of detail at a time with the assurance that the models will clearly reveal the impact of what we are doing.

Chapter 22

Enhancing the Requirements Model

In this chapter, we describe the process of taking the technology-independent requirements model of the system and mapping it into an architecture model, which takes into account both the technology and the physical constraints in which the implemented system must work. As already indicated, this process is an iterative one in which the components of the requirements model are assigned to physical processes, while nonfunctional requirements, such as input and output processing, reliability, and so on, are added.

The purpose of enhancing the functional requirements model is to obtain a technology-nonspecific model of the requirements, which reflects the whole range of general systems concerns. Business policy, compatibility with existing systems in the environment, compatibility with the particular family of products being produced by the company, security, and organizational structure are all factors that must be considered. These additional requirements influence input and output processing, user interface processing, maintenance, redundancy management, and self-test processing.

One way to view this additional processing is with an outside-in approach, as shown in Figure 22.1. By this we mean that we view the system from the vantage point of the environment in which it exists; that is, where it receives data from other systems and transmits data to them; where it may have to interface with users; and where it may have some maintenance, redundancy, and self-test requirements imposed.

In the following sections, we use the architecture template to mold the system into this environment, and to enhance the requirements model to make it technology-nonspecific.

22.1 Input and Output Processing

In creating a system design, we must define communications across the system's boundary that were not addressed while building the requirements

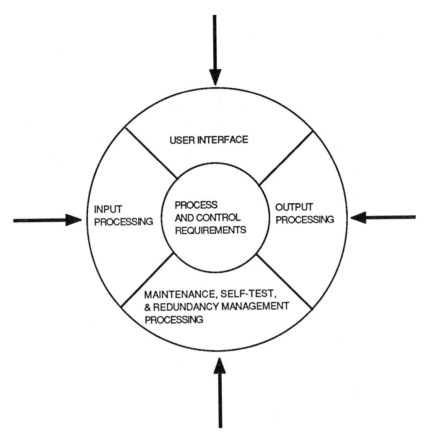

Figure 22.1. Outside-in approach to architecture development.

model. In the requirements model, we mapped information (data and control) flows across the boundary, but we did not address how that crossing will be physically performed. The Automobile Management System has several such flows, two of which are the SHAFT ROTATION input and the THROTTLE POSITION output. These were derived from the following segments of the problem statement for that system given in Chapter 26.

> *The system controls the car through an actuator attached to the throttle. This actuator is mechanically in parallel with the accelerator pedal mechanism, such that whichever one is demanding greater speed controls the throttle.*

> *The system is to measure speed by counting pulses it receives from a sensor on the drive shaft. Count-rate from this sensor corresponds to vehicle miles-per-hour through a proportionality constant.*

In the requirements model for the Automobile Management System, we did not include any processing to convert the physical shaft rotation into numerical values, nor to convert the computed value of the desired throttle position to drive the throttle to that position. Using the architecture template as a guide, we identify this additional input and output processing to make the requirements model technology-nonspecific based on the corresponding technology decisions; in the case of the Automobile Management System, we have to decide how the system will interface with the shaft and the throttle. In general, the added processing is realized as buffers surrounding the requirements model, as illustrated in Figure 22.2.

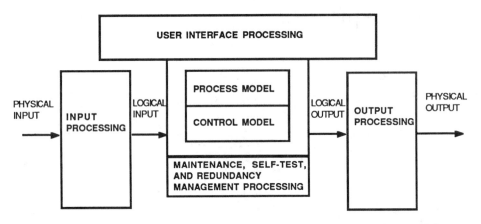

Figure 22.2. Input and output buffers for the requirements model.

Additional processing is added dependent on technology decisions. The input processing accepts physical input from a source and converts it to a logical form usable by the system. The output processing takes the system's logical output and converts it to a physical form acceptable to the output sink.

In the Automobile Management System example, we have to add processes to interpret the shaft rotations and to move the throttle. For example, the shaft might have a magnet mounted on it from which a transducer would count pulses and transmit a voltage proportional to rotations per unit of time. Similarly, we could decide that in order to assure a smooth ride, we can avoid abrupt movement of the throttle by driving it in small steps with a stepper motor. These new processes would be added to the existing requirements model in the input and output processing blocks of the architecture template, as illustrated in the portion of the enhanced DFD shown in Figure 22.3.

The same type of decisions about which technologies to use have to be made for all input and output signals, resulting in further additions to these

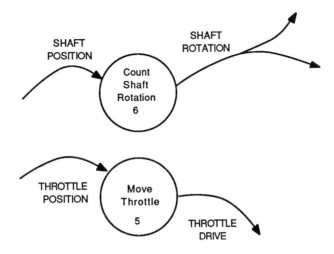

**Figure 22.3. Input and output processes
for the Automobile Management System.**

two blocks of the architecture template. As well as the processes and flows of
the DFDs, control signals and processing may also be modified and extended
as a result of the technology decisions. The input and output processing in its
most general form can be thought of as the encoding and decoding of the
information receivers and transmitters, and can eventually reside in the
hardware, the software, or both.

22.2   User Interface Processing

The system-to-user interface requires the same kinds of technology-based enhancements as we made for the system-to-system interface. So, here again,
we must add the decisions that were omitted from the requirements model on
use of available technology, and on various cost, operational environment,
and other criteria. We must make design tradeoffs to select the physical user-
machine interface.

In the Automobile Management System, many data and control signals
cross the user-system boundary. One technology decision we must make, to
satisfy the following requirements statement from Chapter 26, is to use a
CRT display with a keyboard:

> *The Automobile Management System will have a full numeric key-
> board and a CRT display—The user interface processing for the system
> shall be intelligent, such that all driver entries will be validated by
> checking for reasonableness (i.e., range on fuel tank input) or any other
> appropriate measure for all the other inputs.*

"Intelligence" in the driver interface is interpreted to mean that it must check user inputs for syntactical accuracy and ask for the inputs again if they are not valid. So, if the user were to enter a fuel quantity outside of a predetermined range, then the system would not accept it, and would ask the user to enter a new quantity. The user interface module must also format all the data for display on the CRT screen.

All of these technology decisions enhance the Automobile Management System DFD. Processing is added in the user interface block of the architecture template between the requirements model core and the driver, as illustrated in Figure 22.4. Like all processes, these additional processes can be further decomposed as required. Figure 22.5 shows a DFD and CFD for the driver interface process.

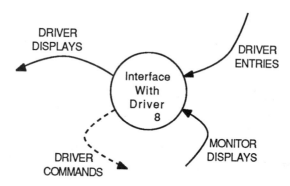

Figure 22.4. Enhancements to the Automobile Management
System DFD for user interface processing.

In the case of the user interface, the additional processing in the architecture template converts physical user inputs (such as keyboard entries) into logical inputs for the requirements model core, and takes the system's logical outputs and converts them into the physical form required for the user interface module. We show this in Figure 22.6.

The user interface processing block is separated from the other input and output processing blocks on the architecture template for the following three reasons:

- Technology for the user interface can be more flexible than that for the system-to-system interface.

- Human factors are a special concern with the user interface block. Separating it allows them to be considered independently of other parts of the system.

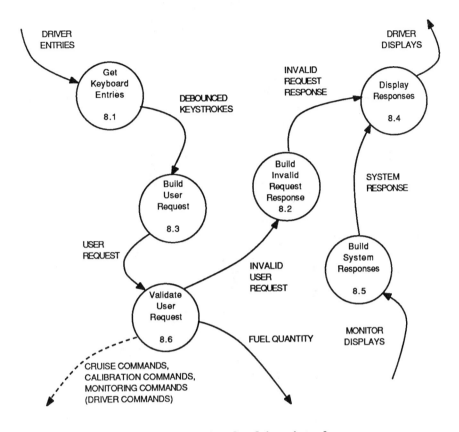

Figure 22.5. DFD/CFD for the driver interface process.

- This separation provides the opportunity to create a user interface model that can be prototyped and validated independently of the main system, while the architecture template as a whole still gives an integrated view of the whole system.

22.3 Maintenance and Self-Test Processing

The systems we develop may have various types of technology-dependent maintenance and self-test requirements. The available technology might also dictate that redundant modules are required, which, in turn, necessitate redundancy management processing. It is clear, then, that we cannot identify these additional requirements for maintenance, self-test, redundancy, or redundancy management until we have selected an implementation technology that meets the system's reliability and performance criteria and analyzed its particular characteristics.

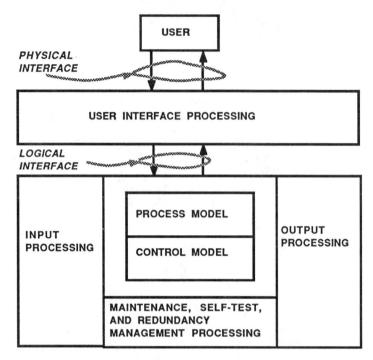

Figure 22.6. User interface buffer to the requirements model.

Suppose in the Automobile Management System that the safety and reliability requirements cannot be achieved by one shaft interface module using available technology. One solution might be to mount two of these units on the shaft, and thus receive two values of shaft rotation. We must then decide on an algorithm to determine which of the two values, or what averaging scheme, to use. Another additional requirement might be our need for a means to change the monitoring schedule so that the driver would be reminded to change the oil and filter every 2,000 miles instead of every 3,000 miles. In either case, we would add processing to the maintenance, redundancy management, and self-test buffer as shown in Figure 22.7.

·In the case of the monitoring schedule, we would not only have to add a data process for updating the store, but also some control flows and control processing to ensure that the system could not control speed or accept any other inputs while the store is being updated. We not only have added processing for the maintenance and self-test block, but have also identified another user interface. Regardless of whether we choose a maintenance scheme, a store-update scheme, or a full-blown built-in self-test, we would have to identify additional processing, as illustrated in Figure 22.8.

This additional processing forms a buffer between the system and other systems or between the system and a maintainer buffer. The maintainer buffer is an important means for automatically gathering maintenance infor-

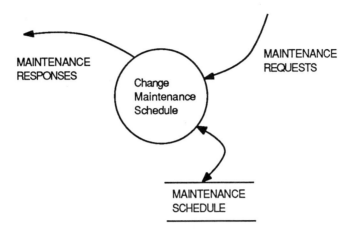

Figure 22.7. Enhancements for maintenance and self-test buffer.

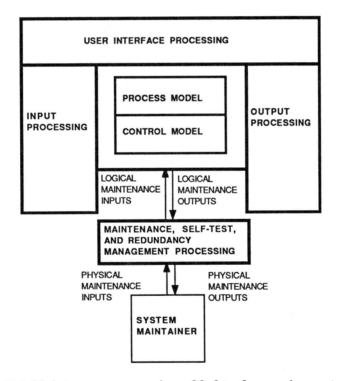

Figure 22.8. Maintenance processing added to the requirements model.

mation, but is often overlooked in systems development. System maintenance and self-test should be clearly identified and given full attention. It is not acceptable for a system to meet all the safety, performance, and other criteria, and yet cause major perturbations to the user because no consideration was given to self-test, fault-isolation, or maintenance-recording capabilities.

Even if the decision is made not to include any additional processing in this block of the architecture template, the maintenance ramifications of design decisions should still be considered.

22.4 The Complete Enhanced Requirements Model

Figures 22.9 and 22.10 group together all the enhancements that we have seen piecemeal in this chapter for the Automobile Management System DFD and CFD. Note that the additional processing in the architecture template completely surrounds the functional requirements model core.

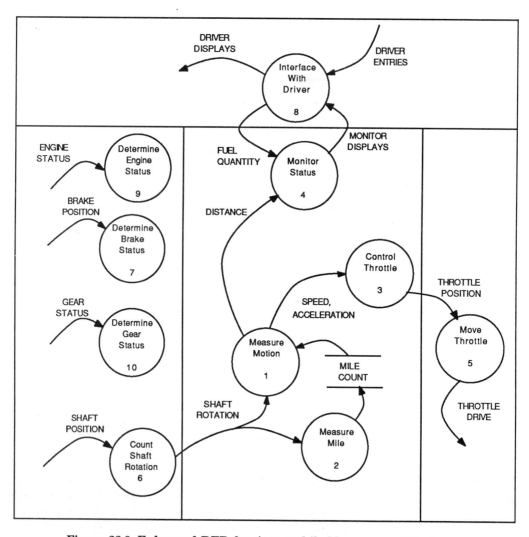

Figure 22.9. Enhanced DFD for Automobile Management System.

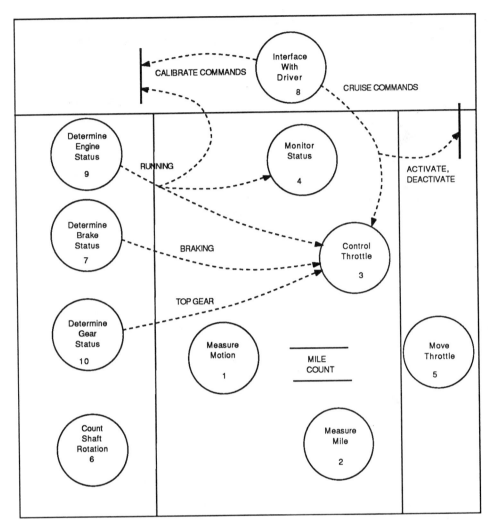

Figure 22.10. Enhanced CFD for Automobile Management System.

Before we leave the example, we want to emphasize the fact that the architecture template should be used as a guide only. Not every system will need additional processing in every block of the template. For example, there are systems that do not interface with other systems, but interface only with users. These types of systems need no processing in the input and output blocks.

22.5 Technology-Independent Versus Technology-Nonspecific

In this chapter, we have described how application of the architecture template transforms our technology-independent requirements model into a technology-nonspecific physical model. The result of this enhancement has been to insert a buffer between the essential requirements model core and the environment, as shown in Figure 22.11.

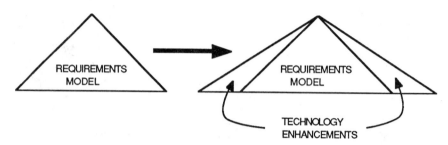

Figure 22.11. Architectural enhancements to the requirements model.

In transforming the requirements model into the technology-dependent model, the essential requirements core must be carried through and preserved wherever possible. There are several reasons for this, as follows:

- We want to be able to change the technology-dependent buffer without perturbing the entire model when interface technology changes.

- We want to be able to locate system requirements and determine the impact when they change.

- In later phases of the life cycle, we want to facilitate the tasks of testing the system's core requirements, both independent of and integrated with technology decisions.

- We want traceability between the essential requirements model and the resulting system.

As you have seen, these enhancements to the essential model have taken into account the system's environment and technology. The process of identifying these technology-dependent requirements is iterative: You may not be able to identify all the additional processing before completing a first-cut architecture model. We discuss this more in the next two chapters.

There are several benefits of the technology-nonspecific model, one of which is the end-to-end visibility it provides. We can view the system in its entirety from input source to output sink. In the Automobile Management System, we have a view of the system from the shaft-mounted sensor through the system functions to the throttle driver module. This provides the basis for some tradeoff evaluations when selecting a specific technology. We could, for example, take the following steps in selecting the appropriate technology for implementing the system:

- Determine which of the end-to-end flows are critical to the system's safety or performance.

- Trace these flows to determine the processes along the input-to-output path.

- Assign mathematical values to critical criteria; for example, if we were concerned about system safety or reliability with available technologies, we could assign reliability figures to each process for each technology.

- Select the technology that meets the system's implementation criteria and other system constraints, including cost.

Some of the above steps are useful in generating evaluations such as Failure Modes and Effects Analyses (FMEA), which are essential for some types of systems (avionics systems, for example). Additionally, the technology-nonspecific model might be used with appropriate simulation tools to execute the model as if it were a working system to evaluate the technology or to prototype the system. Some automated tools on the market today are able to implement parts of these models, but not the whole models. Someday, implementation of whole models will also be possible.

22.6 Organizational Implications

There are several organizational benefits derived from applying the architecture template. One benefit is that it can be used to organize and allocate tasks and responsibilities on a project. For example, the task of specifying system maintenance can be assigned to one group in the development team, while the specification of the user interface can be assigned to a different group, and so on, for the rest of the buffers on the architecture template. Such allocation of tasks can be especially useful to the project because, while each of these buffers requires special knowledge of a particular technology, the architecture template defines the integration and coordination of these different tasks. On the other hand, these different assignments do not necessarily have to go to different people nor does there have to be assignment of team tasks to every buffer on the architecture template. The system being specified and the size of the development team will determine these issues.

The following examples illustrate this division of expertise in accordance with the architecture template:

- Some members of the development team might be human factors' specialists and could work on the user interface without having to be knowledgeable about the input and output technology for the system-to-system interface.

- In some systems, such as an avionics data display and entry system or an automatic bank-teller system, the user interface specification is just as important as the system's functions. In such cases, a special group could specify and prototype the user interface independent of the other parts of the system.

- In some systems, the demands on the technology to interface with external devices equal or exceed those to perform the system functions, and in these cases the project emphasis would go on the interfaces. Such systems are the avionics, which positions control surfaces on an aircraft, or the valve and thermostat controller in a process control system, where the mechanism by which the system either interfaces with other systems or with external devices such as sensors might be the most critical.

The division of the development team along the boundaries defined by the architecture template also has benefits during the implementation, test, and maintenance phases of the system, as follows:

- During implementation, specific hardware and software specialists can address the user interface or the input and output technology.

- The architecture template provides the basis for testing the system both from a technology-independent and a technology-dependent viewpoint.

- Each type of technology can be tested independent of the others; the architecture template provides for cohesiveness of tasks.

- This isolation of different types of technology rolls over as a benefit during maintenance; for example, if the self-test or any other specific feature changes, the technology-nonspecific model shows the impact of that change both on the system and on the organization's resources.

The architecture template, then, provides a mechanism for integrating the tasks of the hardware and software teams. Yes, it can even force them to talk to each other, occasionally. And that can't possibly hurt.

22.7 Summary

- The architecture template maps the requirements model into the architecture model, and helps identify additional, nonfunctional requirements.

- The physical forms of the user-to-system and system-to-system interfaces are established.

- Maintenance and self-test requirements are determined based on system needs and available technology.

- Whereas the requirements model is technology-independent, the architecture model provides a physical system configuration that is still technology-nonspecific.

- The architecture template can be used as a basis for dividing the project assignments, and defines the interfaces between these divided groups.

Chapter 23

Creating the System Architecture Model

In the preceding chapter, we saw how the technology-nonspecific model is created. Now we will use the architecture model to map the enhanced requirements model allocations to architecture modules, using the components described in Part IV.

We will use the architecture context diagram to establish the system's architectural boundary, architecture flow diagrams to identify the modules and the information that flows between them, and architecture interconnect diagrams to define the channels on which the information flows.

23.1   Architecture Context Diagram

The architecture context diagram establishes the architectural boundary between the system and the environment. Figure 23.1 shows the ACD for the Automobile Management System.

Should the architecture context diagram be any different from the data and control context diagrams in the system requirements model? In most cases, the answer is No, the boundary should remain the same. Sometimes, however, technology decisions and enhancements to the requirements model might add some additional functions, which might in turn result in different, additional, or reduced flow across the system boundary.

In determining the architectural boundary between the system and its environment, the areas most likely to be affected are the user interface and the maintenance and self-test blocks. Technology decisions on the user interface can cause some system functions to be enhanced to make it more user-friendly. This is such an important aspect of system design, and one that in the past has often been overlooked, that it may well be worth including, in

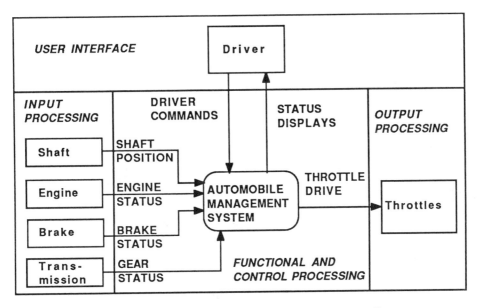

Figure 23.1. ACD for the Automobile Management System.

the original requirements analysis, functions performed by users of the system as well as the functions to be automated. This results in a wider context for the model, which has several benefits.

One such benefit is better specification of the interfaces between the user functions and those to be automated. Another is that this wider scope helps in selecting the most appropriate system-to-user boundary, which is then reflected in the architecture context diagram.

23.2   Architecture Flow and Interconnect Diagrams

To build architecture flow diagrams, we must identify architecture modules and allocate functional and control processing to them. Figure 23.2 shows a generic DFD/CFD/CSPEC. Assume that we will allocate the processes from the DFD to two modules: processes 1 and 2 to one module, and processes 3 and 4 to the other. This allocation decision is based only on the data processing functions, not on the control processing. In allocating the latter, one option is to divide it to correspond exactly with the allocation of the data processing.

We have specified data and control processing, PSPECs, and CSPECs in the requirements model and can ask the following questions:

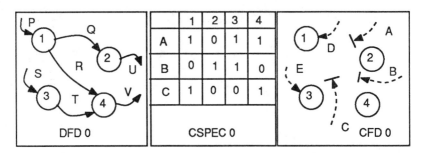

Figure 23.2. Generic DFD/CFD/CSPEC.

• First, does any one module clearly dominate the control of the system's behavior?

• Second, should any data processes be duplicated in more than one module to satisfy the control requirements as well as the technology decisions?

• Third, should all modules contain the control necessary to be self-sufficient? That is, should each module contain the CFD control signals and those parts of the corresponding CSPECs such that it can make its own process activation and deactivation decisions?

If the answer to the third question is Yes, then the simple allocation discussed above applies, but affirmative answers to the first and second questions can produce a different result. If one module, say module 2, is the controller, then we want to assign it overall control of the system, and would allocate CSPEC 0 to it. We still need to control the functions of module 3, so several additional control signals would be created to flow between module 2 and module 3. This results in a split process activation table, which we discussed in Section 19.1.

In general, the allocation process requires looking at both data and control processing from the requirements model, making design decisions, making the allocations based on those decisions, evaluating the design decisions and allocations, and, usually, iterating through the whole process again.

With regard to the order in which the AFD and AID should be drawn, there may be some advantage in drawing the AFD first since that is where the requirements model is mapped into the architecture modules. However, as long as both the AFD and AID are produced as end products, either order will do. In most circumstances, the allocation is to be decided first (hence, the AFD would be created first). But in some instances, the allocation of functions depends on the information flow channel bus loading, which requires creation of the AID first.

23.3   Example of AFD and AID Mapping

The allocation of system requirements into an architecture must take into account all the considerations discussed in Chapter 22. As an illustration, we allocate to architecture modules the enhanced DFD and CFD for the Automobile Management System, developed in the previous chapter. We also create the AFDs and AIDs for this allocation. Seven modules are needed: one each for the shaft, gear, engine, brake interface, user interface, throttle interface, and the automobile management computer. The AFD in Figure 23.3 is based on these modules, and on the flows from the enhanced requirements model.

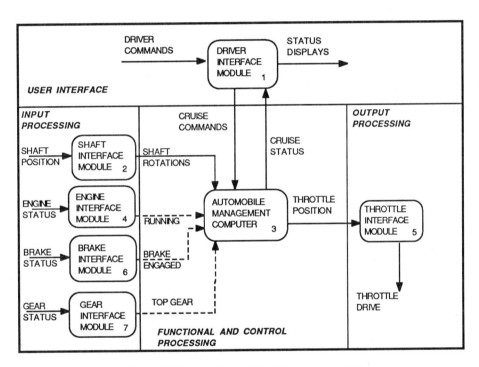

Figure 23.3. AFD 0: Automobile Management System.

The next step is to build the AID. To do this, we will need to select the channels by which information flows between the modules. Usually, we could just as well build the AID first, but in this case, the architecture modules were already available for building the AFD, and so we chose to build the AFD first and the AID second. Selecting the channels is one of the two major decisions being made as the AFD and AID are created, the other being the allocation of functions to architecture modules. The channel decisions for the Automobile Management System are documented in Figure 23.4.

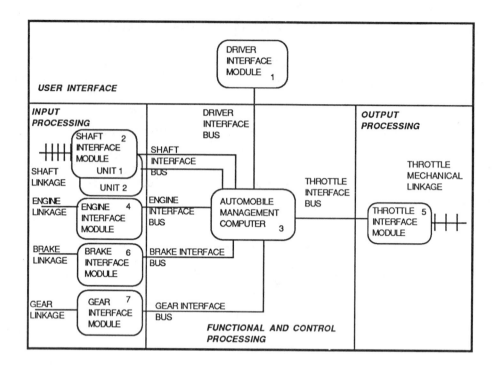

Figure 23.4. AID 0: Automobile Management System.

The combination of the processing required in the enhanced model, and the architecture modules chosen, may result in some modules being unable to fulfill the requirements for system reliability or safety. A solution to this problem might be to duplicate some of the modules to obtain additional reliability through redundancy. In this sense, the enhanced requirements model only provides a partial view of the system's technology dependence.

The introduction of redundant architecture modules may require some processing in the maintenance or self-test buffer of the architecture template to arbitrate the selection of the redundant processes. In our example of the Automobile Management System, we might allocate this processing to the automobile management computer. Now we can build architecture module specifications, architecture interconnect specifications, and the architecture dictionary for the allocation shown in the AFD and AID. The architecture module specifications will document the allocation of processes, and may contain a top-level functional description of the architecture modules. The AMS for the Automobile Management System is shown as a traceability matrix in Figure 23.5, the AIS in Figure 23.6, and the enhancements to the dictionary in Figure 23.7.

ARCHITECTURE MODEL COMPONENTS / REQUIREMENTS MODEL COMPONENTS	SHAFT INTERFACE MODULE	AUTO-MOBILE MANAGE-MENT COMPUTER	THROTTLE INTERFACE MODULE	DRIVER INTERFACE MODULE	GEAR INTERFACE MODULE	BRAKE INTERFACE MODULE	ENGINE INTERFACE MODULE
MEASURE MOTION 1		X					
MEASURE MILE 2		X					
CONTROL THROTTLE 3		X					
MONITOR STATUS 4		X					
DETERMINE ENGINE STATUS 9							X
DETERMINE GEAR STATUS 10					X		
DETERMINE BRAKE STATUS 7						X	
COUNT SHAFT ROTATIONS 6	X						
INTERFACE WITH DRIVER 8.1 8.2 8.3 8.4 8.5				X			
VALIDATE DRIVER REQUEST 8.6		X					
MOVE THROTTLES			X				
CSPEC 0		X					

**Figure 23.5. Architecture module specification
for the Automobile Management System.**

AIS : DRIVER INTERFACE BUS

The driver interface bus is a serial bus that carries information in 32-bit serial data, per the format shown below

8 BIT LABEL	4 BIT STATUS	20 BIT ENCODED DATA

The labels are listed in the architecture dictionary.

**Figure 23.6. Architecture interconnect specification
for the Automobile Management System.**

Name	Composed Of	Type	Origin Module	Destination Module	Channel
Activate	\Driver's cruise control activate command\ 2 values: on, off	C	Driver Interface Module	Automobile Management Computer	Driver Interface Bus
Braking	\Input signal indicating brakes applied\ 2 values: on, off	C	Brake Interface Module	Automobile Management Computer	Brake Bus
Desired Speed	\Desired speed cruise control is to maintain\ units: miles per hour	D	Automobile Management Computer		
Fuel Quantity	\Entered value of fill-up fuel quantity\ units: gallons range: 0-18 gallons	D	Driver Interface Module	Automobile Management Computer	Driver Interface Bus
Throttle Position	\Output signal driving throttle position\ units: volts range: 0-8 volts	D	Automobile Management Computer	Throttle Interface Module	Throttle Bus

Figure 23.7. Architecture dictionary for the Automobile Management System.

23.4   Model Consistency and Balancing

The requirements model components, along with other requirements for the system, must be accounted for in the architecture model. Components of the architecture model must be consistent with each other. The consistency rules, therefore, are designed to ensure a balanced architecture model and to ensure traceability between the requirements model and the architecture model. These consistency rules follow.

Rule 1: *Every architecture module that appears on an AFD must also appear on the corresponding AID.*

The AFD and AID represent two views of the system's architecture: one is from the information flow aspect, and the other from a physical interconnect aspect. These two views may not show any differences between the architecture modules as they both contain the same unique ones, but the AID shows redundant architecture modules, while the AFD does not. AFDs do not need to show them since redundant modules, and their information flows, are assumed to be identical. They are shown on the AID, however, because their physical interconnections may be different. Any nonidentical modules must appear on both diagrams. The names and numbers of the corresponding architecture modules must be the same on the AID and the AFD.

Rule 2: *Every component of an information flow into an architecture module must be used within that module, and every component flowing out must be generated within that module.*

The information that flows into an architecture module must be used by that module in its entirety and the information flow coming out must be generated inside that module. If there is data being received by a module that it does not use, then the implications of this to the maintenance of the system are well-known as the stamp coupling effect of structured design [12], whereby data of one type or category is all grouped together and transmitted whether or not it is all used. For many systems, this might be accepted for efficiency reasons, but those reasons should be clearly recorded. The information that flows into and out of an architecture module must be defined in the architecture dictionary. The information that flows into and out of the architecture module must be the same as the data and control flows into and out of the allocated data and control processes.

Rule 3: *Every architecture interconnect channel must have at least one information flow (data or control) allocated to it.*

Every architecture interconnect channel must have some flows allocated to it. If not, then that channel is presumably not needed.

Rule 4: *Every PSPEC and CSPEC from the requirements model must have a place in the architecture model.*

Every PSPEC and CSPEC must be traceable to the architecture model through the AMSs. There must be a listing of all processes (or their higher-level groupings) in the AMSs. The CSPECs can appear complete or as individual component sheets, as discussed in Part IV.

Rule 5: *Every flow (data or control) in the requirements model must be assigned a place in the architecture model.*

The architecture dictionary is an enhancement of the requirements dictionary. Every data and control flow in the requirements dictionary must be allocated in the architecture model, verifiable through the dictionary. Every requirements dictionary component has one of two options: Either it must be allocated to a module, or it must flow from one module to another. The architecture dictionary has additional fields that represent the origin module, destination module, and architecture communication channel. For those flows that are allocated to a module, the origin module field must be specified. For flows that go from one architecture module to one or more other architecture modules, all three entries must be filled in. The architecture dictionary makes it possible to verify that complete allocation has taken place, and that there is traceability between the requirements and architecture models.

23.5 The Complete Architecture Model

We started out with the requirements model and enhanced it to create the technology-dependent model by taking an outside-in approach of trying to fit the requirements into the environment in which they have to operate. To create each of the modules on the architecture flow diagram and architecture interconnect diagram, we partitioned the enhanced requirements model. After identifying modules to which we allocated processing and flows, we mapped our decisions using architecture module components. We can perform this allocation from the enhanced model in any combination; that is, we could allocate processes that are technology-dependent and technology-independent together or separately. The end result is illustrated in Figure 23.8.

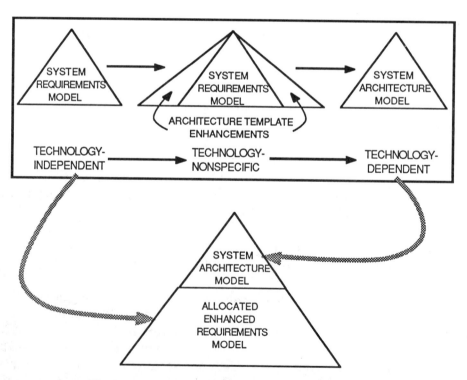

Figure 23.8. Architecture development process.

We have created the top-level architecture for the system in terms of modules and the flow and channels by which these modules communicate, and we have identified and allocated processing and flows to these modules. What we now have is a model for the implementation of the system showing us two important aspects: the allocation of requirements into architecture modules, and the definition of flow channels and flow vectors.

23.6 Summary

- The architecture context diagram establishes the boundary between the system and its environment.

- The architecture flow diagram and architecture interconnect diagram are created by mapping the enhanced requirements model into modules and information channels.

- The modules and channels must be consistent with each other and with the processes and flows from the requirements model.

- The architecture module specification must document the allocation of PSPECs and CSPECs, and the architecture dictionary must document the allocation of data and control flows.

Chapter 24

Creating the Hardware and Software Architecture Models

At the outset of the book we stated that the methods are applicable to the specification of systems, hardware, or software, and earlier in Part V we emphasized the fact that systems come in hierarchies, as illustrated in Figure 24.1. We will now discuss how this hierarchical property helps us create the hardware and software architectures.

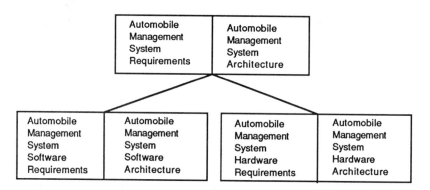

Figure 24.1. Hierarchical nature of the Automobile Management System.

What we have done so far is map system requirements into an architecture, and in the process we have allocated individual system requirements to modules. We must now decide whether each module is going to accomplish its intended function through a hardware or a software implementation. In so doing, we carry the modeling process one step further to make the allocation between the two. Between them, the hardware and software must fulfill all the functions specified for the architecture modules, as we will discuss in greater detail in the rest of this chapter. Figures 24.2 and 24.3 show the DFD and CFD for the allocated requirements of the automobile management computer.

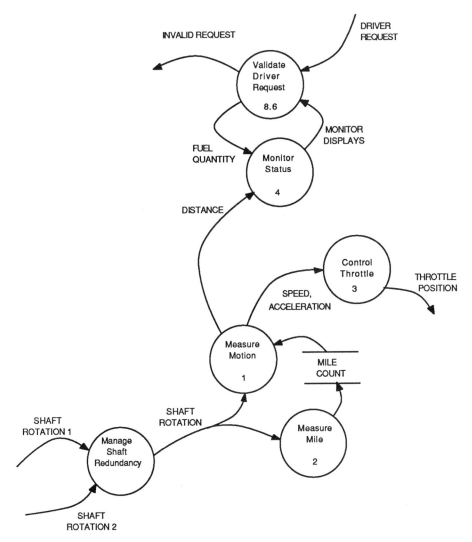

**Figure 24.2. DFD of requirements allocated
to the automobile management computer module.**

The diagrams in Figures 24.2 and 24.3 show that besides the processes allocated from the requirements, we have allocated one more process for handling the redundancy of the shaft interface module. This processing, which resides in the maintenance, self-test, and redundancy management processing buffer for the automobile management computer module, was needed because the system will be receiving two shaft rotation signals as shown in AID 0 in the previous chapter.

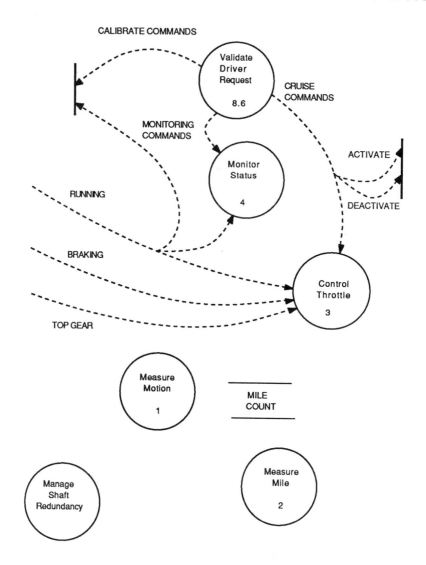

**Figure 24.3. CFD of requirements allocated
to the automobile management computer module.**

24.1 Hardware and Software Partitioning

The process of partitioning the architecture module requirements between hardware and software requires the following steps, which do not necessarily occur in the order listed.

- Hardware functions must be identified.

- Software functions must be identified.

- Hardware (CPUs, memory, and so forth) must be selected to host the software functionality.

The procedure is iterative, requiring tradeoffs and design decisions. The important question from a modeling perspective is, How do we capture these hardware and software partitioning decisions?

Since the requirements model and the resulting enhanced model are, respectively, technology-independent and technology-nonspecific, we are free, as far as the model is concerned, to allocate any part of the requirements either to hardware or software.

There are three basic options for partitioning the requirements of a single module between hardware and software: all hardware, all software, or some of each. Using the Automobile Management System as an example again, assume we have taken the third option, choosing to implement some requirements in software and some in hardware. As a result of the software choice, we will have to develop the requirements and architecture for the hardware on which the software is hosted, as well as for the hardware to perform the system functions.

We can model the hardware architecture using architecture model components. To do this, we need to know the physical interconnections of the system, and these have been established in the system-level AFD and AID. To read shaft rotations, for example, we must design hardware components that will read the shaft interface bus. Similarly, the hardware must be designed to interface with all the buses specified on the system AID.

These decisions, along with the selected CPU and associated hardware, can be modeled by creating a hardware design AID of the automobile management computer module, as shown in Figure 24.4, which illustrates the application of the AFD/AID concept to the modeling of hardware design.

AFDs and AIDs can also capture the *detailed* hardware design. For example, the gear bus receiver from the AID shown could be further defined in an AFD/AID of its own in which the details of the bus interface logic would be specified. We can decompose each of the hardware modules until we reach fundamental physical entities that comprise the system's hardware.

In Figure 24.4, shown on the next page, we have chosen to show the decomposition of the shaft bus receiver since we allocated the redundancy management of the shaft to the hardware. Figure 24.5 shows the requirements allocated to hardware, and Figure 24.6 shows the enhanced hardware requirements.

On the following page, Figures 24.7 and 24.8 show the AFD and AID. Based on the hardware configuration shown for the automobile management computer module, we can start creating the software architecture.

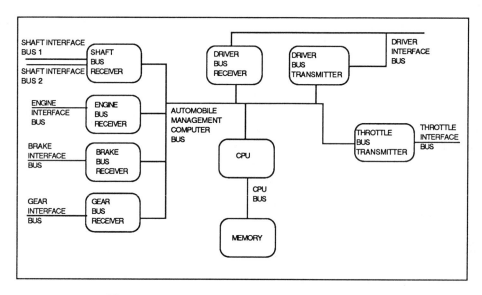

**Figure 24.4. AID for automobile management
computer hardware configuration.**

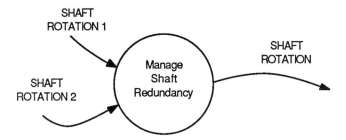

Figure 24.5. Requirements allocated to hardware.

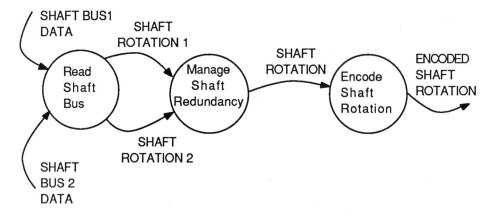

Figure 24.6. Enhanced hardware requirements.

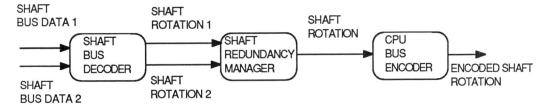

Figure 24.7. AFD for shaft interface module.

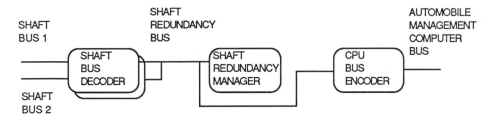

Figure 24.8. AID for shaft bus receiver.

24.2 Applying the Template to Software Requirements

We can use the architecture template once again to identify the system's software requirements, but only after we have decided on the hardware and software partitioning. Once this decision has been made, we must use the AFD and AID to determine how the software in any one subsystem (or architecture module) is going to interface with the other subsystems and with the environment. To do this, we take the DFD and CFD for each architecture module and add the necessary interface processing.

As an example, the automobile management computer module from AFD 0 of the Automobile Management System will receive and transmit data to and from several different modules in the system. The AID defines how this information will be received and transmitted, and defines hardware as a data and control interface with the specified information flow channels. The format chosen for this information will be suitable for processing by the software. For instance, the shaft rotation data coming from the shaft interface module would be received by the hardware in the communication protocol of the shaft interface bus, and converted to a protocol with which the software can perform speed and distance calculations.

One common form of bus is a twisted pair of wires, carrying serial information. With this type of bus, the hardware might be responsible for converting the information to parallel form before transferring it to the software, which would then further transform it into some internally acceptable format. This is the processing that would go into the input processing block of the software architecture template, and we would have been unable to specify it without first deciding on the system architecture.

As we saw in Figure 24.4, there are two shaft interface modules. The software must include the redundancy management processing to decide which signal to use, and this processing will be assigned to the maintenance, redundancy management, and self-test block on the architecture template.

In the same way, we must specify each of the software interfaces in the automobile management computer module and surround with interface processing the central core that was allocated to this module.

The enhanced software DFD and CFD for the automobile management computer are illustrated in Figures 24.9 and 24.10. The same procedure would then be applied to every architecture module in the system architecture flow and interconnect diagrams.

Here are some observations on what these figures illustrate:

- We see that the definition of the system resulted in allocating requirements to subsystems that together perform the system's tasks.

- We see that at both the system- and the software-definition levels, we had to make partitioning decisions at the higher levels before we can determine the specifics of one module's software.

- The general conclusion is that higher levels of the system always provide the requirements for the lower levels. For systems containing hardware and software, this means that we need to know system-level requirements, decide on the system-level architecture, and then decide on the allocation of system requirements to hardware and software before we can establish the software requirements.

This last point is very important and cannot be overstated; there is a common tendency to get too detailed too fast. One of the most important things we have learned using these techniques is to recognize the level of system being specified. It would have been a mistake, for example, to have started with the software requirements. We first had to establish the system requirements, identify the modules within the system, and then work our way down to the software. Systems in general may have several processors, and the above scheme can also be used to map each processor's requirements from the system requirements.

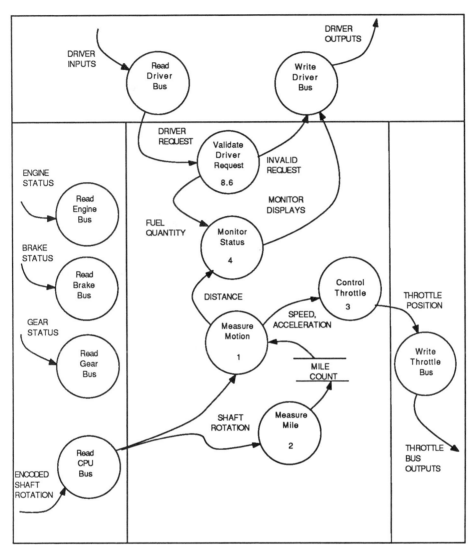

**Figure 24.9. Enhanced DFD for the automobile
management computer software.**

One of the problems we face, especially with embedded systems, is that
we do have to deal with extensive system, architecture, hardware, and software requirements, and it is easy to confuse them and waste significant resources.

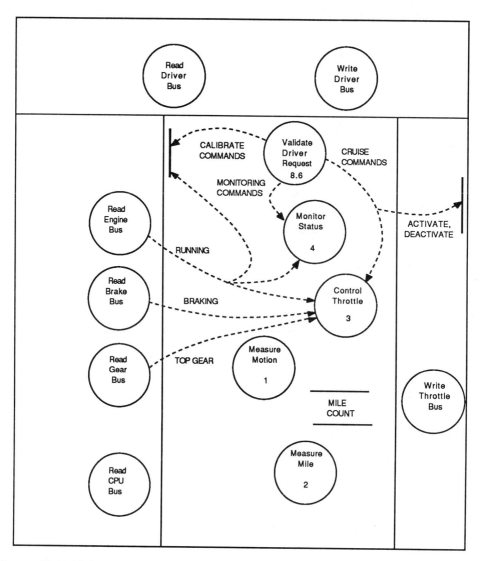

Figure 24.10. Enhanced CFD for the automobile management computer software.

24.3 Developing the Software Architecture

We are now ready to start defining software modules to perform the allocated software requirements. This process repeats all the steps illustrated earlier, but we allocate functions to modules at the software level instead of at the system level.

It is beyond the scope of this book to get into the details of how to create software modules, but there are many different ways to map software requirements into modules. An effective way is to combine the AFD concept with the structure chart of structured design, illustrated in Figure 24.11.

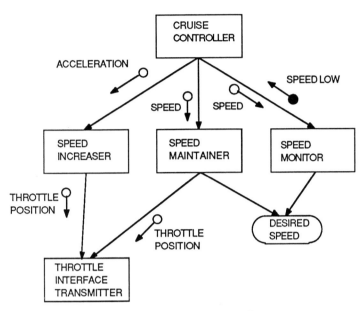

Figure 24.11. A structure chart.

Among the good sources of information on structure charts are Page-Jones [12], Constantine and Yourdon [19], and Myers [11]. There are also several sources on the preferred characteristics of software modules, besides the above structured design references, such as the work by Parnas [13].

The architecture flow diagram shows the software modules connected as a network, while the structure chart shows them connected as a hierarchy. The following steps outline the process for creating a software architecture using AFDs or structure charts, as illustrated in Figure 24.12.

Step 1: Build the top-level software AFD using the architecture template as a guide to allocate tasks within its blocks.

Step 2: Break these tasks into subtasks, using AFDs, until they become single-thread tasks.

Step 3: Take the requirements allocated to each single-thread task and transform them into a structure chart.

What is the point at which we switch from mapping into AFDs to mapping into structure charts? The simple answer is, AFDs are used for mapping

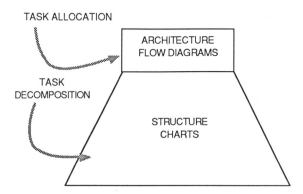

Figure 24.12. Software development structure.

multi-thread processes, while structure charts are used for mapping single-thread processes.

A multi-thread process is one that contains multiple parallel tasks, or that must deal with real-time considerations, such as interrupts, task control, or a multi-tasking executive. A single-thread process is one that has a single entry and single exit.

24.4   The Hardware and Software Architecture Process

In conclusion, we summarize our discussion about system hierarchies and application of the architecture template. To develop the hardware and software architectures, we use the same process we used for the system architecture: Regardless of what level of the system we are specifying, the process remains the same.

When we applied the architecture template at the system level, we identified system processing in each of the blocks of the template. Now, one level below that, we establish *software and hardware requirements,* and identify processing that has to do with the *software and hardware level* of specification.

It is very important to keep your appropriate "hat" on when working on each of these particular levels. In other words, don't start doing software or hardware architecture in the middle of the system architecture. The same is true of requirements modeling: Don't get hung up in hardware or software requirements while working on the system requirements.

Figure 24.13 shows the stages for developing the software and hardware architectures.

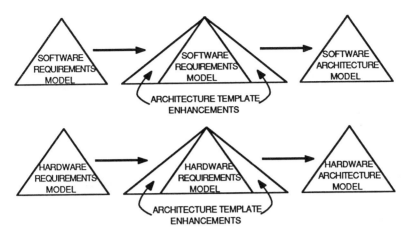

Figure 24.13. Hardware and software architecture development process.

24.5 Summary

- We use the architecture template to allocate functions to hardware and software, just as we used it to allocate system functions.

- Processes from the preceding technology-nonspecific model can be allocated to hardware or to software.

- At this stage, the hardware and software interfaces must be defined.

- The template can then be used again to structure the hardware and software separately.

- Hardware decomposition stops when separate, deliverable units are identified.

- Software decomposition can switch from architecture flow and interconnect diagrams to structure charts when the processes switch from multi-thread to single-thread.

- Keep the levels of specification clearly separated; that is, do not mix the system level with the software level, for example.

Chapter 25

Architecture Development Summary

In this chapter, we summarize how the iterative nature of building the requirements and architecture models supports the iterative nature of systems development. We also summarize the steps used in the modeling process.

The requirements modeling activity is iterative: As the model proceeds from an abstract to detailed definition of the system, refinement of the higher-level abstractions might identify new or different partitionings of flows, processes, or both. Similarly, the architecture modeling activity is iterative: As the requirements model is allocated to specific architecture modules, the refinement of this allocation might identify new or repartitioned modules that better meet the system's architectural requirements. But further, functional partitioning of the system may not be able to proceed in the absence of some architectural considerations; or architecture development might reveal the need for additional functional requirements.

All of this emphasizes that the models cannot be created in a sequential cookbook manner. Rather, the iterations are an essential part of the process, as illustrated in Figure 25.1.

25.1 Partitioning the Modeling Process

The modeling process, like the development process, must begin by capturing the system's requirements and architecture. Probably the most important thing to realize in the early stages is not to get bogged down in too much detail. A number of problems seem to cause this to happen, but the two most prevalent causes are

- the customer or marketing description of the system received by the modeling team contains functional requirements, architectural details, and sometimes even implementation details of particular hardware and software modules, and

- the development team's past system implementation experience seems to overwhelm the situation.

The solution is to try to sort through all the details and to work with what is most important to start the new project. Use the six categories of system requirements, system architecture, software requirements, software architecture, hardware requirements, and hardware architecture to sort the details, and put them in the right category.

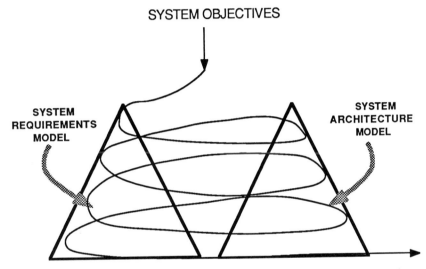

Figure 25.1. Iterative process for developing
system requirements and architecture.

The system model

After completing the first step of deciding where a particular requirement or architectural detail belongs, such as whether you are dealing with a functional requirement or the customer's choice of CPU, the six categories can further be refined. Each contains several subcategories, such as processing and control for the requirements, and the blocks on the architecture template. Begin with some disregard for balancing and rigor: It is easy to get hung up in trying to make a model rigorous too early in the process. Keep both the initial requirements and the architecture models loose, unbalanced, and nonrigorous. Early in the modeling and development process, we don't know all the details of the system; if we did, we could start typing code and soldering printed circuit boards.

This loose model can serve many useful purposes: It can be used to partition modeling and development tasks; to communicate between the development team and the customer; to estimate resources for the project; or to scope out the project. Later it will serve as the starting point for resolving the missing rigor and establishing system requirements and architecture. It will then balance through all its levels and provide the working design specifications that are final deliverables to the customer.

It is not important that either of the models be *created* top-down and level by level—they can go in any direction—but an outside-in approach, using the architecture template, works best. The process is shown in Figure 25.2.

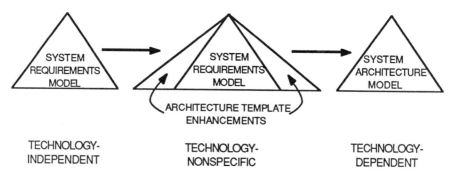

Figure 25.2. System modeling process.

Periodically during the iterative model-building process, the two models should be archived. This serves two purposes: First, it produces intermediate progress deliverables; and second, it preserves previous versions of the models that can be used for reference if there ever is a need to go back and make changes. This archiving should be done, at the least, at major decision points in the modeling process. For example, archive before the first-cut allocation is refined, or when the functional partitioning is changed to accommodate some specific allocation requirement.

The hardware and software models

After the system architecture model has been developed, take the requirements allocated to each module and determine whether that module is going to be implemented in hardware or software. These determinations are illustrated in Figure 25.3. The resulting model defines the hardware and software requirements for each module. At this stage, the software requirements can be evaluated to determine the requirements for the host hardware.

Next, develop the separate architectures for the hardware and the software. Use the same procedures as were used for allocating system-level requirements to system-level modules. This stage is shown in Figure 25.4.

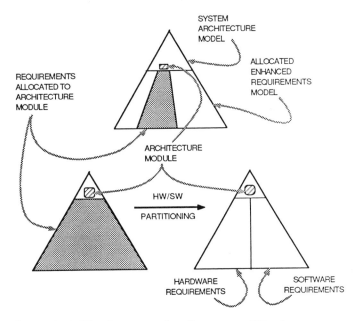

Figure 25.3. Hardware and software partitioning process.

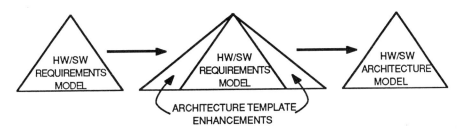

Figure 25.4. Hardware and software modeling process.

Just as the system requirements were enhanced, the hardware and software requirements need to be enhanced, to ensure that they will work with each other, and fulfill the requirements allocated to system architecture modules. The software requirements are enhanced to interface with the hardware. The hardware requirements are enhanced to interface with other architecture modules and with the system environment.

The architecture modeling process we have described in this summary can be applied to arbitrarily large and complex systems, as is being currently done on several very large avionics and process control projects, among others. One such project is the total avionics for an aircraft. The upper-level models capture the requirements and architecture of the total system. The upper-level definition identifies the line replaceable units (LRUs), each of which is an avionics subsystem. The next level of definition defines the requirements and architecture for each of these subsystems. These are then partitioned between hardware and software. Figure 25.5 shows how the process can be applied to the specification of such systems, consisting of many subsystems, which in turn consist of many physical components before reaching the hardware and software level.

In conclusion, when the system, hardware, and software models have been defined, the resulting model will be a single cohesive representation of the system design, as shown in Figure 25.6. The upper levels of this model represent the system architecture, the lower levels represent the hardware and software architectures.

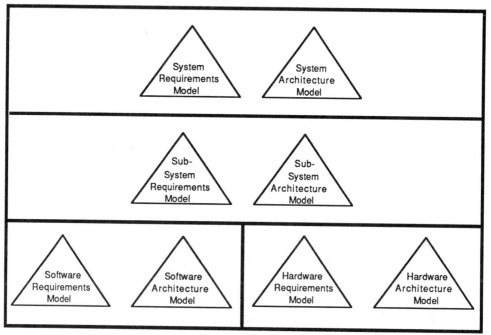

Figure 25.5. Application of requirements and
architecture modeling to large systems.

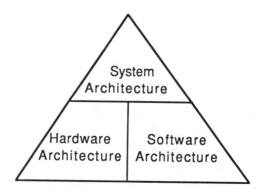

Figure 25.6. Integrated system, hardware, and software model.

PART VI

Examples

Chapter 26

Automobile Management System

This example is derived in part from a problem used at the July 1985 STARS[1] Methodology Conference in Colorado Springs as a basis for comparing several different development methods. The proponents of each method applied that method to the one problem, and presented their results at the conference for the attendees to evaluate.

26.1 Problem Statement

An Automobile Management System is to be developed as an optional extra on some car models. The system is to take care of several routine operation and maintenance tasks, including

- cruise control

- average speed monitoring

- fuel consumption monitoring

- maintenance monitoring

---

[1]STARS is an acronym for the Department of Defense's "Software Technology for Adaptable, Reliable Systems."

A description of these tasks follows. The description represents that which might be provided by the automobile manufacturer to an outside developer, and includes a requirements statement and a system-level configuration.

Cruise control

The cruise control function is to take over the task of maintaining a constant speed when commanded to do so by the driver. The driver must be able to enter several commands, including: Activate, Deactivate, Start Accelerating, Stop Accelerating, and Resume. The cruise control function can be operated any time the engine is running and the transmission is in top gear. When the driver presses Activate, the system selects the current speed, but only if it is at least 30 miles per hour, and holds the car at that speed. Deactivate returns control to the driver regardless of any other commands. Start Accelerating causes the system to accelerate the car at a comfortable rate until Stop Accelerating occurs, when the system holds the car at this new speed. Resume causes the system to return the car to the speed selected prior to braking or gear shifting.

The driver must be able to increase the speed at any time by depressing the accelerator pedal, or reduce the speed by depressing the brake pedal. Thus, the driver may go faster than the cruise control setting simply by depressing the accelerator pedal far enough. When the pedal is released, the system will regain control. Any time the brake pedal is depressed, or the transmission shifts out of top gear, the system must go inactive. Following this, when the brake is released, the transmission is back in top gear, and Resume is pressed, the system returns the car to the previously selected speed. However, if a Deactivate has occurred in the intervening time, Resume does nothing.

Since speed and distance per drive shaft rotation are affected by tire size and wear, the system is to have a calibrate capability. For this purpose, two further controls will be provided: Start Measured Mile and Stop Measured Mile. They are only effective when cruise control is inactive. The driver presses Start Measured Mile at the start of a measured mile, drives the mile, and then presses Stop Measured Mile. The system is to record the number of shaft pulses over this interval, and use this count as its mile reference in all calculations.

Average speed monitoring

The system is to provide the driver with an average speed indication on its display. The driver enters a Start Trip command, and later, whenever he enters an Average Speed request, the system will display the average speed of the car for all the time the engine has been running since the Start Trip. This continues until the next Start Trip.

Fuel consumption monitoring

Whenever the fuel tank is filled, the driver may enter the quantity of fuel added since the last fill-up. The system will then calculate and display the fuel consumption over that period.

Maintenance monitoring

The system will monitor the car's mileage, and notify the driver of required maintenance according to the following schedule:

Oil and oil filter change	5,000 miles
Air filter change	10,000 miles
Major service	15,000 miles

Two hundred and fifty miles before each required service, the appropriate message will appear intermittently; fifty miles before, it will appear continuously, and will remain until the driver enters a Service Complete command.

26.2 Requirements and Architecture Development

The various steps required to develop the requirements and architecture models for the Automobile Management System have been discussed extensively in Parts III and V. We will now present the complete development of those models.

Often, a user's problem statement does not distinguish between system requirements and system architecture. This is certainly true of the problem statement presented in the preceding section. For example, there are several references to the shaft and the throttle, which may or may not be the best places to sense the speed and control the engine. Of course, the user, or whoever is paying for development of the system, is certainly entitled to specify both the requirements and the architecture, but care must be taken that this does not unduly restrict the options of the system developer.

What are some of the options that arise from this problem statement? The driver has to enter commands and receive system responses in the form of displays. The displays could be liquid crystal displays (LCDs), cathode-ray-tube displays (CRTs), or simply light-emitting diodes (LEDs) together with some flashing warning lights. Similarly, the input commands could be entered through individual buttons, or different commands could be just two positions of the same switch. Fuel data entry could be through a full numeric keyboard or a rotary switch with LED indicators.

The requirements and architecture models that follow reflect requirements and architecture decisions that typically would be made in the course
of discussions with the user and the customer. Some of these resolutions are
listed below.

- The system controls the car through an actuator attached to the
  throttle. This actuator is mechanically in parallel with the accelerator
  pedal mechanism, such that whichever one is demanding greater speed
  controls the throttle. The system is to drive the actuator by means
  of an electrical signal having a linear relationship with throttle deflection, with 0 volts setting the throttle closed and 8 volts setting it fully
  open.

- The system is to measure speed by counting pulses it receives from a
  sensor on the drive shaft. Count-rate from this sensor corresponds to
  vehicle miles per hour through a proportionality constant.

- When the system senses that the speed is more than 2 mph above the
  selected speed, it is to completely release the throttle (this situation
  would occur when driving downhill). At any speed below this, it is to
  drive the throttle to a deflection proportional to the speed error until, at
  2 mph below the selected speed, the throttle is fully open (the steep
  uphill situation). The system thus serves as the feedback or control
  part of a servo loop, in which the engine is the feed-forward part. For
  smooth and stable servo operation, the system must update its outputs
  at least once per second.

- To avoid rapid increases in acceleration, the actuator must never open
  faster than to traverse its full range in 10 seconds. It may close at any
  rate, however, since the car just coasts when the throttle is closed. The
  automotive engineers have determined that, with these characteristics,
  the system will hold the car within ± 1 mph of the selected speed on
  normal gradients, and will give a smooth, comfortable ride.

- When the system is accelerating the car, it must measure the acceleration and hold it at 1 mph/sec. Again, the throttle setting will be
  affected by the gradient. If the acceleration reaches 1.2 mph/sec, the
  throttle should be closed; at 0.8 mph/sec, it should be fully open.
  Between these limits, the opening is to be linearly related to acceleration.

- The Automobile Management System will have a full numeric keyboard and a CRT display.

- The user interface module for the system will be "intelligent," such that all driver entries will be validated by checking for reasonableness (for example, range on fuel tank input or other appropriate measures for other inputs).

26.3   Requirements Model

The complete requirements model follows this section. Since this is a complete model, the diagram and specification numbers are sufficient to identify them, and figure numbers are not used. This system must interface with several other systems in the car and with the driver. This is illustrated in the context diagrams in which our system is shown performing the task Control & Monitor Auto, and interfacing with the driver, drive shaft, transmission, engine, brake, and throttle mechanism. These, and the signals shown passing between them, should make sense to you in light of the preceding problem statement.

DFD 0 and CFD 0 show that we chose to divide the model into four major processes: Measure Motion, Measure Mile, Control Throttle, and Monitor Status. Again, these correspond quite closely to the problem statement. Each of them is decomposed down another level or two, and we recommend that you study them in detail to see how the problem has been translated into the requirements model. Better yet, before you look at the whole analysis, try doing it yourself, to see how your results compare to ours. This is by far the best way to learn how to apply the method.

As with all the examples in this part of the book, we do not give a detailed narrative walkthrough of the analysis: Plenty of explanation has been provided throughout the text, but the real point of the method is, of course, that the model will speak for itself.

It is typical during the structuring of a set of system requirements that inconsistencies, omissions, or both are exposed. This example is no exception: In analyzing the problem, we realized that it is not clear whether the driver is supposed to be able to select Start Accelerating when the system is not Cruising, so this possibility is shown with a question mark in CSPEC 3. It was also very obvious that the calibration process must have some default values, so that, if the driver has either never calibrated, or puts in absurd values, the system will default to something reasonable; this is shown in PSPEC 2. In the problem statement, the term "will appear intermittently" requires further definition of how frequently and for how long. All these are topics to be discussed with the customer, and their discovery reaffirms the value of the analysis processes.

A point to be made to the designer, which also became clear during analysis, is that the system will need to have some nonvolatile memory. The Monitor Status and Measure Mile functions need to retain their data when the power is turned off.

This model has provided useful examples throughout the book, and is as big as is warranted for a book of this size, yet it is tiny compared to the typical real application. This has led to at least two drawbacks: The first is that small models do not illustrate very well the benefits of keeping the control specifications at as high a level as possible. Although the CSPECs are, in fact, right where they should be, at levels 1, 2, and 3, those are all the levels there are. Imagine this as just the top three levels of a large model, which incorporates another four or five levels. Such a model probably would be several times thicker than this book. Each of the simple, primitive processes here would be a complex process, a major subsystem in itself. We would be doing well if we could keep the control structure of such a model as simple as it is here.

The second drawback is that the matrix and tabular representations of sequential machines only provide benefit when the machine is so large that the state transition diagram becomes unintelligible. Again, it is not practical to include such a large example here, so only STDs are used. In practice, state transition matrices are by far the most common. Remember, there is no difference in the roles or information content of the different representations; each has its own advantages in different circumstances.

Furthermore, for purposes of illustration, we have used fewer processes per diagram, and gone down more levels, than we would have done on a real project. Where appropriate, we have included comments to the reader (as well as comments that are included with the model for the user) to explain what we have done. Let the modeling begin!

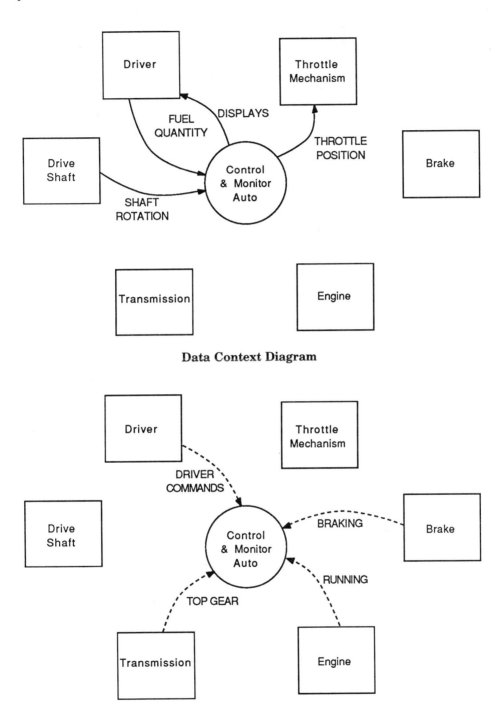

Data Context Diagram

Control Context Diagram

Note: It is optional whether the "unused" terminators are left in. We usually choose to do so as a reminder of their existence.

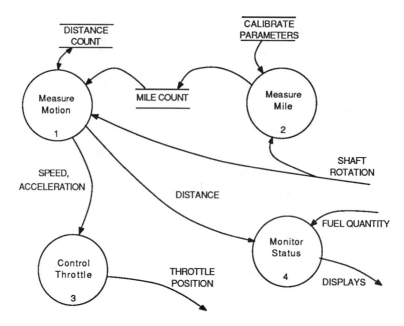

DFD 0; Control & Monitor Auto

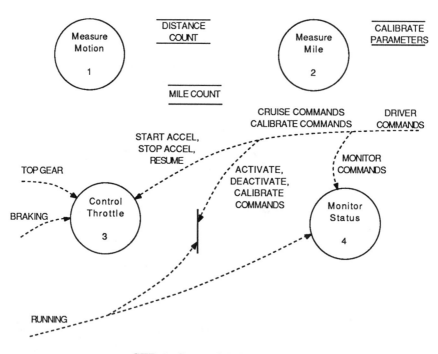

CFD 0; Control & Monitor Auto

Note: The stores may be left out of a diagram in which they are not used. Notice the complex branching and decomposition patterns in the CFD.

CSPEC 0; Control & Monitor Auto

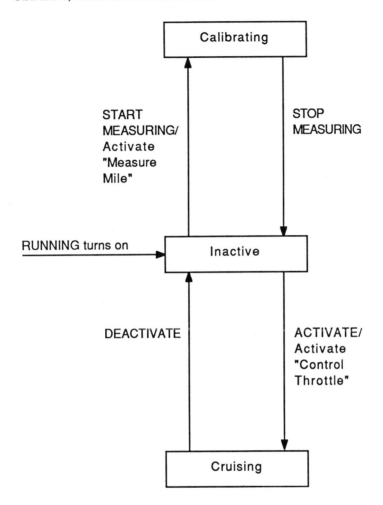

Note: As an exercise, redraw this STD as a matrix and as a table. Also, control the processes through a process activation table. It will be a useful exercise, and will illustrate that none of them is necessary in such a simple CSPEC.

Remember that an action remains in effect until the next transition. So, for example, Measure Mile remains active while the state is Calibrating, then goes inactive when STOP MEASURING occurs, even though no action is shown on that transition. In this method, processes are not "switched on" and "switched off;" they are *held* On by their activators for the duration needed.

TIMING SPECIFICATION

INPUT	EVENT	OUTPUT	EVENT	RESPONSE TIME
ACTIVATE	Turns On	THROTTLE POSITION	Goes to selected cruise value	0.5 sec. max.
RESUME	Turns On			
DEACTIVATE	Turns On	THROTTLE POSITION	Goes to null condition	0.5 sec. max.
TOP GEAR	Turns Off			
BRAKING	Turns On			
START ACCEL	Turns On	THROTTLE POSITION	Goes to acceleration value	0.5 sec. max.
STOP ACCEL	Turns On while THROTTLE POSITION at acceleration value	THROTTLE POSITION	Goes to cruise value	0.5 sec. max.
RUNNING	Turns On	THROTTLE POSITION	Goes to null value	0.5 sec. max.
SHAFT ROTATION	Rotation rate changes	THROTTLE POSITION	Corresponding change in value	1 sec. max.
	Distance since last maintenance exceeds maintenance warning distance	MAINT NEEDED	Displayed	10 sec. max.
FUEL QUANTITY	Entered	FUEL CON-SUMPTION	Displayed	1 sec. max.
AV SPEED RQST	Turns On	AV SPEED	Displayed	1 sec. max.
START TRIP				No time-critical outputs
START MEASURED MILE				
STOP MEASURED MILE				

PSPEC 1; Measure Motion

For each pulse of SHAFT ROTATION:

add 1 to DISTANCE COUNT

then set:

$$\text{DISTANCE} = \frac{\text{DISTANCE COUNT}}{\text{MILE COUNT}}$$

At least once per second, measure pulse rate of SHAFT ROTATION in pulses per hour, and set:

$$\text{SPEED} = \frac{\text{Pulse rate}}{\text{MILE COUNT}}$$

At least once per second, measure rate of change of SHAFT ROTATION pulses in pulses per hour per second, and set:

$$\text{ACCELERATION} = \frac{\text{Rate of change}}{\text{MILE COUNT}}$$

SHAFT ROTATION is in arbitrary angular units per pulse. The units are arbitrary because they are always divided into each other, and so cancel out.

PSPEC 2; Measure Mile

Each time activated, start counting SHAFT ROTATION pulses.

While LOWER LIMIT ≤ pulse count ≤ UPPER LIMIT

set MILE COUNT = pulse count,

otherwise

set MILE COUNT = DEFAULT COUNT.

Sets MILE COUNT to the count of shaft rotation pulses if that number is within the range that reasonably represents a measured mile. Otherwise, sets it to the default value.

SHAFT ROTATION is in arbitrary angular units per pulse. The units are arbitrary because they are always divided into each other, and so cancel out.

Note: No mention is made of *how* the process is activated. This is an important part of the information hiding and nonredundancy principles. The PSPEC does not know how or why it is activated, only what to do when it is. Likewise, the CSPEC does not know what the PSPEC does, only how to activate it. The user (who is familiar with the method) knows exactly where to look for this information.

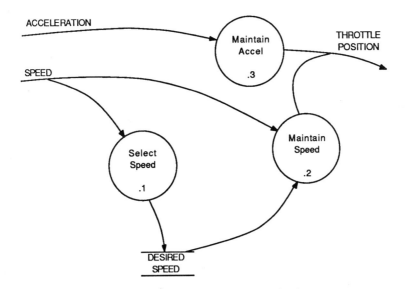

DFD 3; Control Throttle

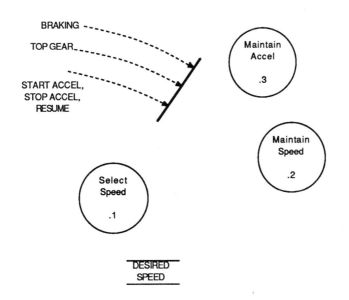

CFD 3; Control Throttle

Note: This whole process, and its CSPEC, are deactivated whenever CSPEC 0 is not in the Cruising state. When deactivated, all its outputs are null, and the driver has complete control of the throttle.

CSPEC 3; Control Throttle

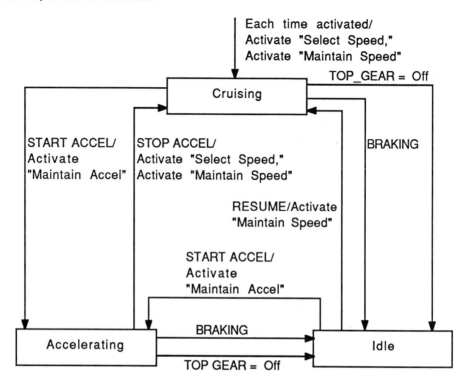

Note: Again, with such a simple CSPEC, neither the matrix forms nor a PAT are needed. Their message would be less intuitively obvious than the simple STD.

Notice that CSPEC 0 activates process 3 and hence also activates CSPEC 3. This is what "Each Time Activated" refers to.

PSPEC 3.1; Select Speed

Issue DESIRED SPEED = SPEED

PSPEC 3.2; Maintain Speed

Set:

$$
V_{Th} = \begin{cases} 0; & (S_D - S_A) > 2 \\ 2(S_D - S_A + 2); & -2 \le (S_D - S_A) \le 2 \\ 8; & -2 > (S_D - S_A) \end{cases}
$$

subject to:

$$
\frac{dV_{Th}}{dt} \le .8V/\text{sec.}
$$

where:

$$
\begin{aligned}
V_{Th} &= \text{THROTTLE POSITION} \\
S_D &= \text{DESIRED SPEED} \\
S_A &= \text{SPEED}
\end{aligned}
$$

Varies throttle opening from closed to fully open as speed varies from 2 mph above desired speed, to 2 mph below it. Restricts rate of opening to .8V/sec.

PSPEC 3.3; Maintain Accel

Set:

$$
V_{Th} = \begin{cases} 0; & A > 1.2 \\ 20(1.2 - A); & 0.8 \le A \le 1.2 \\ 8; & 0.8 > A \end{cases}
$$

subject to:

$$
\frac{dV_{Th}}{dt} \le .8V/\text{sec.}
$$

where:

$$
\begin{aligned}
V_{Th} &= \text{THROTTLE POSITION} \\
A &= \text{ACCELERATION}
\end{aligned}
$$

Varies throttle opening from closed to fully open as acceleration varies from 1.2 mph/sec to 0.8 mph/sec. Restricts rate of opening to .8V/sec.

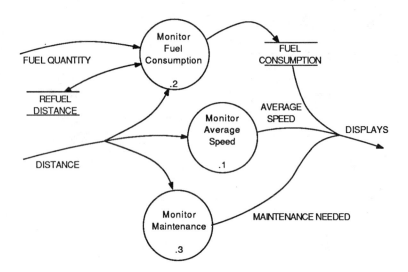

DFD 4; Monitor Status

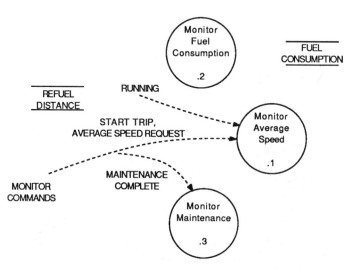

CFD 4; Monitor Status

Note: Again, the "unused" stores may be omitted if preferred.

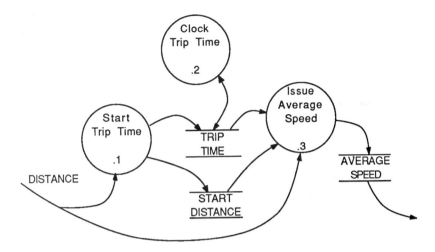

DFD 4.1; Monitor Average Speed

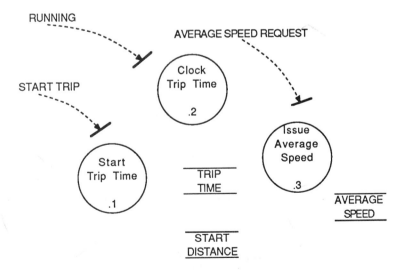

CFD 4.1; Monitor Average Speed

CSPEC 4.1; Monitor Average Speed

START TRIP activates process 4.1.1; START TRIP
RUNNING activates process 4.1.2; CLOCK TRIP TIME
AV SPEED RQST activates process 4.1.3; ISSUE AVERAGE SPEED

PSPEC 4.1.1; Start Trip Time

Issue TRIP TIME = 0
Issue START DISTANCE = DISTANCE

PSPEC 4.1.2; Clock Trip Time

Every second process is on, add 1 second to TRIP TIME

PSPEC 4.1.3; Issue Average Speed

Issue:

$$AVERAGE\ SPEED = \frac{DISTANCE - START\ DISTANCE}{TRIP\ TIME}$$

PSPEC 4.2; Monitor Fuel Consumption

Issue:

$$FUEL\ CONSUMPTION = \frac{DISTANCE - START\ DISTANCE}{FUEL\ QTY}$$

then set:

$$REFUEL\ DISTANCE = DISTANCE$$

Note: With simple one-to-one activation, as in CSPEC 4.1, a PAT is not worthwhile. They are needed only when there is a one-to-many relationship between inputs and activators.

Frankly, we went too far with the children of process 4.1—it should have been a primitive—but we wanted to add depth to the example. Try redrawing it the way it should be, and writing a single PSPEC.

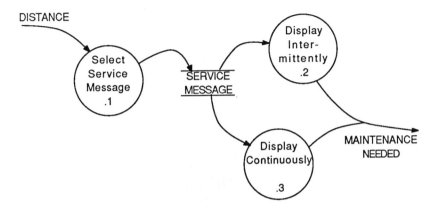

DFD 4.3; Monitor Maintenance

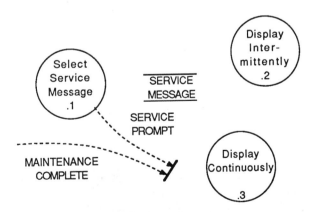

CFD 4.3; Monitor Maintenance

CSPEC 4.3; Monitor Maintenance

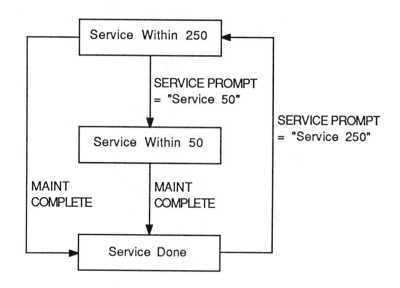

INPUT	PROCESS	
STATE	.2; Display Intermittently	.3; Display Continuously
Service Within 250	1	0
Service Within 50	0	1
Service Done	0	0

Note: Here we have used a PAT. We have also used the states as STD outputs (the Moore convention). Rework this CSPEC using the Mealy convention. You will discover why we did it the Moore way.

PSPEC 4.3.1; Select Service Message

Whenever DISTANCE+250 miles is a multiple of			Issue SERVICE MESSAGE=	Issue SERVICE PROMPT=
5,000	10,000	15,000		
Yes	No	No	"Change oil and oil filter"	SERVICE 250
	Yes	No	"Change oil, oil filter, and air filter"	
		Yes	"Major service needed"	

Whenever (DISTANCE + 50 miles) is a multiple of 5,000, issue:
    SERVICE PROMPT = SERVICE 50

PSPEC 4.3.2; Display Intermittently

[Intermittently?] issue MAINT NEEDED = SERVICE MESSAGE

Need to discuss frequency and duration of intermittent display with manufacturer

PSPEC 4.3.3; Display Continuously

Set MAINT NEEDED = SERVICE MESSAGE

REQUIREMENTS DICTIONARY

		Data (D) or Control (C)
ACCELERATION =	\Measured vehicle acceleration\ Units: Miles per hour per second	D
ACTIVATE =	\Driver's cruise control activate command\ 2 Values: On, Off	C
AV SPEED =	\Calculated average trip speed\ Units: Miles per hour	D
AV SPEED RQST =	\Driver's request to display average trip speed\ 2 Values: On, Off	C
BRAKING =	\Input signal indicating brakes applied\ 2 Values: On, Off	C
CALIBRATE CMDS =	([START MEASURED MILE | STOP MEASURED MILE])	C
CALIBRATE PARAMETERS =	LOWER LIMIT + UPPER LIMIT + DEFAULT COUNT	D
CRUISE CMDS =	([ACTIVATE | DEACTIVATE | RESUME]) + ([START ACCEL | STOP ACCEL])	C
CRUISE CTRL STATE =	\State of cruise control process\ 3 Values: Inactive, Cruising, Accelerating	C
DEACTIVATE =	\Driver's cruise control deactivate command\ 2 Values: On, Off	C
DEFAULT COUNT =	\Constant = *TBD;* Default value of calibrated mile count\ Units: Dimensionless *Need to get this value from auto manufacturer*	D
DESIRED SPEED =	\Speed cruise control is desired to maintain\ Units: Miles per hour	D
DISPLAYS =	(FUEL CONSUMPTION) + (MAINT NEEDED) + (AV SPEED)	D
DISTANCE =	\Calcualted distance traveled by vehicle\ Units: Miles	D
DISTANCE COUNT =	\Count of shaft rotation pulses over life of vehicle\ Units: Dimensionless	D
DRIVER CMDS =	CRUISE CMDS + MONITOR CMDS + CALIBRATE CMDS	C
FUEL CONSUMPTION =	\Calculated vehicle fuel consumption\ Units: Miles per gallon	D

FUEL QTY = \Entered value of fill-up fuel quantity\   D
Units: Gallons

INACTIVATE = \Driver's cruise control inactivate   C
command\
2 Values: On, Off

LOWER LIMIT = \Constant = *TBD*; Lower limit of   D
calibrated mile count\
Units: Dimensionless
*Need to get this value from auto
manufacturer*

MAINT COMPLETE = \Driver's indication that required   C
maintenance has been completed\
2 Values: On, Off

MAINT NEEDED = \Display messages indicating type of main-   D
tenance needed\
3 Values: "Change oil and oil filter,"
"Change oil, oil filter, and air filter," "Major
service needed"

MILE COUNT = \Count of shaft rotation pulses over mea-   D
sured mile\
Units: Dimensionless

MONITOR CMDS = (START TRIP) + (MAINT COMPLETE) +   C
(AV SPEED RQST)

REFUEL DISTANCE = \Calculated distance to next refuel\   D
Units: Miles

RESUME = \Driver's cruise control resume command\   C
2 Values: On, Off

RUNNING = \Input signal indicating engine running\   C
2 Values: On, Off

SERVICE MESSAGE = \Display messages indicating type of   D
maintenance needed\
3 Values: "Change oil and oil filter,"
"Change oil, oil filter, and air filter,"
"Major service needed"

SERVICE PROMPT = \Prompt for service advisory message\   C
2 Values: Service-250, Service-50

SHAFT ROTATION = \Input pulse stream corresponding to   D
angular rotation of drive shaft\
Units: Arbitrary angular unit per pulse

SPEED = \Calculated vehicle speed\   D
Units: Miles per hour

SPEED LOW = \Speed below cruise control target range\   C
2 Values: True, False

START ACCEL = \Driver's command to start accelerating\   C
2 Values: On, Off

START MEASURED MILE = \Driver's command to start measuring mile\
2 Values: On, Off — C

START TRIP = \Driver's command to restart trip calculations\
2 Values: On, Off — C

STOP ACCEL = \Driver's command to stop accelerating\
2 Values: On, Off — C

STOP MEASURED MILE = \Driver's command to stop measuring mile\
2 Values: On, Off — C

THROTTLE POSITION = \Output signal driving throttle position\
Units: Volts, Range: 0–8 — D

TOP GEAR = \Input signal indicating transmission in top gear\
2 Values: On, Off — C

TRIP TIME = \Elapsed time since start of trip\
Units: Seconds; Range: 0–10,000 — D

UPPER LIMIT = \Constant = *TBD;* Upper limit of calibrated mile count\
Units: Dimensionless
Need to get this value from auto manufacturer — D

26.4 Architecture Model

The architecture developed for the Automobile Management System requirements, captured in the requirements model and the problem statement, is shown in the diagrams that follow. The creation of this architecture followed the steps of Part V.

The architecture flow diagram shows that the system will interact with the driver through a user interface module. The shaft is provided with a shaft interface module, which will sense the rotation mechanically, convert it to an electrical signal, and transmit this signal to the cruise control computer module.

The engine status and brake status are provided, through their respective interface modules, by sensing ignition switch position and brake position.

The driver enters commands to the system through the driver interface module. This module does all the communications with the driver and only sends valid commands to the computer. It contains the processing necessary to validate the driver commands, which it then transmits to the computer; it receives and displays the cruise control and monitoring status.

The throttle is moved via the throttle interface module. It drives it to a position proportional to the desired position calculated by the computer, with a voltage of 0 for the closed position and 8 for fully open.

The cruise control computer interconnects to each of these modules by independent electrical buses. The shaft and throttle modules, being very critical to the whole operation, have to be made redundant. These redundant modules are linked by redundant buses to the automobile management computer module, which contains the necessary processing to perform the redundancy management.

Development of the architecture model required the creation of an enhanced requirements model, which is shown in the enhanced DFD and CFD. The architecture module specifications and the architecture interconnect specifications show the allocation of the requirements model to the architecture modules. The architecture dictionary sample shown enhances the requirements dictionary to allocate flows from the requirements model.

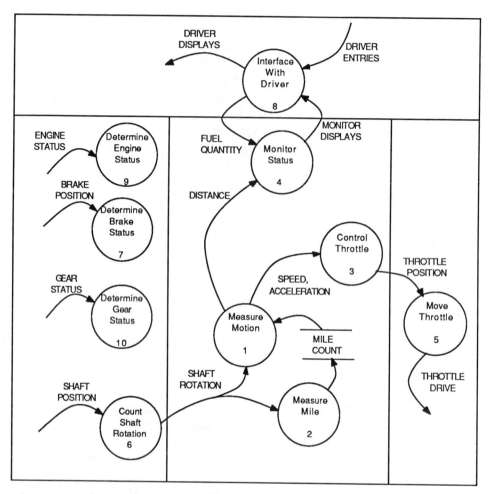

Enhanced DFD 0 for the Automobile Management System.

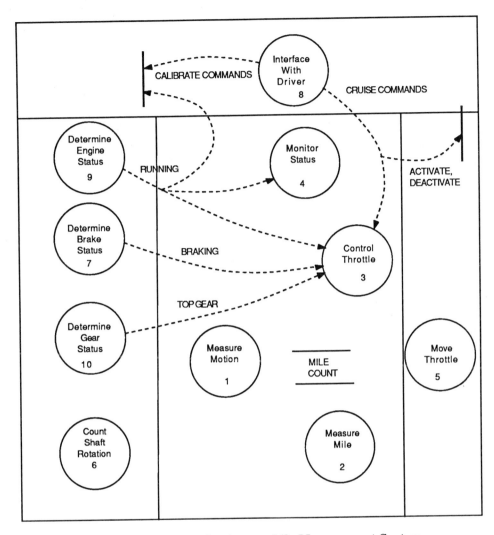

Enhanced CFD 0 for the Automobile Management System.

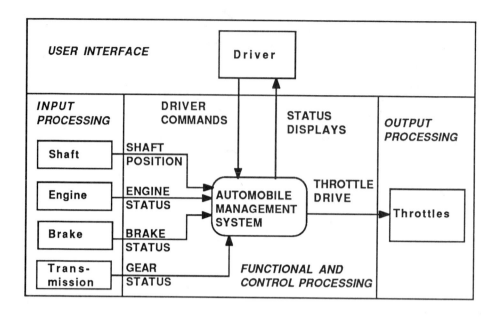

Architecture context diagram.

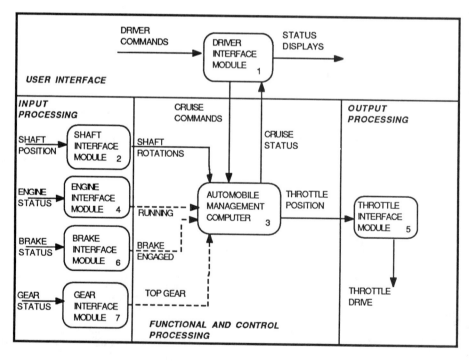

Architecture flow diagram.

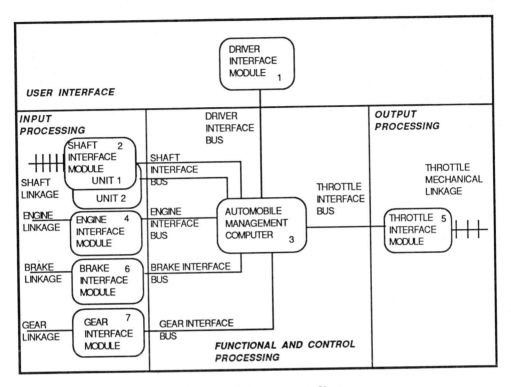

Architecture interconnect diagram.

ARCHITECTURE MODEL COMPONENTS / REQUIREMENTS MODEL COMPONENTS	SHAFT INTERFACE MODULE	AUTO-MOBILE MANAGE-MENT COMPUTER	THROTTLE INTERFACE MODULE	DRIVER INTERFACE MODULE	GEAR INTERFACE MODULE	BRAKE INTERFACE MODULE	ENGINE INTERFACE MODULE
MEASURE MOTION 1		X					
MEASURE MILE 2		X					
CONTROL THROTTLE 3		X					
MONITOR STATUS 4		X					
DETERMINE ENGINE STATUS 9							X
DETERMINE GEAR STATUS 10					X		
DETERMINE BRAKE STATUS 7						X	
COUNT SHAFT ROTATIONS 6	X						
INTERFACE WITH DRIVER 8.1 8.2 8.3 8.4 8.5				X			
VALIDATE DRIVER REQUEST 8.6		X					
MOVE THROTTLES			X				
CSPEC 0		X					

AMS for the Automobile Management System.

AIS : DRIVER INTERFACE BUS

The driver interface bus is a serial bus that carries information in 32-bit serial data, per the format shown below:

8 BIT LABEL	4 BIT STATUS	20 BIT ENCODED DATA

The labels are listed in the architecture dictionary.

AIS for driver interface bus.

ARCHITECTURE DICTIONARY

Name	Composed of	Type	Origin Module	Destination Module	Channel
Activate	\Driver's Cruise Control Activate Command\ 2 Values: On, Off	C	Driver Interface	Automobile Management Computer	Driver Interface Bus
Braking	\Input Signal indicating brakes applied\ 2 values: On, Off	C	Brake Interface	Automobile Management Computer	Brake Bus
Desired Speed	\Desired speed Cruise Control is to maintain\ Units: Miles per hour	D	Automobile Management Computer		
Fuel Qty	\Entered value of fill-up fuel quantity\ Units: Gallons Range: 0-18 gallons	D	Driver Interface	Automobile Management Computer	Driver Interface Bus
Throttle Position	\Output signal driving throttle position\ Units: Volts Range: 0-8 volts	D	Automobile Management Computer	Throttle Interface	Throttle Bus

Chapter 27

Home Heating System

In a panel session at the 1986 IEEE COMPSAC Conference, the following Home Heating System example[1] was used to compare several different real-time requirements methods. Prior to the conference, the system had been analyzed using each of the methods, and the results were presented for comparison.

27.1 Problem Statement

Note that this unedited statement, the figure, and the terminology, are almost exactly as given at the conference. It is typical of real-life problem statements, which may be ambiguous, vague, or even misleading. This is why we want to analyze them using a structured method before proceeding with a design.

Heating system overview

The system is summarized in the figure below. A temperature-sensing device compares the difference between the temperature t_h, sensed in the house, and the reference temperature t_r, which is the desired house temperature. The difference between these two, the error in the temperature, is measured and sent to the controller. The controller signals the furnace; the furnace produces heat, which is introduced to the house at rate Q_i; the house loses heat at the rate Q_o. If insufficient heat is supplied to the house, the temperature t_h falls. If the amount of heat going into the house exceeds that flowing out by natural means, the temperature of the house rises. The purpose of the feedback mechanism is to keep the difference between the reference temperature, t_r, and the temperature of the house, t_h, within desired limits if possible. A

---

[1]We are indebted to Stephanie White for preparing the original problem statement.

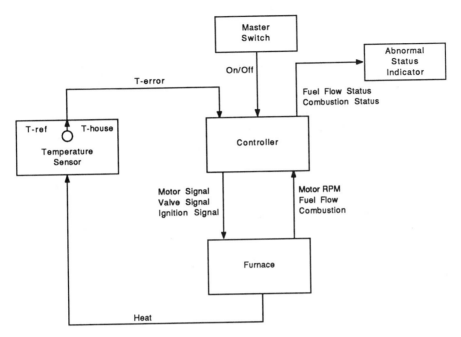

Home Heating System block diagram.

high outdoor temperature with a resultant heat flow into the house is possible but no air conditioner is present in the current system.

Temperature control device

A computer system interacting with a temperature sensing device is used to control the desired temperature of the house. A master switch can be set at Heat or Off. With a Heat setting, the furnace will operate as in the description. With an Off setting, the furnace will not operate. The homeowner is also allowed to select a desired temperature setting.

For purposes of comfort and furnace efficiency, the total change of temperature allowed in the house will be 4 degrees. If a room temperature of 70 degrees is desired, the furnace must operate so that the temperature never falls below 68 degrees or rises above 72 degrees (unless the outside temperature is greater than 72 degrees).

Note that if the comfort interval (bandwidth) is too small, the frequency with which the furnace oscillates between On and Off will be too rapid to be efficient. If the bandwidth is too great, the house will sometimes be too cold, and sometimes too warm.

The temperature sensing device does not have great precision and accuracy. It will detect temperature variations of the order of magnitude of one degree. It also has a time lag of the order of one minute.

The furnace subsystem

The oil furnace, which is used to heat the house, has a motor that drives a fan to supply combustion air, and also that drives a fuel pump.

When the house gets too cold, the motor is activated. When the motor reaches normal operating speed, the ignition is activated and the oil valve is opened. The fuel is ignited at this time and the furnace begins to heat the water, which circulates through the house. A fuel flow indicator and an optical combustion sensor signal the controller if abnormalities occur.

The furnace is alternately activated and deactivated by the controller to maintain the temperature within the required limits. When the furnace is deactivated, first the oil valve is closed, and 5 seconds later (to allow for the valve lag-time), the motor and ignition are deactivated. There is a 3-second lag-time before the motor stops.

Controller

Inputs to the controller

- Heating system master switch setting, which can be Off or Heat.

- Error between the house temperature and the temperature setting (t_h-t_r).

- Motor RPM status, which is a discrete[2] indicating whether or not the motor is at normal operating speed.

- Combustion status, which is a discrete indicating whether combustion is taking place or not.

- Fuel flow status, which indicates whether adequate fuel flow exists or not.

Outputs from the controller

- Valve signal, which is a discrete signaling the valve to open or close.

- Motor signal, which is a discrete directing the motor to start or stop.

- Ignition signal, which is a discrete directing ignition to start or stop.

- Signals to indicate abnormal status for combustion and fuel flow.

---

[2]A discrete is a hardware binary switch providing input to a control system or computer.

Controller requirements

When the master switch is On and outside temperature permits,

$$t_r - 2 \leq \text{house temperature} \leq t_r + 2$$
$$\text{where } t_r = \text{temperature setting}$$

Furnace input control signals shall be generated in a manner compatible with furnace operation described in the furnace subsystem description.

Minimum time for furnace restart after prior On interval is 5 minutes.

Furnace turn-off shall be initiated within 5 seconds after either

1. Master switch is turned Off.

2. Fuel flow rate falls below adequate level.

3. The optical detector indicates the absence of combustion.

To minimize the extent of house temperature overshoots and undershoots beyond the desired limits, the timing of furnace signals initiating or terminating calls for heat shall be based on the rate of temperature change during the corresponding interval.

The controller shall send signals to a status indicator device when abnormal conditions exist, such as inadequate fuel flow or lack of combustion.

In addition to the above requirements for a single residence, the customer wishes the controller to be used for a group of five condominiums. Each condominium has the same temperature control device, furnace system, abnormal status indicator, and heating requirements described above. However, all use oil from a single oil tank. It has been determined that the oil flow will allow at most four furnaces to operate simultaneously.

27.2 Requirements Model

The following are issues that arose while analyzing the Home Heating System. Reasonable assumptions have been made to complete the analysis, but in real life, they should all be discussed with the customer.

- The restriction that only four furnaces may operate simultaneously raises further questions: When all homes are requesting heat, which one should be denied, and for how long? For the sake of this analysis, we have assumed that no home should be denied heat for more than ten minutes, and that they should all have equal probability of being denied.

- No information is given on motor startup or ignition delay. We need to know these in order to know how long to wait for the fuel flow and ignition status signals to go normal after starting the motor. Values of $T1$ and $T2$ have been shown in the analysis.

- Related to the previous item, we have assumed that the status signals are in the abnormal state when the furnace is Off. To assume otherwise would imply sensors that are more sophisticated than is usual in heating systems.

- What if the motor *never* comes up to speed? There is no indicator provided to show this situation, which could be quite dangerous.

- We *are* given the stop time of the motor, but there does not seem to be any use for this information. If we make the reasonable assumption that the oil flame is self-supporting once ignited, then there is no point in keeping the ignition signal On while the motor runs down.

- How long should we wait after an abnormal condition before attempting to restart the furnace? We have assumed in the analysis that it must be manually restarted after such an event by operating the master control.

- It is not clear what the temperature sensor accuracy specification means. It is stated that "temperature variations of the order of magnitude of 1 degree" presumably means "about 1 degree," but that, in turn, could mean ±.5 degrees or ±1 degree. Also, does it mean both the precision *and* the accuracy have this same value? This could double the effective error. In the analysis, we have assumed that the accuracy is ±.5 degrees, and that the precision is significantly better than this, say .1 degrees. The total variation then is ±.6 degrees, so to keep the temperature variations within the desired ±2 limits, we have set the thresholds at ±1.4 degrees. This means the temperature variation could be as little as ±.8 degrees. A third unknown in this equation is *repeatability* of the sensor, and this is not mentioned. We assume it is good enough to be negligible.

This system is an example of a model in which the control requirements predominate. It is not as control intensive as the systems discussed in Section 12.9, but notice that the flow diagrams only extend to level 2 in order to separate the CSPECs for each residence.

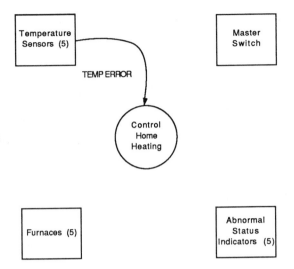

Data context diagram: Home Heating System.

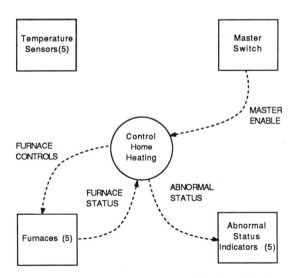

Control context diagram: Home Heating System.

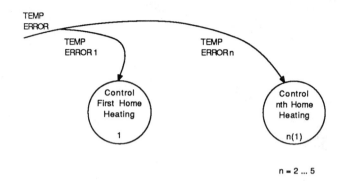

DFD 0: Control Home Heating.

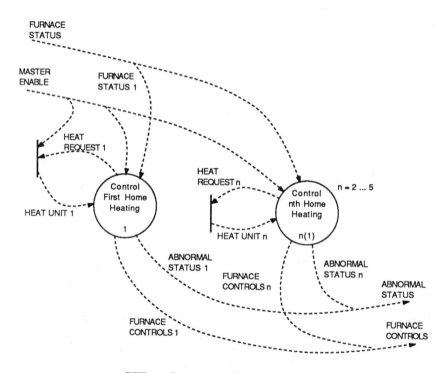

CFD 0: Control Home Heating.

Note: Here we have five duplicate processes, and use the approach of expanding only one, while referring the others to that one.

TABLE 1

HEAT REQUEST 1	HEAT REQUEST 2	HEAT REQUEST 3	HEAT REQUEST 4	HEAT REQUEST 5	ENABLE ALL
On	On	On	On	On	Off
Any other condition					On

TABLE 2

MASTER ENABLE	HEAT REQUEST 1	ENABLE ALL	ENABLE 1	HEAT UNIT 1
Off				Off
	Off			Off
Heat	On	On		On
Heat	On	Off		On
Heat	On	Off	Off	Off

TABLE (n+1), n = 2 ... 5

MASTER ENABLE	HEAT REQUEST n	ENABLE ALL	ENABLE n	HEAT UNIT n
As Table 2				

CSPEC 0: Control Home Heating. Sheet 1 of 2.

Note: ENABLE ALL is a signal internal to the CSPEC. It does not appear on any flow diagram.

While ENABLE ALL is Off, set ENABLE 1 through ENABLE 5 On or Off according to the following rules:

- One and only one will be Off at any time.

- None of them will be Off continuously for more than 10 minutes.

- The Off time will be shared equally among them.

CSPEC 0: Control Home Heating. Sheet 2 of 2.

Note: This CSPEC is a good example of keeping strictly to requirements. It is very tempting here to specify an algorithm for achieving these requirements (in fact, on our first approach, that is what we did). There are many algorithms that might meet the requirement, *but they are all designs and should not appear in this model*. The statement given is the true requirements statement.

TIMING SPECIFICATION

INPUT SIGNALS	EVENT	OUTPUT SIGNALS	EVENT	RESPONSE TIME
MASTER ENABLE	Off	VALVE CONTROL 1 . . . . VALVE CONTROL 5	All Off	5 sec max
FUEL FLOW STATUS n or COMBUSTION STATUS n	Abnormal	VALVE CONTROL n	Off	5 sec max
		n = 1 ... 5		

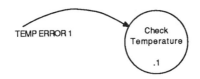

DFD 1; Control First Home Heating.

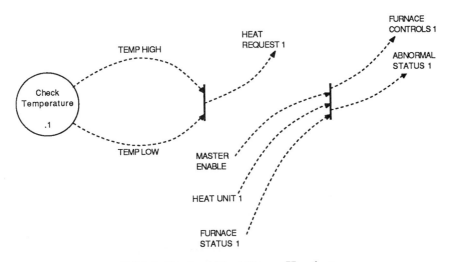

CFD 1; Control First Home Heating.

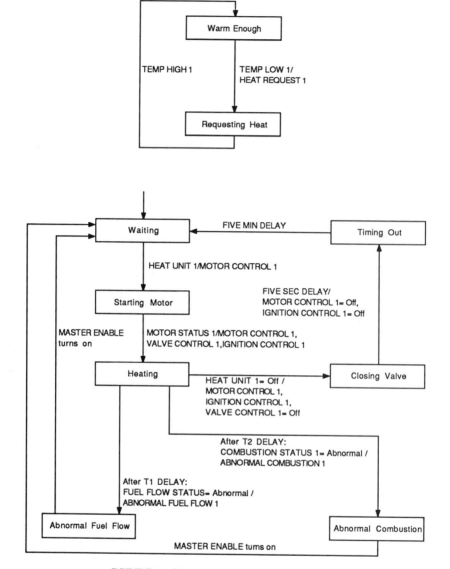

CSPEC 1; Control First Home Heating.

Note: Here, effective use is made of the universal availability of time in PSPECs and CSPECs. Remember, as in the Automobile Management System, that an action remains in effect until the next transition, so does not need to be explicitly turned off. Also recall from the discussion of naming control signals that stating their names alone implies their On state.

PSPEC 1.1; Check Temperature

Measure rate of change of TEMP ERROR 1 $= \frac{dT}{dt}$.
Then, while TEMP ERROR 1 $+ (\frac{dT}{dt} \times 1 \text{ minute}) > 1.4$ degrees

> set TEMP HIGH 1 $=$ True

> while TEMP ERROR 1 $+ (\frac{dT}{dt} \times 1 \text{ minute}) < -1.4$ degrees

> set TEMP LOW 1 $=$ True

Takes account of 1 minute delay in temperature sensor by predicting threshold crossings 1 minute ahead.

PSPEC n, $n = 2 \ldots 5$; Control nth Home Heating

As process 1, with the following correspondences:

$$\text{ABNORMAL STATUS n} \Rightarrow \text{ABNORMAL STATUS 1}$$
$$\text{HEAT UNIT n} \Rightarrow \text{HEAT UNIT 1}$$
$$\text{HEAT REQUEST n} \Rightarrow \text{HEAT REQUEST 1}$$
$$\text{TEMP ERROR n} \Rightarrow \text{TEMP ERROR 1}$$

REQUIREMENTS DICTIONARY

		Data (D) or Control (C)
ABNORMAL STATUS =	$\sum_{n=1}^{5}$ ABNORMAL STATUS n	C
ABNORMAL STATUS n =	COMBUSTION STATUS n + FUEL FLOW STATUS n, $n = 1 \ldots 5$	C
HEAT UNITS =	$\sum_{n=1}^{5}$ HEAT UNIT n	C
FURNACE CONTROLS =	$\sum_{n=1}^{5}$ FURNACE CONTROLS n	C
FURNACE CONTROLS n =	VALVE CONTROL n + MOTOR CONTROL n + IGNITION CONTROL n, $n = 1 \ldots 5$	C
FURNACE STATUS =	$\sum_{n=1}^{5}$ FURNACE STATUS n	C
FURNACE STATUS n =	MOTOR STATUS n + COMBUSTION STATUS n + FUEL FLOW STATUS n, $n = 1 \ldots 5$	C
TEMP ERROR =	$\sum_{n=1}^{5}$ TEMP ERROR n	D

Note: For the sake of brevity, the primitive definitions are not given; only the group flows are defined. We use the Σ sign to signify a string of + operations. Remember, the meaning is still "together with" with no ordering implied.

27.3 Architecture Model

The architecture model for the Home Heating System was essentially suggested in the problem statement by the block diagram. Since our decision was to use the problem statement as provided by the conference, we simply show here the architecture diagrams that capture the architecture of the system as suggested. The figure on the following page shows the architecture flow diagram for the Home Heating System. This diagram essentially represents the block diagram shown earlier using our symbols for capturing the system architecture.

The architecture interconnect diagram shown on the following page also captures the system's physical configuration using our symbols for the architecture model. These two diagrams would be much more meaningful if the problem statement were modified to make the architecture more interesting, but they are true to the problem statement as provided for the conference, which only asked for capturing the requirements for the controller and not the entire system.

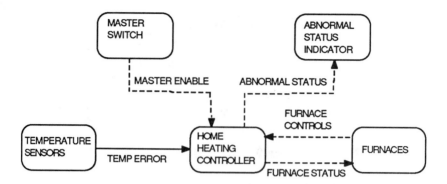

Architecture flow diagram: Home Heating System.

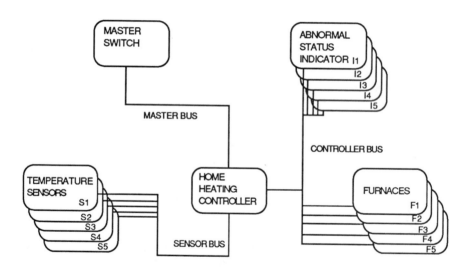

Architecture interconnect diagram: Home Heating System.

Chapter 28

Vending Machine

This example is an extension of a problem that we presented at the Structured Development Forum in San Francisco, February 1986. The problem statement and the resulting models were developed interactively as a dialogue between a customer and an analyst. Below is the outline of this dialogue and the resulting requirements and architecture models.

28.1 Customer Dialogue

The customer started by outlining to the analysts that he is faced with crooks as customers who try putting junk into the coin slots of his vending machines hoping to get something for nothing. Some even try to enter coin-like slugs to fool the machines. They also try to vandalize the selection register to get products free. These are major problems for the vending machine operators because they do business on a narrow margin, which disappears very quickly. The machine is to do the following:

- Accept objects from the customer in payment for their purchase.

- Check each object to make sure it is not a slug. This is to be done by validating the size, weight, thickness, and serrated edges.

- Accept nickels, dimes, and quarters. Any other coins are to be treated as slugs and returned to the customer.

- Only initiate payment computation or product selection process after a valid coin is detected. The system is to be difficult for people to trick.

- Accept product selection from the customer.

- Check to see whether the selected product is available (check product dispenser to make sure it is not empty), and if not available, then return coins automatically and notify the customer.

- Accept a variety of products, which will change from time to time. Hence, as a maintenance feature, the product prices should be changeable.

- Return the customer's payment on request if he or she decides not to make a selection.

- Dispense the product to the customer if it is available and the amount is sufficient.

- Return the correct change to the customer if the amount deposited is greater than the product price.

- Disable the product selection after the product is dispensed and until the next validated coin is received (remember those crooked customers).

- Make deposited coins available for change.

Based on these statements, a requirements model and an architecture model were developed. The remainder of this chapter contains these models.

28.2 Requirements Model

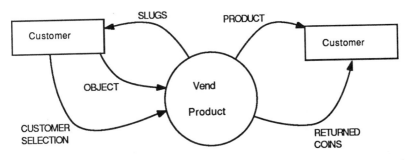

Data Context Diagram.

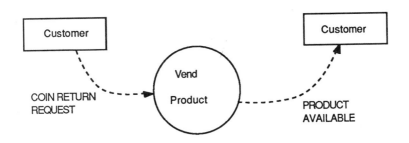

Control Context Diagram.

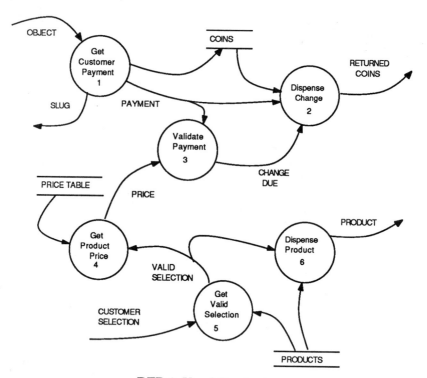

DFD 0: Vend Product.

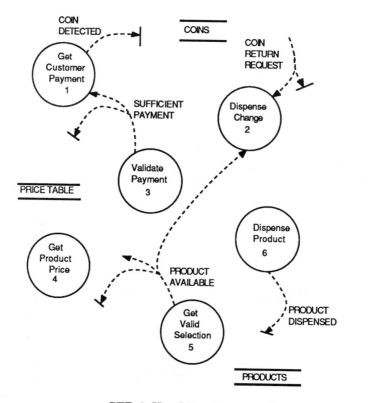

CFD 0: Vend Product.

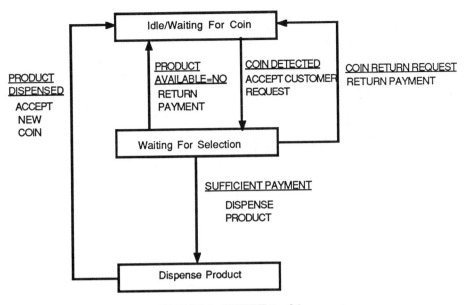

CSPEC 0: SHEET 1 of 2.

Process Activated / Control Action	Dispense Change	Dispense Product	Get Valid Selection
Accept Customer Request	0	0	1
Return Payment	1	0	0
Accept New Coin	0	0	0
Dispense Product	1	1	0

CSPEC 0: SHEET 2 of 2.

TIMING SPECIFICATION

INPUT	EVENT	OUTPUT	EVENT	RESPONSE TIME
OBJECT	Inserted	SLUGS	Ejected	2 sec. max.
CUSTOMER SELECTION	Entered	PRODUCT AVAILABLE	Displayed	0.5 sec. max.
		PRODUCT	Dispensed	5 sec. max.
COIN RETURN REQUEST	Entered	RETURNED COINS	Returned	2 sec. max.

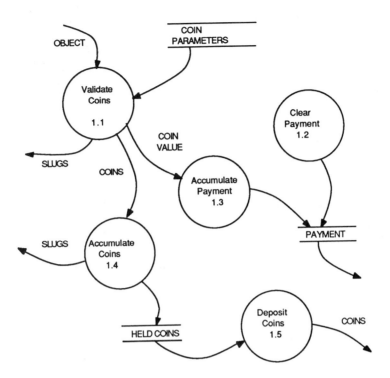

DFD 1: Get Customer Payment.

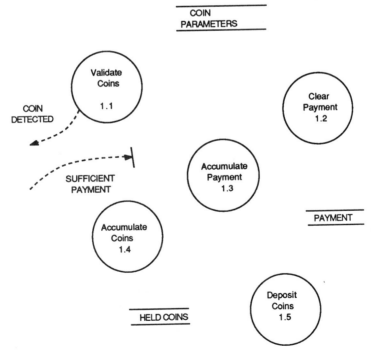

CFD 1: Get Customer Payment.

SUFFICIENT PAYMENT	CLEAR PAYMENT
TRUE	1
FALSE	O

CSPEC 1: Get Customer Payment.

PSPEC 1.1; Validate Coins

Examine OBJECT to see if it matches any set of COIN PARAMETERS

    If so:
        accept OBJECT as COIN

    otherwise:

        return OBJECT as SLUG.

PSPEC 1.2; Clear Payment

    Issue PAYMENT = 0.

PSPEC 1.3; Accumulate Payment

    Add COIN VALUE to PAYMENT.

PSPEC 1.4; Accumulate Coins

If HELD COINS ≤ HOLD CAPACITY then:

    return COIN as SLUGS

otherwise:

    Add COIN to HELD COINS.

PSPEC 1.5; Deposit Coins

Transfer HELD COINS to COINS

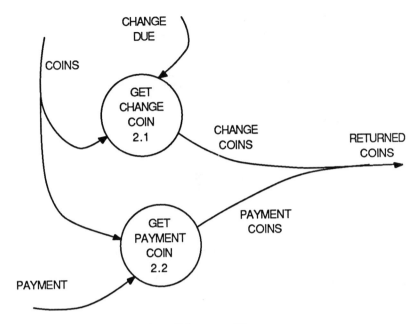

DFD 2: Dispense Change.

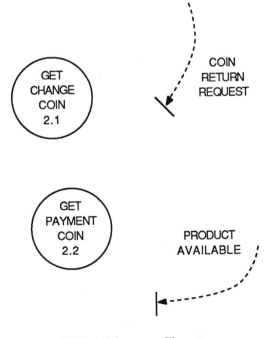

CFD 2: Dispense Change.

CONTROL INPUTS		ACTIVATE PROCESS	
COIN RETURN REQUEST	PRODUCT AVAILABLE	GET CHANGE COIN 2.1	GET PAYMENT COIN 2.2
TRUE	NO	0	1
D/C	YES	1	0

CSPEC 2: Dispense Change.

PSPEC 2.1; Get Change Coin

From COINS extract CHANGE COINS = CHANGE DUE

PSPEC 2.2; Get Payment Coin

From COINS extract PAYMENT COINS = PAYMENT

PSPEC 3; Validate Purchase

If PAYMENT ≥ PRICE then:

   Issue SUFFICIENT PAYMENT = Yes
   Issue CHANGE DUE = PAYMENT − PRICE

otherwise:

   Issue SUFFICIENT PAYMENT = No

PSPEC 4; Get Product Price

From PRICE TABLE issue PRICE corresponding to VALID SELECTION

PSPEC 5; Get Valid Selection

If CUSTOMER SELECTION is available in PRODUCTS then:

    Issue PRODUCT AVAILABLE = Yes
    Issue VALID SELECTION = CUSTOMER SELECTION

otherwise:

    Issue PRODUCT AVAILABLE = No.

PSPEC 6; Dispense Product

From PRODUCTS, select PRODUCT corresponding to VALID SELECTION

PARTIAL REQUIREMENTS DICTIONARY

	Data (D) or Control (C)
COINS = 0{[QUARTERS | DIMES | NICKELS]}8	D
CUSTOMER SELECTION = [SODA | CANDY | CRACKERS | GUM]	D
OBJECTS = [COINS | SLUGS]	D
QUARTERS = \U.S. Currency Coin Value with Standard Weight, Size, and Composition\ Units: Dollar/4	D

28.3   Architecture Model

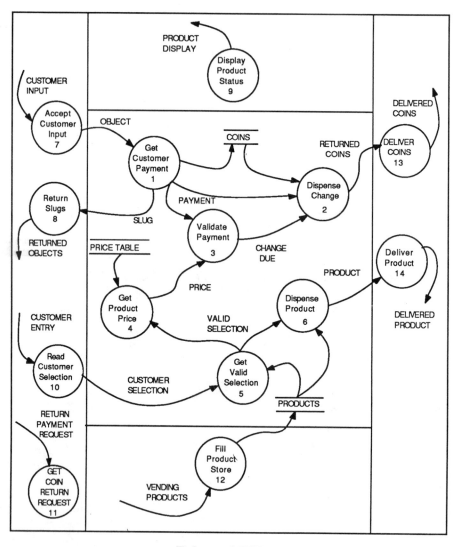

Enhanced DFD 0.

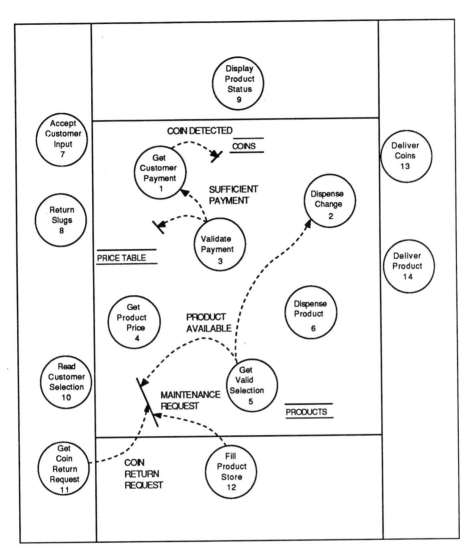

Enhanced CFD 0.

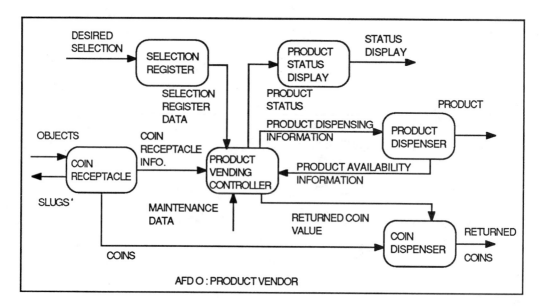

AFD 0.

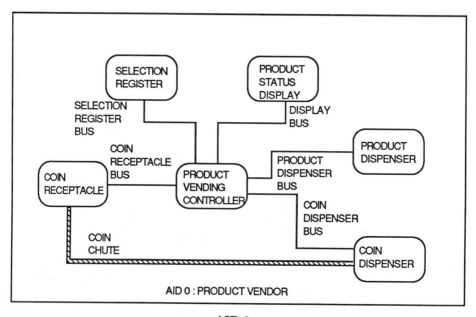

AID 0.

ARCHITECTURE MODEL COMPONENTS / REQUIREMENTS MODEL COMPONENTS	COIN RECEP-TACLE	PRODUCT VENDING CONTROL-LER	SELECTION REGISTER	COIN DISPEN-SER	PRODUCT STATUS DISPLAY	PRODUCT DISPENSER
GET CUSTOMER PAYMENT	X					
DISPENSE CHANGE 2				X		
VALIDATE PAYMENT 3		X				
GET PRODUCT PRICE 4		X				
GET VALID SELECTION 5		X				
DISPENSE PRODUCT 6						X
ACCEPT CUSTOMER INPUT 7	X					
RETURN SLUGS 8	X					
DISPLAY PRODUCT STATUS 9					X	
READ CUSTOMER SELECTION10			X			
GET COIN RETURN REQUEST 11			X			
FILL PRODUCT STORE 12						X
DELIVER COINS 13				X		
DELIVER PRODUCT 14						X
CSPEC 0		X				
COIN STORE				X		
PRODUCT STORE						X

Traceability Matrix.

FLOW NAME	COMPOSED OF	ORIGIN	DESTINATION	CHANNEL
OBJECTS	COINS + SLUGS	EXTERNAL	COIN RECEPTACLE	EXTERNAL
COINS	QUARTERS + NICKELS + DIMES	COIN RECEPTACLE	PRODUCT VENDING CONTROLLER	COIN RECEPTACLE BUS
PRODUCTS	[SODA CANDY GUM]	PRODUCT VENDING CONTROLLER	PRODUCT DISPENSER	PRODUCT DISPENSER BUS

Partial Architecture Dictionary.

```
AIS : PRODUCT DISPENSER BUS

The information on this bus will be sent
as a discrete signal containing 8 serial
bits. The product information will be encoded
into the 256 combinations.

The characteristics of this bus will be

      High = 5 +/- 0.2 Volts
      Low = Ground
```

Sample Architecture Interconnect Specification.

Appendix A

Standard Symbols
and Definitions

A.1 Introduction

The purpose of Appendix A is to establish definitions for the symbols and components within the requirements and architecture models. Meant to be a summary of the two models, this Appendix is a quick reference guide to all definitions and rules presented within the text. Appendix A represents the core symbols, components, and rules for the use of the structured methods on any program or project. Guidelines that can be changed from time to time to allow program flexibility without affecting the methods have not been included.

A.2 Standard Symbols

This section defines the allowed standard symbols for use with creating the requirements and architecture models.

A.2.1 Data flow

Definition: A data flow is a pipeline through which data of known composition flows. It may consist of a single element or a group of elements.

Naming Rules: The name of a data flow must not imply any processing. There must be no verbs in data flow names, only nouns and adjectives.

SHAFT DATA

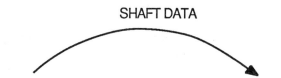

Figure A.1. Data flow: A solid arc with a name.

A.2.2   Control flow

Definition: A control flow is a pipeline through which control information of known composition flows. It may consist of a single element or a group of elements.

Naming Rules: The names of control flows must not imply any processing. There must be no verbs in control flow names, only nouns and adjectives.

CRUISE COMMANDS

Figure A.2. Control flow: A dashed arc with a name.

A.2.3   CSPEC bar

Definition: A CSPEC bar is a symbol used on a CFD to indicate the interface between the CFD and its CSPEC.

Naming Rules: CSPEC bars are not labeled, since it is understood the CSPEC inherits the name and number of the CFD and DFD.

Figure A.3. CSPEC bar: A short unlabeled bar.

A.2.4 Process

Definition: A process indicates the transformation of incoming data flow(s) into outgoing data flow(s). It is also used to map the paths along which control signals flow, but does not indicate control processing.

Naming Rules: The process name must be a verb acting upon a specific object.

Figure A.4. Process: A circle with a name and a number.

A.2.5 Store

Definition: A data or control store is simply a data or control flow frozen in time. The data or control information it contains may be used any time after that information is stored and in any order.

Naming Rules: A store name must be indicative of its contents—a name that groups together all the flows to and from the store. A store name must be a noun; there should be no processing implied in the store name; and it must be defined in the dictionary.

Figure A.5. Store: A pair of parallel lines containing a name.

A.2.6 Terminator (source or sink, also external)

Definition: A terminator represents an entity outside the context of the system that is a net transmitter or receiver of system data.

Naming Rules: The terminator name must include a noun, and must not imply any processing.

ENGINES

Figure A.6. Terminator: A rectangle containing a name.

A.2.7 Architecture module

Definition: An architecture module is a physical entity that either is a grouping of other physical entities or is a fundamental physical entity to which logical flows and processes have been allocated. This physical entity could be a hardware unit, such as the cruise control system or the cruise control computer (that is, it can be used to represent any level of system entity). Or, it could be a software module to compute airspeed by a specific algorithm or a group of software modules that together perform the navigation function.

Naming Rules: An architecture module must be named as a noun (no verbs in architecture unit names).

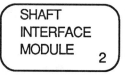

SHAFT
INTERFACE
MODULE   2

Figure A.7. Architecture module: A rounded rectangle containing a name and number.

A.2.8 Information flow vector

Definition: An information flow vector is a grouping of all the information that flows between any two architecture modules. These flows may contain any number of data and control flows that constitute the interface between the two architecture modules.

Naming Rules: The name of an information flow vector must be representative of its contents, and must not contain any verbs.

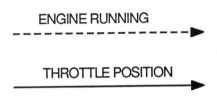

Figure A.8. Information flow vector: A solid or dashed line with a name.

A.2.9 Information flow channel

Definition: An information flow channel represents the physical means by which an information flow travels from one architecture module to another. This channel may be constructed of any material or energy carrier, for example, it may be electrical, mechanical, optical, or radio waves. There can be different symbols for different mediums of transmission.

Naming Rules: The name of an information flow channel must be a noun that indicates the medium of information transmission.

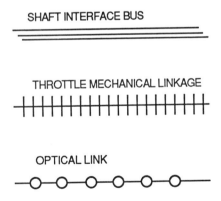

Figure A.9. Architecture information flow channels.

A.3 Requirements Model

The requirements model consists of the components in Figure A.10. The requirements model comprises both graphical and textual components. The components of a requirements model are: data context diagrams; control con-

text diagrams; data flow diagrams; control flow diagrams; process specifications; control specifications; timing specifications; and the requirements dictionary. The model also incorporates a set of balancing or self-consistency
rules.

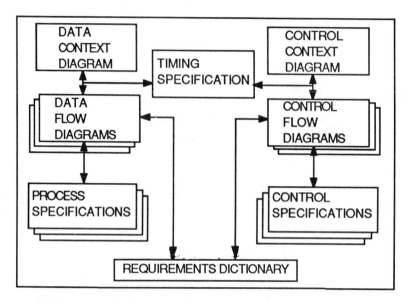

Figure A.10. Components of the requirements model.

A.3.1   Context diagrams

DATA CONTEXT DIAGRAM

Definition: The data context diagram establishes the data boundary between
  the system under study and the environment. It is used to show the
  communications between the system and the environment and the entities in the environment with which the system communicates. The
  data context diagram is the highest-level data flow diagram for that
  system.

Elements:

- one process

- terminators

- data flows

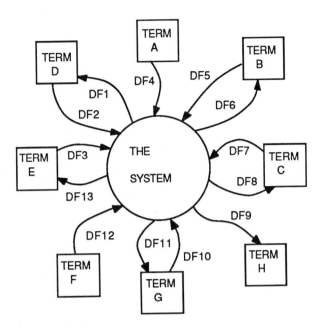

Figure A.11. Sample data context diagram.

Drawing Rules: The only absolute rule for the drawing of the data context diagram is that it must contain only one process (representing the system). Any number of terminators and flow elements are allowed.

CONTROL CONTEXT DIAGRAM

Definition: The control context diagram establishes the control boundary between the system under study and the environment. It is used to show communication between the system and the environment and the entities in the environment with which the system communicates. The control context diagram is the highest-level control flow diagram for the system.

Elements:

- one process (representing the system)

- terminators (same as those on DCD)

- control flows

Drawing Rules: All the rules for the data context diagram apply also to the control context diagram. All the same terminators should be drawn on

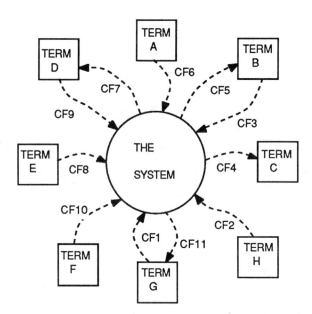

Figure A.12. Sample control context diagram.

both the context diagrams regardless of whether data or control flows or both exist between those terminators and the system.

A.3.2   Flow diagrams

DATA FLOW DIAGRAM

Definition: A data flow diagram is a network representation of a system's functional requirements. The system could be automated, manual, or mixed. The DFD portrays the requirements in terms of their functional component parts, with all interfaces among the parts indicated.

Elements:

- processes

- data flows

- data stores

Drawing Rules: A DFD can be drawn with any number of processes, data flows, and stores, but the guideline is to limit the processes in the range of 7 ± 2, unless the diagram is very complex or very simple. A store may appear on one diagram only; it must not be repeated on any other data flow diagram.

Naming and Numbering Rules: A data flow diagram must be named and numbered the same as the parent bubble it describes (see Figure A.14). The process numbers on that diagram must start with the number of the parent bubble, with .1, .2, .3, and so forth, appended.

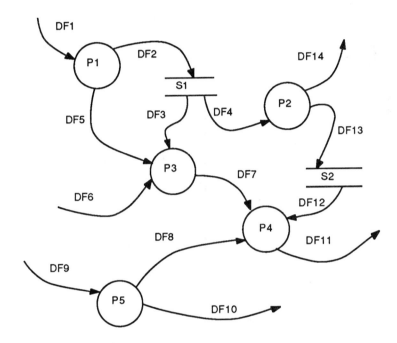

Figure A.13. Sample data flow diagram.

CONTROL FLOW DIAGRAM

Definition: A control flow diagram mirrors the processes and stores from the DFD, but shows control flows instead of data flows. The CFD is constructed simply to constrain the control signals to flow along the same paths as the data signals may flow.

Elements:

- processes (same as a DFD)

- stores (same as a DFD)

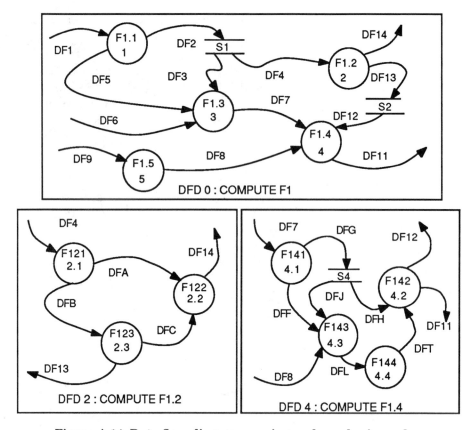

Figure A.14. Data flow diagram naming and numbering rules.

- control flows

- bar symbol representing the control specification

Drawing Rules: All the rules that apply to a DFD apply to the CFD. There are no special rules concerning CFDs and the only additional symbol added, the bar symbol, represents the control specification. This bar may be drawn anywhere on the CFD, and may be duplicated or varied in length. The stores on a CFD are repositories of control signals.

Naming and Numbering Rules: The components (processes and stores) on a CFD, and the CFD itself, should be named and numbered identically with its DFD, as shown in Figure A.16.

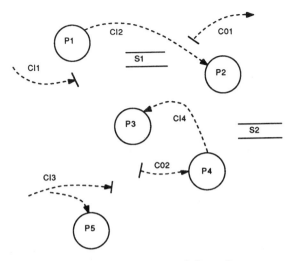

Figure A.15. Sample control flow diagram.

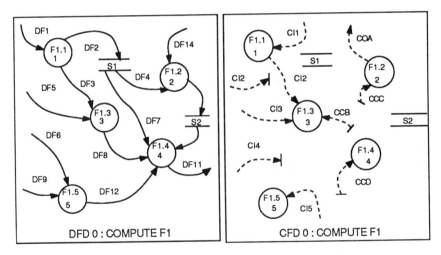

Figure A.16. DFD and CFD naming and numbering.

A.3.3 Process and control specifications

PROCESS SPECIFICATION

Definition: A process specification must be written for every functional primitive process on a data flow diagram. A functional primitive process is defined as a process that is not further decomposed into a child DFD, but is described in a PSPEC.

Elements: Process specifications can be written or drawn (that is, they can consist of text or graphics) to satisfactorily and unambiguously describe what that process has to do. They may be constructed using structured English, graphics, charts, mathematical equations, block diagrams, decision tables, or any other elements that specify the processing requirements.

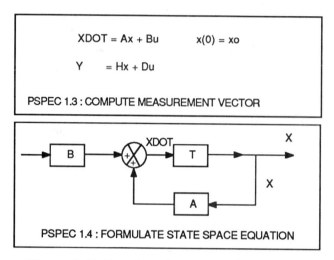

Figure A.17. Samples of process specifications.

Process Specification Rules: Process specifications must describe how their output signals are generated from their input signals—nothing more and nothing less. There are no other specific rules regarding the procedural content of a process specification although for any given project other rules may be implemented, such as,

- format of process specification

- size of process specification

- method of setting up procedural description

Naming and Numbering Rules: The process specification name and number should be the same as the parent process it describes (see Figure A.18).

CONTROL SPECIFICATION

Definition: Control specifications convert input signals into output control signals or into process controls. Control specifications have two roles, one to show control processing and the other to show process control.

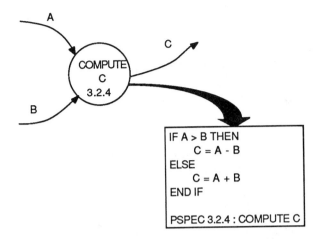

Figure A.18. Process specification naming and numbering rules.

Elements:

- state transition diagrams

- state transition tables

- state transition matrices

- decision tables

- activation tables

Control specifications may contain combinational machines, or sequential machines, or both. The elements used to represent a combinational machine are decision tables and process activation tables. Figure A.19 illustrates the concept for a combinational machine CSPEC. Figure A.20 shows an actual example.

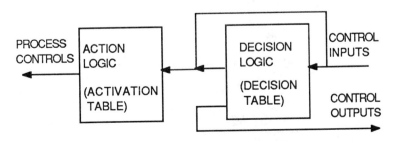

Figure A.19. Generic CSPEC for combinational system.

A decision table is used to show control signal processing; it creates a mapping of input control signals into output control signals.

An activation table for a combinational machine shows process control. Via this table, control signals are mapped into process activators. The control processing and process control for a combinational machine may further be combined into one table, as illustrated in Figure A.20.

The concept of a sequential machine CSPEC is illustrated in Figure A.21. The event logic can be represented by decision tables. The se-

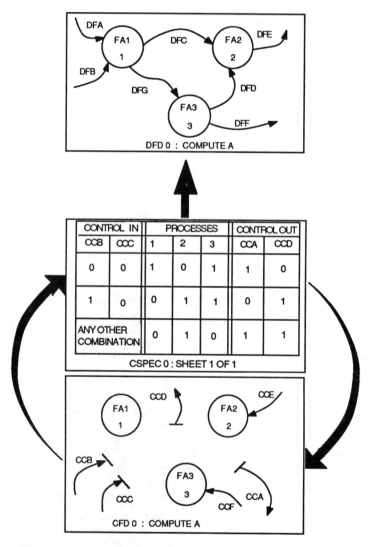

Figure A.20. Sample CSPEC for combinational system.

quential machine can be represented by state transition diagrams, state transition tables, or state transition matrices. The action logic can be represented by decision tables or process activation tables.

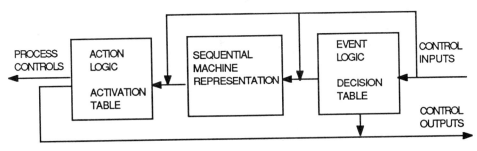

Figure A.21. Generic CSPEC for sequential system.

In the example shown in Figure A.22, a state transition diagram is used to show the sequential behavior of the system.

Control Specification Rules: A control specification can consist of any number of sheets, there is no limitation. It is given the same number as the corresponding DFD and CFD. As illustrated in Figure A.20, the CSPEC that goes along with DFD 0 and CFD 0 is numbered CSPEC 0. In addition, if the CSPEC consists of multiple sheets, it is given sheet numbers, as for example, "Sheet M of N," or "SHT M of N."

A.3.4 Timing specifications

TIMING SPECIFICATION

Definition: The timing specification is a list of system input events and their resulting system output events, both expressed in terms of the system input and output signals that represent them. The timing relationships are listed for each input-to-output event pair.

Elements: The timing specification consists of a list or lists in any tabular or other format appropriate for the particular system. It may be supplemented with timing diagrams as needed.

Timing Specification Rules: Every primitive system input and output signal must be listed at least once in the timing specification, even if its timing is listed as noncritical. Every signal listed in the timing specifica-

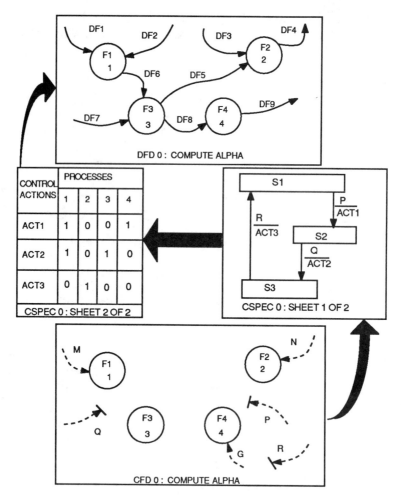

Figure A.22. Sample CSPEC for sequential system.

tion must be defined in the requirements dictionary and must be a member of a context diagram flow.

A.3.5   Requirements dictionary

Definition: The requirements dictionary is an ordered list of data and control flow names and data and control store names, each with a definition in terms of its components and structure. Every data flow, control flow, and store on the flow diagrams must be defined in the dictionary down to its primitive elements.

Elements: The dictionary is to be constructed using the following symbols:

=	*means*	composed of
+	*means*	together with
{ }	*means*	iterations of
[|]	*means*	select one of
( )	*means*	optional
" "	*means*	literal
* *	*means*	comment field
\\ \\	*means*	description of primitive element

Examples:

> PERF PRDNS = TRIP PRDNS +
> [HLDG TIME AVLBLE | STEP PRMTRS +
> STEP CLB SVGS | SAVINGS]

The following are *instances* of the above definition:

> PERF PRDNS = TRIP PRDNS

> PERF PRDNS = TRIP PRDNS + HLDG TIME AVLBLE

> PERF PRDNS = TRIP PRDNS + STEP PRMTRS +
> STEP CLB SVGS

> PERF PRDNS = TRIP PRDNS + SAVINGS

Naming Rules: Every data flow, control flow, and store described in the dictionary must have exactly the same name as used in the data flow diagrams, control flow diagrams, process specifications, control specifications, data context diagrams, and control context diagrams.

A.3.6   Requirements model balancing rules

Balancing is the practical means of verifying that the requirements model is rigorously defined and that all of its components are linked consistently. The rules for balancing a requirements model are listed below, and then are detailed in the paragraphs that follow.

Rule 1: *Every DFD must balance with its parent process.* In addition, each of its children must balance with it. Each process on a DFD must be broken down further or described in a process specification. The context diagram contains the parent bubble for the level 1 DFD and each of the level 1 bubbles is the parent of a diagram below it.

Every data flow that flows into a parent process must completely map into the child diagram. A parent flow may be decomposed into subflows on a child DFD, but every element in the parent flow must match the elements of that flow in the child diagram. For example, if the parent flow were composed of three elements, but the child diagram only used two of those elements, then the DFD is unbalanced.

Rule 2: *Every PSPEC must balance with the functional primitive process it describes.* The name and number of the process specification should be the same as the functional primitive they describe. The PSPEC must use all the elements flowing into the functional primitive process. Process specifications must specify the input-to-output transformation.

Rule 3: *Every CFD must balance with its parent process.* CFD balancing is the same as DFD balancing. Every control signal flowing into or out of a process must appear on the child CFD. On the child CFD, the control flow may flow into or out of a CSPEC represented by a bar symbol or it may flow into or out of a process indicating use or generation at a lower level.

Rule 4: *Every CSPEC must balance with its associated CFD.* Control flows flowing into a bar on the CFD must appear as inputs to the control specification, and control flows out of a bar must be generated in the control specification. A signal flowing into a bar on a CFD must show up as an input to a decision table, activation table, or as an event on a state transition diagram in the CSPEC. A signal flowing out of a bar on a CFD must appear as an output from a decision table or an activation table.

Rule 5: *Every CSPEC must only show activation and deactivation of processes on the DFD having the same number as the CSPEC.* Processes on a given DFD may be controlled only from the control specification of the same number as that DFD. Thus, processes in different DFDs cannot be controlled from the same control specification: For example, the activation table that goes with the DFD 0 and CFD 0 may only control the process on DFD 0. A control signal may not control, directly or indirectly, the PSPEC or CSPEC that generated it, nor any ancestor process of that PSPEC or CSPEC.

Rule 6: *The derivation of control signals from data signals (data conditions) can only be specified in a PSPEC for a functional primitive process.* Control signals may be generated from data signals in process specifications. They appear as outputs from primitive processes in the control flow diagrams. They flow only on the CFD, not on the DFD.

Rule 7: *Every data flow, control flow, and store must be defined, and must be decomposed to its primitive elements, in the requirements dictionary.* Every flow must be defined in the dictionary in terms of its components, and they, in turn, must be defined in the dictionary in the same way. This procedure must continue until every component of the original flow is decomposed into primitive elements, as illustrated in Figure A.23. Every dictionary entry must have a unique name (no aliases).

$$A = [B + C|D + E]$$

$$B = 0\{Q + R\}4$$

$$C = S + T$$

$$D = [N|M]$$

$$E = G + (H)$$

$$G = \cdots$$

$$H = \cdots$$

$$Q = \cdots$$

$$R = \cdots$$

$$S = \cdots$$

$$T = \cdots$$

$$M = \cdots$$

$$N = \cdots$$

**Figure A.23. Illustration of flow decomposition
in the requirements dictionary.**

A.4 Architecture Model

The architecture model consists of both graphical and textual components. These components are the architecture context diagram, the architecture flow diagram, the architecture interconnect diagram, the architecture module specification, the architecture interconnect specification, and the architecture dictionary. The architecture model is shown in Figure A.24, and is derived from the requirements model by applying design criteria that map the functional requirements into an architecture. The architectural representation of a system must fit the categories shown in Figure A.25. These categorizations can be applied to any system as well as to its component subsystems.

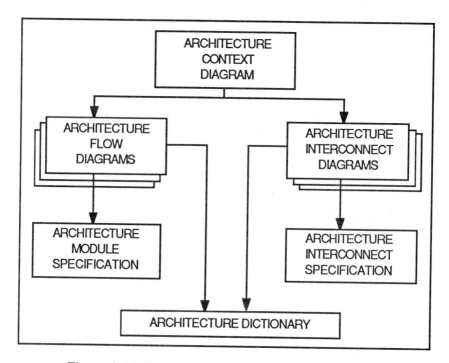

Figure A.24. Components of the architecture model.

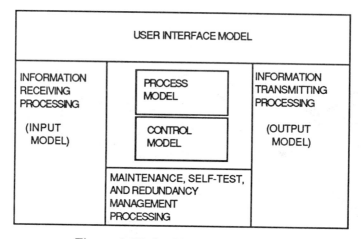

Figure A.25. Architecture template.

A.4.1 Architecture context diagram

Definition: The architecture context diagram establishes the information
boundary between the system and the environment. It is used to show
communication between the system and entities in the environment

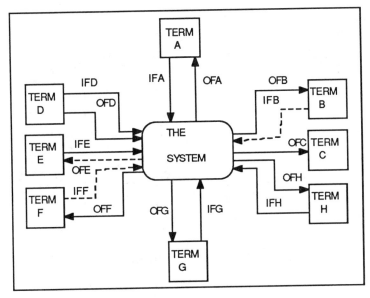

Figure A.26. Sample architecture context diagram.

outside the system. The architecture context diagram is the highest-
level architecture diagram for that system.

Elements:

- one architecture module

- terminators

- information flow vectors

Drawing Rules: The only absolute rule for drawing the ACD is that it may
not contain more than one architecture module, representing the system. Any number of information flow vectors and external entities are
allowed.

A.4.2   Architecture flow and interconnect diagrams

The architectural representation scheme must show two aspects of the architecture: It first must show the information flows between the various architecture modules, and second, the channels on which this information travels.
These two aspects may be shown on two separate diagrams: the architecture
flow diagram and the architecture interconnect diagram. Or, the two may be
combined on one diagram: the architecture flow and interconnect diagram.

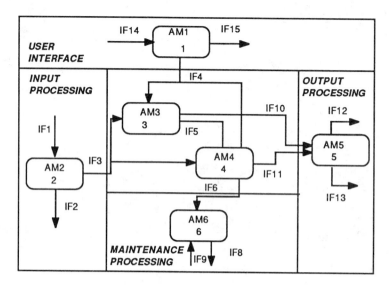

Figure A.27. Sample architecture flow diagram.

ARCHITECTURE FLOW DIAGRAMS

Definition: An architecture flow diagram is a network representation of a system configuration. The AFD represents a set of DFD and CFD flows and processes grouped into one architecture module. The architecture modules are represented by the architecture module symbol, and the communications between the architecture modules are represented by information flow vectors.

Elements:

- architecture modules

- information flow vectors

Drawing Rules: An AFD can be drawn with any number of architecture modules and information flow vectors. It can be drawn to show the configuration of an entire system in terms of its component subsystems or to show the expansion of any component subsystem.

Naming and Numbering Rules: An AFD must be named and numbered the same as the parent module it describes (see Figure A.28). The modules on that diagram must be numbered with the number of the parent module with .1, .2, .3, and so on, appended for the child modules.

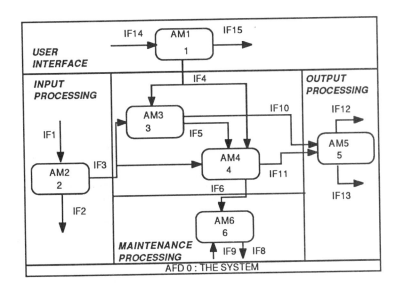

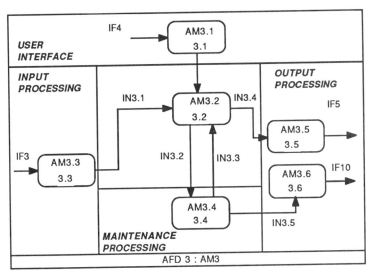

Figure A.28. AFD naming and numbering rules.

ARCHITECTURE INTERCONNECT DIAGRAM

Definition: An architecture interconnect diagram is a representation of the channels by which the architecture modules communicate. The channels represent the physical means by which the information travels from one architecture module to another. The physical means might be any material or energy medium such as electrical buses, mechanical linkages, or an optical link.

Elements:

- architecture modules

- information flow channels

Drawing Rules: An AID is created corresponding to each AFD. The AID shows the communication channels for the architecture modules of the AFD, and shows the redundancy of the architecture modules and the channels that link them. Architectural redundancy, module redundancy, or channel redundancy are shown on the AID only, not on the AFD. Figure A.29 shows an AID.

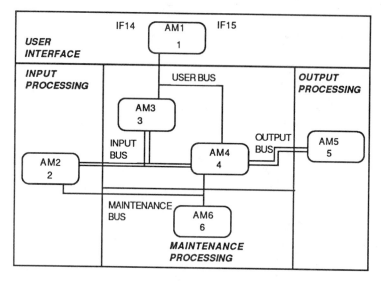

Figure A.29. Sample architecture interconnect diagram.

Naming and Numbering Rules: The AID and its components are named and numbered the same as the modules on the corresponding AFD, with additional notation added for redundant modules. Some examples of how redundancy may be indicated are "L," "C," and "R" for left, center, and right, or "LANE 1," "LANE 2," and "LANE 3." Either of these is suitable notation for a triple-redundant set of modules.

A.4.3. Architecture module and interconnect specifications

Textual specifications must be written for each architecture module for two purposes: first, to specify the information and processing allocation, and second, to specify the characteristics of the channels by which the architecture modules communicate. The allocation is specified in an architecture module specification and the channel characteristics are specified in an architecture interconnect specification.

ARCHITECTURE MODULE SPECIFICATION

Definition: An architecture module specification must be written for every architecture module in the architecture model (see Figure A.30). The purpose of the AMS is to state the information and processing allocation for that architecture module along with a description of the architecture module in narrative or graphical form.

ARCHITECTURE MODULE SPECIFICATION 0 : TRACEABILITY MATRIX							
	ARCHITECTURE MODEL COMPONENTS						
REQUIREMENTS MODEL COMPONENTS	AM1	AM2	AM3	AM4	AM5	AM6	AM7
1	X					X	
2			X		X		
3		X		X			
4					X		
5							X
CSPEC 0						X	

Figure A.30. Sample architecture module specification.

Elements:

- narrative or graphical description

- traceability matrix for functional allocation

ARCHITECTURE INTERCONNECT SPECIFICATION

Definition: The architecture interconnect specification establishes the characteristics of the physical media connecting the architecture modules.

Elements:

- graphical or textual characteristic definitions

  Since the channels may be constructed of any medium, such as electrical, mechanical, or optical, the characteristics of each of the channels must be defined appropriately.

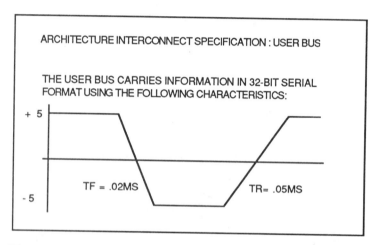

Figure A.31. Sample architecture interconnect specification.

A.4.4 Architecture dictionary

The architecture dictionary is a listing of all the data and control flow elements on the architecture flow diagrams. The architecture dictionary is an enhancement of the requirements dictionary with the appropriate supplementary information. There must be traceability between the two dictionaries. When logical processes are allocated to architecture modules, the flows between them and the channels on which they flow must be specified in the architecture dictionary. Figure A.32 shows the minimum content required in an architecture dictionary to completely and uniquely specify the architecture flows. Other attributes may be added as needed by the particular system. The bus information must be provided for every primitive element, and may be provided for groupings that flow in their entirety along one channel.

NAME	COMPOSED OF	TYPE	ORIGIN MODULE	DESTINATION MODULE	CHANNEL
X	X1+X2 + X3	D			
X1		D	AM2	AM4 AM5	USER BUS
X2		D	AM2	AM3	OUTPUT BUS
X3		D	AM2	AM6	OUTPUT BUS

Figure A.32. Example of enhancements to dictionary.

A.4.5 Balancing rules

Architecture model components must be consistent with each other. In addition, the requirements model components along with other requirements for the system must be accounted for in the architecture model. The rules fall into two categories: those rules that help in the creation of a balanced architecture model, and those that create traceability between the requirements model and the architecture model.

Rule 1: *Every architecture module that appears on an architecture flow diagram must also appear on the corresponding architecture interconnect diagram.* In addition, the names and numbers of the corresponding architecture modules must be the same on the AFD and the AID. The AFD represents the system architecture from an information flow aspect, while the AID represents it from a physical interconnect aspect. These two diagrams contain the same architecture modules: The only difference between them is that the AID shows redundant modules, while the AFD does not need to show them because redundant architecture modules and their information flows are identical. The reason redundant modules need to be shown on the AID is that their physical interconnects may be different. If two modules are not identical, that is, if the processing allocated to them differs, or their information flows differ, then they are not considered redundant, and must be uniquely defined both on the AFD and the AID.

Rule 2: *Every component of an information flow into an architecture module must be used within that module.* The information that flows into an architecture module must be used by that architecture module in its entirety and the information flow coming out of an architecture module must be generated inside that module. The information that flows to and from an architecture module must be accounted for in the architecture dictionary. The information that flows to and from the architecture module must be the same as the data and control flows to and from the allocated data and control processes.

Rule 3: *Every architecture interconnect channel must have at least one information flow (data or control) allocated to it.* Every architecture interconnect channel must have some flows allocated to flow along it. If that is not the case, then that architecture interconnect channel should not exist.

Rule 4: *Every PSPEC and CSPEC from the requirements model must have a place in the architecture model.* Every PSPEC and CSPEC must be traceable to the architecture model through the architecture module specifications. There must be a listing of all processes (or their higher-level groupings) in the AMSs. The CSPECs can be allocated as complete units, or divided into separate parts.

Rule 5: *Every data or control flow in the requirements model must be assigned a place in the architecture model.* This allocation must be verifiable through the architecture dictionary, which is an enhancement of the requirements dictionary. The architecture dictionary has additional fields that represent the origin module, destination module, and architecture communication channel.

Every requirements dictionary component has one of two options: Either it must be allocated to a module, or it must flow from one module to another. For those components that are allocated to a module, the origin module field must be filled in; for components that go from one architecture module to one or more other architecture modules, all three entries must be filled in. In this way, it will be possible to verify from the architecture dictionary that complete allocation has taken place and that there is traceability between the requirements and architecture models.

Appendix B

Making the Models into Documents

B.1 Organizing the Models

When you have completed the requirements and architecture models, and assuming they are not just for your own immediate group's consumption, you probably will be faced with the issue of how to transform this stack of diagrams and specifications into presentable documents. In many cases, they will be deliverable items to your customers, and may have to fit into their or your standard document formats. If your customer is a government agency, you will have to conform with whichever government standard documentation specification is imposed by your contract.

The problem is, all these formats and standards were designed to provide structure where none existed—to give structure to a narrative specification. It can be hard to fit a graphic model into a narrative format, and the two structures often conflict.

At the time of writing this text, we have had considerable experience in putting the requirements model into document format, but much less with the architecture model. Nevertheless, we do include a suggested documentation format for the architecture model.

First, we will discuss the sequence in which the model itself should go together, then we will go into some of the standard document formatting issues. There are two basic ways in which the model might be sequenced: numerically or top-down. Since our methods use a top-down approach, this arrangement of the model is appealing. It is arranged in the following order: context diagrams; level 1 diagrams and specifications; level 2 diagrams and specifications, and so on; followed by the dictionary and any appendices. This sequence has the attractive property that a subset of the model can be taken off the top of the document down to any desired level. This subset provides a complete summary of the requirements down to the corresponding level of detail. The problem with this arrangement, which we have found insurmountable in practice, is that it is *not* in numerical order, and people using it get very confused. It seems that numerical ordering is a deeply ingrained convention in our minds.

The other approach, then, is to arrange the model in straightforward numerical order, starting, again, with the context diagram, followed by the level 1 diagrams and specifications (process 0), then by process 1 and all of its descendants, then process 2 and all of its descendants, and so on. Obviously, the disadvantage here is that it is *not* top-down: The last descendant of process 2—PSPEC 2.8.6.6.7, for example—will be followed immediately by DFD 3. But most people can find their way around it, so it seems to be the practical way to go. But whichever order is chosen, as long as the user is aware of that order and of the numbering conventions of the method, then the resulting document is self-indexing. Given the process number on any particular sheet, it is easy to find your way to the parent and children, and to their parents and children. In principle, this means that page numbering and section or paragraph numbering is redundant, but again, we have found that traditions are hard to break, especially in the military community, and a superstructure comprised of these other numbering systems is required.

Throughout the main document structure described above, the local structure is simple and repetitive. Each DFD is immediately followed by its CFD (if any), then its CSPEC (if any). Where a DFD's decomposition ends, this whole package is replaced by a PSPEC (since PSPECs do not have CFDs or CSPECs associated with them). Arranging these groups of related items together in this way keeps all the information about one part of the system neatly packaged in one place.

For a long time to come, we should assume that many users of structured specifications are newcomers to them, and need some introduction to their use. For this reason, two additions should be included with the model: a top-level textual system description (more or less a verbal description of the level 1 diagrams and specifications); and a brief description of the method itself, which includes references to more complete information. The top-level description allows the new user to see the system described both in the familiar way, and in the structured way.

The whole structure of a typical document is, then,

> top-level system description
> introduction to structured specifications (how to read and use them) plus
>   references
> data context diagram
> control context diagram
> level 1 data flow diagram (process 0)
> any level 1 control flow diagrams
> any level 1 control specifications
> timing specification

Next, the following block of items is repeated for all n, either in numerical or in top-down order:

> data flow diagram n
> control flow diagram n (if any)
> control specification n (if any)

> OR

> process specification n

followed by

> system requirements dictionary
> appendices

For the control intensive systems discussed in Section 12.9, the local repetitive structure would have to be changed to allow a CFD, optionally with a CSPEC, but without a corresponding DFD. For very large systems, the document might need to be divided among several volumes. A practical way to do this is to assign a high-level process, usually a level 1 process, to each volume. If this is done, then the context and level 1 diagrams and specifications should be duplicated in each volume to make it self-contained. Thus, in Volume 2 we might have

> data and control context diagrams
> DFD 0, CFD 0, CSPEC 0
> DFD 2, CFD 2, CSPEC 2
> DFD 2.1, CFD 2.1, CSPEC 2.1
> DFD 2.1.1, CFD 2.1.1, CSPEC 2.1.1
> and so on

Only Volume 1 would contain all the introductory material: the top-level system description, and the users' guide. If the model is supported by a good automated tool, it might be practical, and would certainly be useful, to generate a sub-dictionary for each volume containing just those flows appearing in that volume. Appendices referenced by PSPECs or CSPECs should be attached to the volume in which they are referenced.

The architecture model can also follow a very similar documentation scheme. Here again, the architecture diagrams can be arranged in a top-down layering or a strictly numerical layering. But, since the architecture model reflects the physical configuration of the system, it might be better to use a top-down layering of the diagrams. The architecture module specifications can be incorporated into the whole layered scheme outlined below or the traceability matrix can be placed along with the context diagram if only one traceability matrix has been built to capture the entire allocation. In some instances, the traceability matrix is built to give a comprehensive picture of the allocation, rather than fragmenting it into smaller pieces to go with each AFD layer.

The whole structure of a typical document is, then,

> top-level system description
> introduction to structured specifications (how to read and use them, plus references)
> architecture context diagram
> level 1 architecture flow diagram
> level 1 architecture interconnect diagram
> level 1 architecture module specifications
> level 1 architecture interconnect specifications

Next, the following block of items is repeated for all n, in numerical or top-down order:

> architecture flow diagram n
> architecture interconnect diagram n
> architecture module specification n
> architecture interconnect specification

followed by

> system architecture dictionary
> appendices

B.2 Military Standards

All of the above applies to situations that are not constrained by the rigors of military standards. We are in the early days of introducing structured specifications to military programs, and while some success has been achieved in embedding them into the standard formats, we cannot claim to have the ultimate answers.

Military standards demand rigid paragraph, table, and figure numbering, all of which is, to some degree, inconsistent with the numbering of the requirements and architecture methods. A first step toward getting relief is to request an exception from the standard. This is usually granted if the contracting agency is convinced that you have a reasonable alternative, which is clearly defined in an in-house standard and meets the spirit of the basic standard.

Some of the more usual standards called out are MIL-STD-483, MIL-STD-490, and more recently, MIL-STD-483A, MIL-STD-490A, and DOD-STD-2167. The last three invoke Data Item DI-MCCR-80025, which specifies the actual document format. They all have the characteristic of surrounding the requirements section itself with boilerplate sections such as Scope, Applicable Documents, and so on.

The requirements section itself is not well-oriented to the true functional requirements represented in the model, but more toward design requirements, with paragraphs for programming requirements, programming language, design standards, and similar items.

The sections that do address functional requirements are segmented into separate subparagraphs for the inputs, processing, and outputs of each process. This format can be followed fairly well by embedding each major process of the model into one of these functional paragraphs. The input and output paragraphs can either reference the dictionary, or can contain the appropriate subset of the dictionary. With care, the paragraph numbering and process numbering can be made to relate to each other. For example, in a MIL-STD-483 specification, Paragraph 3.2 is Detailed Functional Requirements, and its subparagraphs can be arranged so that Paragraph 3.2.N contains process N, where N may be a multi-digit number. Thus, Paragraph 3.2.4.1.7 would contain process 4.1.7, and if this is a detailed enough level to provide a useful table of contents, it would also contain all the descendants of 4.1.7. Similar arrangements can be made with the other standard formats.

DOD-STD-2167 specifically calls for a top-down approach using structured requirements analysis tools and techniques. As this new standard moves into widespread use, methods such as those described here will become mandatory.

The dictionary naturally fits into an appendix, but, as described above, parts of it might be duplicated within the body of the document. The idea of having a sub-dictionary for each volume of a multi-volume specification is not easily integrated into the standards: They specifically call for appendices to be at the end of the whole set.

Table and figure numbering are particularly difficult issues. Since they all have numbers assigned by the method, the numbering called for by the standards can become very confusing, and can clutter the model hopelessly. We have found that by not calling them figures or tables at all, but simply referring to them as DFD 3.4.2, CSPEC 4.7.1.1, and so on, the numbers from the standard might be avoided (Be warned; there is no guarantee that all government agencies will accept this, or any other suggestions we make here).

The numbers used in the requirements and architecture models are at risk of being confused with the document paragraph numbers. To avoid this, always prefix them with the object identifier. For example, PSPEC 5.2.9.8, CSPEC 4.2, DFD 3.5.7, CFD 9.1.

Much work needs to be done before the worlds of structured methods and military standards are as one with each other. Since the government is becoming increasingly aware of the need for better and more reliable software, we are hopeful that this will come about rather quickly.

Appendix C

Information Modeling: The Third Perspective

In this book, we have covered the development of the system requirements and architecture models from the process and control perspectives. There are other perspectives from which the system may be modeled. Although these are beyond the scope of the book, we shall outline how one of them, the information model, fits into the overall scheme.

The requirements model, as we present it, represents system requirements in terms of processing and control functions. Another aspect of the requirements can be represented by the information model. For stored data systems, the data and control information structure, and the access relationship of that structure to the process and control models, need to be specified. Several such information models exist and are in use. Most notable among these is the entity-relationship approach described by Flavin [5] and by Schuldt [16]. The requirements model captures the process and control aspects; the information model may be added as a third aspect, as shown in Figure C.1.

We purposely do not include the information model with the requirements model, nor do we address its allocation to the architecture model, because there currently is no formal method for integrating the three projections shown in Figure C.1 into a larger framework.

Nevertheless, it seems appropriate to add a word here about integration and the larger framework into which the models fit. Integration does not mean that we must build a rigid and inflexible superstructure; it simply means that all the components must fit together nonredundantly to specify the system. The components of the models must link with each other and must have reasons for their existence, that is, they must serve a useful role in the model. In other words, integration means we will not allow redundant, ambiguous, or incorrect specifications.

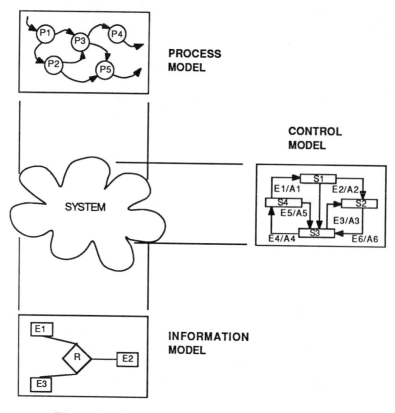

Figure C.1. Requirements projections of a system.

We will now return to our discussion of the addition of the information perspective to requirements modeling and its impact on the architecture model. The architecture model was created by the successive use of the architecture template. This is a general-purpose template: It does not apply in its entirety to all systems. It may be modified to accommodate the third requirements modeling aspect as shown in Figure C.2.

To use this modified template, what aspects of the system and what parts of the requirements model need to be modeled, and which buffers from the architecture template should be used? We will consider some examples.

- An alarm clock and a four-function calculator are two simple examples of real-time systems that contain data and control processing. The stored data in such systems is trivial enough that we could sufficiently specify them using just the requirements and architecture models.

- An automatic bank-teller system requires all three aspects. The screen displays and the customer interactions with the system could be sufficiently represented by the requirements and architecture models, but

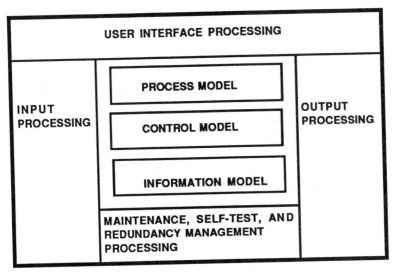

Figure C.2. Architecture template with three requirements projections.

the stored data aspect of the system, that is, the customer data base specification and the access of that data base, would require information modeling.

- A customer billing system might also require all three aspects. Process and control modeling would capture the computation and billing cycle requirements, while the information model would represent the customer data base.

The rationale for raising the topic of information modeling so late in the book is to emphasize three points about which we feel very strongly. First, you cannot apply the modeling techniques without giving thought to what type of a model you are trying to create. Not every system needs requirements modeling from all three aspects, nor even from the two aspects covered in detail in this book, but in general, all three aspects are present to some degree in any system. The question is, What is the purpose of building these models? the answer, The models are built to better understand the system under specification.

The second point is that the modeling components must integrate into an overall framework for specifying the system. The reasons for this are that each requirements or architecture modeling component must demonstrably contribute toward capturing the system specification, and that each of these modeling components must link together into a cohesive, integrated system specification.

The third point is that the complete specification model must integrate with the project development life cycle.

We discussed integration above. To illustrate this concept, let us look at the process of building a house. Many different tools are needed—hammer, saw, square, level, tape measure, plane, sanding block, and others. If any one of the tools were missing, it would be hard to accomplish what that particular tool is designed to do. Conversely, any tools not needed to build a house would be an unnecessary investment, a useless burden in your toolkit.

We like to think of the requirements and architecture methods as an integrated toolbox, each modeling component being an integral part of the overall set of tools, useful for some specific purpose, and not creating any extra burdens.

Taking the house building analogy further: The process requires many steps, including agreement on a specification, selecting the proper materials, choosing a contractor, purchasing the materials, and so on. All of these steps must follow a master plan whereby everything happens at its proper time in the process: For example, the paint should not be delivered when the foundation is being laid.

In this same way, the methods provide the specifications for building the system, and it is imperative that the modeling process fit into the grand scheme of the development life cycle. The methods should be applied at the proper times and, like the house building tools, only those methods should be used that are appropriate. They can and should be evaluated, adopted, or adapted for use to suit the system to be specified.

References

[1] Boehm, Barry W. "A Spiral Model of Software Development and Enhancement." *ACM SIGSOFT Software Engineering Notes,* Vol. 11, No. 4 (August 1986).

[2] Booth, Taylor L. *Sequential Machines and Automata Theory.* New York: John Wiley & Sons, 1967.

[3] Date, C. J. *An Introduction to Database Systems, 3rd ed.* Reading, Mass.: Addison-Wesley, 1986.

[4] De Marco, Tom. *Structured Analysis and System Specification.* Englewood Cliffs, N.J.: Prentice-Hall, 1978.

[5] Flavin, Matt. *Fundamental Concepts of Information Modeling.* Englewood Cliffs, N.J.: Prentice-Hall, 1981.

[6] Hofstadter, Douglas R. *Gödel, Escher, Bach.* New York: Random House, Vintage Books, 1980.

[7] Hopcroft, John, and Jeffrey Ullman. *Introduction to Automata Theory, Languages and Computation.* Reading, Mass.: Addison-Wesley, 1979.

[8] Martin, James. *Computer Data-Base Organization.* Englewood Cliffs, N.J.: Prentice-Hall, 1975.

[9] McMenamin, Stephen M., and John F. Palmer. *Essential Systems Analysis.* Englewood Cliffs, N.J.: Prentice-Hall, 1984.

[10] Miller, George A. "The Magical Number Seven, Plus or Minus Two." *The Psychological Review,* Vol. 63, No. 2 (March 1956).

[11] Myers, Glenford J. *Reliable Software Through Composite Design.* New York: Van Nostrand Reinhold, 1975.

[12] Page-Jones, Meilir. *The Practical Guide to Structured Systems Design, 2nd ed.* Englewood Cliffs, N.J.: Prentice-Hall, 1988.

[13] Parnas, David L. *On the Criteria to Be Used in Decomposing Systems into Modules.* Technical Report CMO-CS-71-101; AFOSR-TR-74-0095. Pittsburgh, Penn.: Carnegie-Mellon University (August 1971).

[14] _____, and Paul C. Clements. "A Rational Design Process: How and Why to Fake It." *IEEE Transactions on Software Engineering,* Vol. SE-12, No. 2 (February 1986).

[15] Putnam, Lawrence H. *Software Cost Estimating and Life-Cycle Control: Getting the Software Numbers.* Los Alamitos, Calif.: Computer Society Press, 1980.

[16] Schuldt, Gary. "ER-Based Access Modeling." *Proceedings of the Fifth International Conference on Entity-Relationship Approach.* Centre de Recherches en Informatique de Dijon, Dijon, France: University of Burgundy (November 1986).

[17] Swartout, William, and Robert Balzer. "On the Inevitable Intertwining of Specification and Implementation." *Communications of the ACM,* Vol. 25, No. 7 (July 1982).

[18] Ward, Paul T., and Stephen J. Mellor. *Structured Development for Real-Time Systems.* Englewood Cliffs, N.J.: Prentice-Hall, 1985.

[19] Yourdon, Edward, and Larry L. Constantine. *Structured Design: Fundamentals of a Discipline of Computer Program and Systems Design.* Englewood Cliffs, N.J.: Prentice-Hall, 1975.

Additional information

[20] Seminars on the requirements and architecture models are available through Systems Methods, 2422 Dexter Avenue North, Suite 303, Seattle, WA 98109, and through System Strategies, 5321 Queensbury Drive Southeast, Kentwood, MI 49508.

[21] CASE tools currently supporting the requirements model are made by Cadre Technologies, Iconix, Index Technology, Interactive Development Environments, Mentor Graphics, and StructSoft.

Index

Actions, 15–17, 78–85, 87–88, 92, 168–69
  logic, 89–90, 173–74
  naming, 178
Activation table: *see* Process activation table
Architecture communication channels:
  AIS and, 217–19
  redundancy of, in AID, 209–10
Architecture context diagram (ACD), 193–
  94, 200–201, 248–49, 358–59
  components in, 200
  example, 201, 202, 359
  for Automobile Management System,
  249, 304
Architecture dictionary (AD), 20, 24, 193–94,
  213–14, 220–21, 364–65
  of Automobile Management System, 221,
  307
  of vending machine example, 21, 22, 337
Architecture flow diagram (AFD), 19–20,
  23–24, 193–94, 202–208, 249–54
  decomposition of, 206–207
  examples, 203, 204, 205, 341
  naming and numbering rules, 360–61
  of Automobile Management System, 205,
  207, 251, 263, 304
  of vending machine example, 20, 336
  structure chart and, 267
Architecture interconnect diagram (AID), 21,
  23–24, 193–94, 202, 208–12, 249–54,
  361–62
  decomposition of, 206
  layering rules, 210
  naming and numbering rules, 210, 362
  of Automobile Management System, 262,
  263, 305
  of vending machine example, 21, 336
  redundancy in, 208–11

Architecture interconnect specification (AIS),
  21, 22, 24, 193–94, 217–19, 362–64
  of Automobile Management System, 219,
  306
  of vending machine example, 22, 338
Architecture model, 6–7, 12, 19–25, 94,
  357–66
  Automobile Management System,
  301–307
  balancing, 225, 254–56, 271–72, 344,
  365–66
  components, 192–94
  decomposition of, 206–207
  hierarchy of, 196–97
  illustration, 23
  implementation of, in hardware and
  software, 222–26
  of Home Heating System example,
  321–22
  summary, 22–24, 193–99, 225–26
  symbols of, 197–99
  vending machine example, 334–38
Architecture model, 19, 197–98
  automobile management computer
  module example, 222–23, 258–62,
  265–66
  decomposition of, 206–207
  defined, 342
  implementation of, 222–23
  in ACD, 200
  in AID, 208–12
  naming rule, 197–98, 342
  number in AFD, 202–203
  partitioning of requirements, 258–69
  redundancy of, 208–209
  symbols, 197–98, 342
  timing constraints and, 219–20

379

Architecture module specification (AMS),
19–20, 214–17
  of Automobile Management System, 253,
  306
  of vending machine example, 20
  traceability matrix and, 214, 217–18
Architecture template, 194–97, 204, 234–47,
263–66, 358, 375
  benefits of, 245–47
  for Automobile Management System,
  196
  software requirements and, 263–66
Automobile management computer module,
222–23, 259–62, 265–66
Automobile Management System, 277–307
  ACD example, 202, 304
  AD example, 221, 307
  AFD example, 205, 207, 304
  AID example, 211, 305
  AIS for, 306
  Automobile Management System
  example, 215, 306
  architecture model of, 226, 301–307
  architecture template for, 196
  control diagram for, 283
  CSPEC for, 285, 290, 294, 296
  data vs. control issues, 120–22
  enhanced CFD for, 243, 303
  enhanced DFD for, 242, 302
  flow names in, 140–41
  hierarchical nature of, 258
  input and output processing for, 234–37
  PSPEC of, 152, 287–88, 291, 294, 297
  RD for, 298–300
  response time specification, 95
  safety requirements in, 231
  sequential machine in, 170–72
  STD in, 81–82
  STM in, 83–85
  system context, 123–26
  timing specification, 286
  top-level partitioning, 126–29
  traceability matrix for, 217
  transient signal in, 155
  user interface processing, 237–39
Automated tools, 6, 378
  used for balancing, 46–47, 133, 158
  used for dictionary, 102, 133, 186, 188,
  369
Avionics system example, 4–6

'kus-Naur form, 100–101, 185–88

Balancing:
  architecture model, 254–56, 365–66
  requirements model, 46–47, 108, 116,
  355–57
  (see also specific entries)
Balzer, R., 132, 378
Bar symbol, 63–64, 68, 85, 87–88, 174, 340,
348
Boehm, B., 28, 377
Boolean equation form, 76, 92, 162, 187
Booth, T., 82, 163, 377

CASE tools, 6, 378
Combinational control specification, 85–87,
160–67
Combinational machine, 75–78, 92, 109, 145,
148, 160–67
  CSPEC for, 351–52
Comment:
  in PSPEC, 52, 158
  in requirements dictionary, 101–102
Conditional construct, 158
Consistency checking, 5, 36
  of architecture model, 254–56
  of CSPECs, 68
  of DFDs, 46–47
  of requirements model, 36, 47, 50–51,
  108–109
Constantine, L., 5, 267, 378
Context diagram:
  context process in, 130
  control, 38, 41, 59–61, 72, 283, 345–46
  data, 38, 41–44, 59–61, 283, 344–45
  level 1 and, 124
  nonprimitive flows and, 100
  primitive flows in, 64–66, 101, 102
  timing requirements and, 93–94
  (see also Control context diagram, Data
  context diagram)
Context process, 43, 60–61, 130
Continuous (analog) machine, 74–75, 92
  digital computer and, 75
  PSPECs and, 74
Continuous signals, 64–66, 74–75, 99, 119,
121, 156
  example of primitive in RD, 99, 183–85
Control context diagram (CCD), 38–39, 41,
59–61, 72, 283, 345–46
  of Automobile Management System, 283
  of vending machine example, 325
Control flow, 15–16, 41, 59–66, 98

defined in requirements dictionary, 64, 98, 109
determined in requirements model, 119–23
graphic convention, 59–61, 63, 64, 340
naming, 340
types and attributes, 183–86
Control flow diagram (CFD), 14–19, 35, 61–64, 73, 108–109, 347–49
allocation in architecture model, 214–17
balancing, 61, 108
composite example of, 127
control flow on, 14–15, 64–66
control signals and, 14–15, 64–66
control store on, 67, 73, 142, 341
decomposition of, 39, 62–63
interface with CSPEC (bar symbol), 61–64, 67–68, 85, 87, 175, 340, 348
leveled, 39, 61, 108
link to DFD, 66–67
naming and numbering, 61, 108, 348 –49
of automobile management computer module, 260, 266
of Automobile Management System, 243, 284, 289, 292, 293, 295, 303
of vending machine example, 15, 326, 329, 331, 335
sample, 349
Control model, 13–19, 40, 59–73
control-intensive system and, 144–45
implementation details and, 143–44
purpose of, 144
vending machine example, 14–17
Control outputs, 70
(see also Process controls)
Control signal, 15–16, 64
RD and, 17
symbol for, on CFD, 15–16
(see also Control flow)
Control specification (CSPEC), 15–17, 18, 39–40, 61–64, 67–70
balancing, 89, 344, 356
bar symbol on, 63–64, 68, 85, 87, 174, 340, 354
combinational vs. sequential control, 85–87, 160–68, 351–52
composite, 87–89, 174
decision table and, 162–65
finite state machines and, 39, 70, 85–92, 178
floating, 176, 177

interface with CFD, 63–64, 68, 85, 174, 340
multi-sheet conventions for, 89–91, 109, 172–75
naming and numbering, 68, 108
of Automobile Management System, 285, 290, 294, 296
of combinational machine, 161–67, 351–52
of vending machine example, 16, 19
PAT in, 165
placement of, in model, 175–76
primitive, 145
process controls and, 70–73, 86
purpose of, 68–70, 108–109, 160
rule for allocation in architecture model, 215
state transition diagram and, 62, 87
timing requirements in, 176–77
transaction center and, 71–72, 165–67
user's guide for, 90, 109, 145, 175
Control store, 67, 73, 142
(see also Data store)
naming, 67, 142, 341
Control structure, 5
balancing, 73
determining in requirements model, 106–108, 119–23
illustrated, 60, 107
Cruise control system example: see Automobile Management System

Data abstraction, 130, 199
(see also Information abstraction)
Data condition, 17–18, 66–67, 73, 108
example, 66
Data context diagram (DCD), 38, 41–44, 344–45
external primitive flows in, 179–80
of Automobile Management System, 283
of vending machine example, 325
Data flow, 41–45, 49–51, 57
arcs, 49–50
balancing, 46–47, 56, 133–36
consistency checking of, 46, 47, 51
data stores and, 51, 142
decomposition of, 50, 136
defined, 339
determined from user requirements statement, 118–23
graphic conventions, 43, 49–51, 133–38, 340

in requirements dictionary, 14, 98, 109, 137–38
naming rules, 45, 49–50, 133–36, 140–41, 339
primitive, 49
splitting and merging, 50, 136
types and attributes, 183–86
Data flow diagram (DFD), 13–19, 35, 44–51, 108–109, 346–49
allocation in architecture model, 214–17
composite example of, 127
data signal and, 66
decomposition of, 39, 45, 46
leveling and balancing, 39, 45, 46–47, 56, 108
link to CFD, 66, 68
naming and numbering, 47–49, 346–48
of automobile management computer module, 259, 265
of Automobile Management System, 284ff.
of vending machine example, 13
parent/child relationship, 45, 46–49
sample, 44, 347
Data modeling: see Information modeling
Data process, determining, 121
Data store, 51, 57, 142
defined 44–45, 341
flows and, 142
naming rules, 51, 142, 341
symbol, 45
Data structure:
determined in requirements model, 118–23
Date, C., 183, 377
Decision table (DT), 70, 76–79, 85–86, 92, 109, 158, 351
Home Heating System example, 77, 79
in CSPEC, 162–65
luggage lock example, 76
PAT, 86, 165
STM and, 83–84
transaction center and, 165–67
Decomposition, 36, 130–31
of flows, 133–40
of processes, 45, 133–40
7 ± 2 principle, 131–32
DeMarco, T., 5, 35–37, 54, 89, 377
structured analysis method of, 5, 89
Design, 229–30
constraints, 193

internal timing requirement and, 93, 96, 109, 179
phase, 145–47
Discrete signal, 64–65, 74–75, 98, 99, 119, 121, 156, 185
example of primitive in RD, 98–99, 184–85
Don't care condition, 78, 162–65, 178, 183

Entity, in ACD, 200
Equation, in PSPEC, 151–53
Event, 17, 78–85, 87–91, 167–69
asynchronous, 142
logic, 89–91, 174
naming, 178
response time, 94–97

Feedback control loop, 68–70, 109
Finite state machine, 74–92, 119, 145
combinational, 76–78, 145, 148, 160–67, 351–52
control model and, 40, 67–70
control structures and, 5, 108
CSPEC and, 15, 39, 70, 85–92
model, 74
sequential, 78–85, 87, 92, 167–72, 351–54
theory, 5, 36, 85
Flavin, M., 377
Flight management system example, 75
response time specification, 95
Flow arcs, 42–44, 49–51
symbol on CFD, 63
symbol on DFD, 49–52
Flow diagram: see Control flow diagram, Data flow diagram
Flows:
allocation in AMS, 214–17
balancing, 133–40
(see also Control flow, Data flow)
Functional primitive: see Primitive process
Functional requirements, 3–10, 13, 19–20
(see also Control model, Process model, Timing requirements)
Fundamental entity, 197

Hardware design, 260–63
requirements allocated to hardware, 261–62
Hardware/software implementation of architecture model, 222–23, 260–63
example, 223

Hardware/software models, 272–74
Hierarchical representation, 4, 9–10, 26–27, 38, 231–33
    of Automobile Management System, 258
Hofstadter, D., 208, 377
Home Heating System example, 308–22
Hopcroft, J., 82, 377

Implementation, system, 10, 12, 55–56, 108
    architecture, 214–17
    of process model, 56
    timing constraints and, 219–20
Information abstraction, 5, 36, 108, 130–31
Information flow channel, 199, 201
    in AFD and AIS, 23–24
    in AID, 208
    naming rule, 199, 343
    symbol, 199, 343
Information flow vector, 198–99
    defined, 342
    in ACD, 200
    naming rule, 199, 343
    symbol, 198, 343
Information hiding, 36, 130, 175
Information modeling, 13, 373–76, 378
Input and output processing, 25, 194–97
Input-to-output response time, 94–97, 108
Interface, 7, 25, 193–97, 237–39, 240, 246
Iteration:
    of architecture model, 193, 270–74
    of development process, 10, 24–25, 26–31
    of requirements model, 115–17, 132

Leveling:
    CFDs, 39, 61, 108
    DFDs, 39, 45, 46–47, 56, 108
    PSPECs, 52, 67
Logical function, 43

Maintenance processing, in architecture model, 25, 194–97, 239–42
Martin, J., 183, 377
McMenamin, S., 12, 142, 377
Mealy sequential machine model, 82, 296
Mellor, S., 82, 378
Methods Team, 6
Military standards (documentation), 370–72
Miller, G., 131–32, 377
Modeling process, 270–74
Module, 19–25

automobile management computer example, 259
    software, 266–69
    (see also Architecture flow diagram)
Module specification: see Architecture module specification
Moore sequential machine model, 82, 296
Myers, G., 5, 267, 377

Naming rules:
    abbreviations used, 141
    in AFD, 360–61
    of processes and flows, 45, 140–41, 339–44
Numbering system:
    of flow diagrams, 47, 346–53
    of multi-sheet CSPECs, 89–92, 108

Objects (flows), naming, 45, 140
Operational requirements specification, 181

Page-Jones, M., 122, 267, 377
Palmer, J., 12, 142, 377
Parnas, D., 36, 130, 132, 267, 377
Partitioning, 29
    in Automobile Management System, 126–29
    modeling process, 270–74
    of architecture model for hw/sw implementation, 222–23, 260–63, 273
    of requirements model, 108
Physical configuration, 24–25
Physical modules, 193–99
Physical requirements, 3–4, 7, 43, 193–99
Primitive flow, 64–66, 98–100
    attributes of, 98–100, 185–86
    decomposing groups of, 133
    defined, 98, 183
    examples of, 99
    grouping, 133, 183
    symbol in dictionary, 101
Primitive network, 57, 107
Primitive process, 13, 39, 46, 51, 56, 58, 106–109
    CFD and, 62
    network of, 56, 106–108
    PSPEC and, 13, 62
Process, 45
    allocation in Automobile Management System, 214–17
    controls, 70–73, 106
    data, 122

defined, 341
functionally identical, 142–43
naming rule, 45, 140–41, 341
numbering system, 47–49
on CCD, 59–61
on CFD, 61–64
physical, 195ff.
primitive, 13, 39, 46, 51, 56, 58, 106–109
symbol for, 41, 43
timing requirements, 180
Process activation table (PAT), 15, 86, 165,
   351–52
   example, 86
   of vending machine example, 16, 19
Process activators, 70
   CSPEC and, 176
Process controls, 70ff., 85–87
   in leveled DFDs, 70
Processing, input and output:
   Automobile Management System,
   234–37
   in architecture model, 234–37
Processing, user interface, 25, 237–39
Process model, 13–14, 40, 41–58
   interpreting, 54–56
Process specification (PSPEC), 14, 19–20, 35,
   40, 51–54, 58, 349–50
   balancing, 51–52, 151, 158
   comment in, 52
   conditional statement in, 119–20
   continuous machines and, 74
   data condition and, 66–67
   data signal and, 66
   examples, 53, 123, 350
   functional primitives, 51–52
   leveling and balancing, 52, 67
   naming and numbering rules, 350
   of Automobile Management System, 152,
   287, 288ff.
   of vending machine example, 14, 349ff.
   role of, 150–51
   structured English in, 52–54, 157–58,
   159
   transient signal in, 154–56
   types of, 151–54
   user requirements and, 52, 150
Process structure:
   categories, 121
   in requirements model, 108
Project dictionary:
   abbreviations and, 141
   list of word types, 158

Prototyping, 29
Putnam, L., 378
Putnam model, 6, 378

Real-time systems, 36
   characteristics of, 3, 74, 93
   development methods for, 11ff.
Redundancy requirement, 25
   data store and, 51
   in AFD, 208
   in AID, 208–209, 212
   in Automobile Management System, 262
Reliability requirement, 210, 229
Requirements:
   data vs. control, 119–23, 144
   defined, 10, 12
   functional, 3, 94
   physical, 3, 23
   processing, in PSPECs, 150–59
   timing, 39, 93–97, 108–109, 179–82,
   219–20
Requirements dictionary (RD), 14, 18, 35, 38,
   98–103, 354–55
   attributes of, 183–86
   cockpit display example, 100
   data flow types in, 183–85
   flow decomposition in, 357
   flows in, 64, 98, 109
   in a computerized data base, 102, 103,
   183
   indented explosion of, 102–104
   naming rules, 355
   of Automobile Management System,
   298–300
   of vending machine example, 14, 17,
   333, 337
   primitives in, 98–100
   symbols in, 101, 105, 187–88, 355
   timing signals in, 179–80
Requirements model, 4–6, 13–19, 24, 40,
   106–109
   adding physical constraints, 234–47
   allocation of components in Automobile
   Management System, 213–17
   builders, 114–17
   components of, 37–40, 108–109, 343–57
   consistency checking of, 36, 46–47,
   50–51, 108–109
   decomposition and, 46, 116, 130–31
   enhanced, 234–47
   implementation details and, 144

leveling and balancing, 46–47, 108, 355–57
naming and numbering in, 47ff., 108
of Home Heating System, 311–21
of vending machine example, 325–33
overview of, 17–19, 35–40, 106–109
primitives in, 107, 108
redundancy and, 25, 51
role of automata theory, 85
self-indexing, 5, 36, 108
signals in, 154–56
timing in, 179–82
tools of, 35
users, 113–14
Response time specification, 14, 18, 94–96, 97, 109
(see also Timing specification)

Schuldt, G., 13, 378
Self-test processing, 25, 27, 239–42
Sequential control specification, 87, 88, 90ff.
Sequential machine, 75, 78–85, 87, 89–92, 108, 148, 167–72, 351–53
combination lock example, 78–79
CSPEC for, 352, 353
math representation, 168–69
Mealy and Moore models, 82, 168–69
Seven-plus or-minus-two principle, 131–32, 168, 203, 346, 377
Signals:
attributes, 185–86
continuous vs. transient, 154–56
control vs. data, 64–66, 67, 73, 106–107
discrete vs. continuous, 64–66, 73, 98–99, 156
external primitive, 94, 99
types, 121, 184
Sink, 41, 44
Software architecture, 258ff., 266ff.
Source, 41, 44
Specification model, system, 22, 24–25
STARS Methodology Conference, 277
State, 81–85, 92, 167
naming, 178
State transition diagram (STD), 17, 62, 70, 78–82, 87–92, 168, 351–54
of Automobile Management System, 171, 172, 285
of combination lock example, 78–79
of vending machine example, 16, 19
State transition matrix (STM), 17, 70, 82–85, 87, 89, 92, 109, 168, 351

examples, 84
multi-sheet CSPECs and, 172–75
State transition table (STT), 17, 70, 82–85, 92, 109, 168, 351–53
example, 83
Store: see Control store, Data store
Structure chart, 267
Structured analysis, 5, 35–37, 43, 52, 89
control requirements and, 178
leveling and balancing principles of, 89
primitive network and, 107
process model and, 40
Structured design, 5, 36–37, 267
Structured documentation, 367–72
Structured English, 52–54, 55
examples, 55
in PSPECs, 151, 157–58
structure of, 55
Structured methods:
defined, 11ff., 31
history of, 4–6, 36–37
iteration and, 26–30
Structured programming, 36–37
Swartout, W., 132, 378
System analysts, role of, 114–17
System context, 43, 123–26
System design:
building the architecture model, 229–31
factors, 229–33
System life cycle, 8–10, 28–30
cost, 29
implementation phase, 8, 30, 56, 246
requirements definition phase, 56, 114–15
System maintenance, 25, 27
cost, 10
phase, 246
System model, 271–72
Systems:
control-intensive, 144–45
hierarchy of, 3, 8, 10, 26–27, 231–33
System scope, 43–44, 115, 123–26
Systems development process:
illustration of, 24
iteration and, 10, 24, 26, 132–33
life cycle of, 26–30
System specification:
hierarchical nature, 3, 26–27
leveled, 3–4, 26–27, 38–39
methods of, 3ff.
model, 22, 24–25

(*see also* Architecture model,
Requirements model)

Tabular PSPEC, 14, 153
   (*see also* Process activation table, State
   transition diagram)
Technology-dependent model, 12, 24–25, 230,
   243–45
   (*see also* Architecture model)
Technology-nonspecific model, 234–47
   (*see also* Requirements model)
Terminator, 341–42, 345, 359
   defined, 341
   naming, 342
   on ACD, 200
   on CCD, 59–60
   on DCD, 41–42, 44
   symbol, 41
Testing requirements, 8, 25, 27–29
   phase, 246
Timing diagram, 96, 109
Timing requirements, 39, 93–97, 109,
   179–82
   in architecture model, 216–17, 219–20,
   230
   in CSPEC, 156, 176–77, 179
   in PSPEC, 156, 179
   in requirements model, 39, 93–97,
   108–109
   repetition rate, 94, 97, 109, 176–77,
   179–82
   response time, 94–97, 109, 179–82

Timing specification, 30, 39, 109, 179–82,
   216–17, 219–20, 353–54
   balancing, 182
   of Automobile Management System, 286
   of vending machine example, 328
   (*see also* Response time specification)
Traceability matrix, 214, 216, 217, 363
   of Automobile Management System, 217
   of vending machine example, 337
Transaction center, 45–46
   control, 71–72, 165–67
Transient signal, 154–56
Transition arcs, 81, 82, 169
Truth table: *see* Decision table

Ullman, J., 169, 377
User interface:
   in Automobile Management System,
   237–39
   processing, 25, 237–39
   specification of, 246
User requirements, 37, 93, 113–17, 118
   PSPEC and, 52, 150
Users' guide, to CSPECs, 90, 109, 145, 175

Vending machine example, 12–22, 323–38

Ward and Mellor convention, 82, 378
Ward, P., 82, 378

Yourdon, E., 5, 267, 378